PACKINGHOUSE DAUGHTER

MIDWEST REFLECTIONS

Memoirs and personal histories of the people of the Upper Midwest

PACKINGHOUSE DAUGHTER

A Memoir

CHERI REGISTER

MINNESOTA HISTORICAL SOCIETY PRESS
ST. PAUL

MIDWEST REFLECTIONS
*Memoirs and personal histories
of the people of the Upper Midwest*

Publication of this book was supported, in part, with funds provided by the June D. Holmquist Publication Endowment Fund of the Minnesota Historical Society. Promotion of this book is supported, in part, by a Minnesota Writers Career Initiative grant from the Loft Literary Center.

www.mnhs.org/mhspress

Manufactured in Canada.

10 9 8 7 6 5 4 3 2

International Standard Book Number
0-87351-391-6

∞ The paper used in this publication meets the minimum requirements of the American National Standard for Information Sciences—Permanence for Printed Library Materials, ANSI Z39.48-1984.

*Library of Congress
Cataloging-in-Publication Data*

Register, Cheri, 1945–
  Packinghouse daughter : a memoir / Cheri Register.
    p. cm.
  ISBN 0-87351-391-6
    (cloth : alk. paper)
  ISBN 0-87351-392-4
    (pbk. : alk. paper)
  1. Register, Cheri, 1945—Childhood and youth.
  2. Albert Lea (Minn.)—Biography.
  3. Albert Lea (Minn.)—Social life and customs—20th century.
  4. Packing-houses—Minnesota—Albert Lea—History—20th century.
  5. Strikes and lockouts—Minnesota—Albert Lea—History—20th century.
  6. Working class—Minnesota—Albert Lea—Biography.
  I. Title.

F614.A27 R44   2000
977.6'18—dc21
[B]   00-040214

"The Blue Workshirt" originally appeared in *Hungry Mind Review* (Spring 1995) and was reprinted as "The Workshirt Manifesto" in the *University of Chicago Magazine* (August 1995). An additional excerpt, published under the title "A Ph.D. (Packinghouse Daughter) Examines Her Legacy," appears in *Is Academic Feminism Dead?* (New York University Press, 2000). Thanks to the editors for permission to reprint.

For Mom and Dad

The one irrevocable limitation is that
we cannot go back to where we were.
We must face the new horizons.

PEARL S. BUCK
quoted on the cover of the
1963 commencement program,
Albert Lea High School

PACKINGHOUSE DAUGHTER

Unfair

Legacy

PACKINGHOUSE DAUGHTER

THE PLANT

Prologue: The Blue Workshirt

The early evening train pulled into Albert Lea with brakes squealing and slowed to a crawl alongside the Wilson & Co. meatpacking plant. The lamps at the corners of the parking lot cast the packinghouse itself in shadow, reminding me of a prison-break scene in some movie I had otherwise forgotten—a Hollywood movie, not one of the foreign films I now preferred. As we crossed the channel where I used to watch for giant goldfish while Mom waited in the car for Dad to get off work, I could see the depot glowing up ahead. My folks—the word "parents," like "my father," still sounded haughty to me—were standing outside, shivering in the December cold and wearing the self-conscious smiles that hold back tears. I knew my dad had already made the rounds to tell everyone whom he was expecting: his youngest daughter, that smart girl who won all the scholarships, the one who got her picture in *Wilson Certified News*. She was coming home, on break from the University of Chicago.

I stepped off the train looking like something you might pull out of a cocoon that had cracked open mid-metamorphosis. My hair was growing out of the bubble-do still fashionable at Albert Lea High School, but it was not yet long enough to pull back in a barrette at the nape of my neck. Living in a dormitory full of New Yorkers had put an edge of affectation on my southern Minnesota corn-belt speech, and I was wearing dangly clip-on earrings while I worked up the courage to get my ears pierced. I had an errand to complete over the holidays: buy a blue workshirt—one I could knot at the waist above the new jeans that I wore rolled in a wide cuff halfway up my calf, usually over leather sandals.

I hadn't expected the University of Chicago to require a fashion statement. I had already created an identity for myself, in high school, that needed no uniform: Girl Intellectual. I had thought myself well suited for the Life of the Mind that the brochures and catalogs promised. By the end of fall quarter, though, I learned that I would have to dress more deliberately. Manhattan-style sophistication was beyond my capacity, so I opted for quick identification. The workshirt would ally me with the campus radicals, who used fashion to decry fashion. The serviceable blue denim of workshirt and jeans was a political statement, a mark of allegiance with the workers of the world. I could be comfortable in that, I thought. Getting the workshirt in Albert Lea would be less trouble than shopping in Chicago. I figured I could buy one from my dad's sister Vivian at Montgomery Wards.

My dad was the focus of another vacation project. A packinghouse millwright who had always trusted the union and Hubert Humphrey's Democratic-Farmer-Labor Party (DFL), he was, I knew, just waiting to be awakened to a broader vision. Hadn't he taught me that rich people aren't happy, that

Republicans will do you in for money, that "we . . . the little guys . . . the ordinary working people" are little and ordinary precisely because we are too moral to do what it takes to get rich? I had come home eager to discuss with him the socialist ideas that were beginning to satisfy my longings for a just and responsible life.

My first week in college, I had met a boy named Len—short for Lenin, my dormmates guessed—who was a real socialist and not just toying with the label. He had joined the Young People's Socialist League in high school, and he pedaled his bicycle around Hyde Park, the university neighborhood, nearly every night, going from meeting to demonstration to party. I rode on his handlebars, wondering whether I was to be a girlfriend or a comrade or the unthinkable both-at-once. One night we squeezed into the backseat of a Volkswagen bug in front of the Student Peace Union office and drove the expressways to O'Hare Airport, where we met Madame Nhu, the powerful sister-in-law of President Ngo Dinh Diem of South Vietnam, as she disembarked from her plane. "Down with Diem!" we chanted. "Diem or democracy!" It was October 1963. Within a week, Diem had been assassinated and the escalating war in Vietnam had become a political issue on campus. With a teenager's grandiosity, I felt personally responsible.

Three weeks later, John F. Kennedy was assassinated. That night I sat on the floor of the dorm hallway with a string of other young women in a spontaneous vigil. My friendship with Len was strained a little by my guilt at having betrayed my Democratic heritage. I had dared to question the efficacy of President Kennedy's liberalism and now he was dead and I was in mourning. Nevertheless, as I left campus for home in December, Len entrusted me with his treasured collection of socialist literature: a green net shopping bag full of classic

Marxist documents and pamphlets by Hal Draper and Harvey Swados. I promised to show them to my dad.

I don't remember now whether I got Dad to look at any of the pamphlets that I pulled out of the bag and arrayed on the living-room coffee table. When I try to remember, I can only imagine the gold rims on his teeth flashing at my naïveté. But I will never forget what happened with the blue workshirt.

One late afternoon after Christmas, I met Dad in the kitchen as he came in from work. He was still jingling the car keys in his hand.

"Is it okay if I drive uptown?" I asked. "I need to go to Wards and buy a workshirt."

He peered at me through his glasses, one bushy eyebrow raised. "A workshirt?"

"Yeah. I want one to take back to school."

"Just a regular workshirt?"

"Uh-huh," I nodded. "A blue one, you know. People wear those at UC. They have them at Wards, don't they?"

"Aw, save your money," he said. "I can get you a workshirt if you want one."

There was a smirk at the corner of his mouth, but it appeared so often, prompted by so much in life, that I thought nothing of it. I went back to my spot behind the drop-leaf dining table at the end of the living room and huddled in front of the heat register with *The Brothers Karamazov*, trusting that my errand would get done.

The next afternoon I was too engrossed to jump up at the sound of the car in the driveway. It could have been Dmitri Karamazov's footsteps in the kitchen, for all the attention I was paying. Dad's voice roused me.

"Got a present for you," he said.

He was standing in the doorway with a piece of clothing

rolled under his arm. Light blue mottled with white—there was no mistaking what it was. He held it out toward me, still rolled, and I felt the cotton as I reached to take it. It was soft to the touch, not so stiff that it would stand out among my classmates' shirts as one newly acquired. Just as I grabbed for it, Dad's eyes squinted shut the way they do when he is struggling to contain laughter or tears, and he let the shirt unfurl in front of me. It was stained with hog blood.

My memory stops there. I can't say what happened next. I don't know if my mother cried, "Gordon! Get that smelly thing out of here," as I imagine she would have. I don't remember Dad rolling the shirt back up again and laying it on the breezeway table until the next morning, when he could tuck it back in his locker at the plant. If I took it, I didn't pack it with the rest of my clothes.

All I know for certain is that at this moment I realized I had truly left home. I would never have to take a job on the sliced bacon line, which was women's work in the meatpacking industry, nor would I live in dread of a phone call telling me that my husband was on his way to the hospital in an ambulance, having been hit in the head with a carcass or wounded by an errant blade sharp enough to sever joints and slice through bone. But neither could I leave home behind me entirely. When I wore the clean, blue workshirt that I ended up buying anyway, I did not feel like the girls from the Long Island suburbs who swished by me in the cafeteria line, looking chic in theirs. They had never seen a workshirt put to its intended use.

Like many of my peers, I struggled to get to the simple truth at the core of complex social issues, but everything I saw was refracted through a bloodstain that would not allow simplicity. I often felt as though I were invisible and watching from the sidelines as privileged white suburban kids playacted at being less fortunate than they were. When students occupied the administration building to protest the University of Chicago's complicity in submitting grade point rankings to the selective service (local draft boards drew from the bottom of the rankings to fill their quotas), I stayed outside, wondering how the nurse's aides who had cared for me as a patient in the University hospital were getting by without their paychecks. Yet, when the speakers at rallies on the administration building steps spoke in the name of the working class, I said nothing to identify myself. Playacting or not, the issues were critical. One of the few laborers' kids I had gotten to know dropped out in our junior year and was immediately drafted. His name is inscribed on The Wall in Washington, D.C.

If I count up the meetings I attended, the protests I marched in, the feminist position papers I wrote, I have sound enough credentials to qualify as a sixties activist. And the diploma on my bookcase confirms that Girl Intellectual simultaneously mastered the Life of the Mind. Yet I read "Ph.D." as "Packinghouse Daughter." I find that I still experience the world as a working-class kid away from home. I walk the line between a feisty fidelity to the people of my childhood and a refined repugnance for the work they had to do. And I can't recall the politically charged days of my young adulthood without also remembering my ambivalence, the dark blotch of reality on my sky blue illusions.

Introduction: The Setting

On certain workday mornings when the sky is overcast and his mood just as cloudy, Bill Yost has a little trick he plays to remind himself of his good fortune. He slides into the driver's seat of his car, turns the ignition key and sighs aloud, "Well, I'm off to the plant."

I remember Bill, my high school classmate and fellow Lutheran confirmand, as a dark-haired, serious boy with a sometimes brooding look, even though he hung out with the Southside pranksters who were frequent objects of my vain crushes. I suspected that Bill was a lot smarter, in the sense of school smarts, than he dared let on, and my hunch was right. The "plant" he drives to on bleak mornings is the Eisenhower Hall Theatre at the United States Military Academy, West Point, where he oversees musical and dramatic events in his position as the cultural arts director. But the plant that looms in his memory on those occasional days when work is uninviting is the same one that occupies mine: the Wilson & Co.

packinghouse in Albert Lea, Minnesota, where our fathers earned the wages that kept us clothed and fed and full of dreams.

I had not seen Bill in thirty years when I spotted his nametag on a balding, gray-bearded man at our class reunion. Our conversation leapt immediately to our shared experience of escape.

"Today when I drove into town past the packinghouse," Bill began, "I thought, 'Did I really live here? And how did I get away?'"

His dad, who died at fifty-four, worked at the plant for twenty-five years, but Bill still doesn't know exactly what he did there. He could only guess from the striped coveralls that his dad wore home and shut away in a closet reserved for his workclothes. The clothes' smell made him "a walking billboard for smoked meats." His dad rarely talked about his workday, but Bill got the message contained in his silence: The work itself was dreadful, but the certainty of a daily five A.M.–to–three P.M. shift and a weekly paycheck was good luck to a man whose farmer parents had lost their livelihood in the Depression. That hard-won financial security helped launch Bill, like me, into a clean job that indulges his interest in the arts.

We belong to a generation of working-class children propelled into the middle class by postwar prosperity, higher education, and our parents' determination to spare us the spirit-wrenching disappointments they endured as the youth of the Great Depression. We lived the American Dream, but now its nightmare aspect keeps us tossing: to be successful, which means free from grueling labor, the children of blue-collar families must be driven from home, away from the familiar and secure. We make our parents proud, yet also mystify them with our alien ways: Why haul your kids across town to play soccer when there's a park down the street? Why eat that paper-thin deli turkey when a frozen turkey loaf is a much better buy? What's so funny about Garrison Keillor anyway? My dad once paid this great compliment to my brother-in-law: "Rog is such a nice guy you'd never even know he was educated."

We have *felt* alien, caught between the blue-collar values of the communities we left behind and our new status as the "rich people" we used to scoff at. We watch and listen for the secret evidence that will reveal who among us shares this confusion. Who else never owned a summer cabin? Who else eats apples down to the core? Who else wears the same old sweatpants at home to keep from wearing out their "good" clothes? Camaraderie is a rare joy, a relief from pretending to be something we know we aren't. That's why I have held in memory, for several years, the last line of Deborah Galyan's essay about growing up working-class in Bloomington, Indiana: "And the pure sensation of hurtling up and out of the past that used to thrill me disconcerts me now, with its sheer speed and the unsettling sense that something important is always dropping away."* Those discarded stages of the rocket lie scattered like debris around us, and we sort through them for salvageable mementos of home. The place we meant to escape has formed us nonetheless.

When I set out to write, I thought that the sixties, with its generational collisions and upending of received values, would be the subject of this book, but I was wrong. My working-class upbringing made me a stranger among those who take credit for that myth-ridden decade: the affluent suburban kids away at college who discovered inequality and the moral hollowness

* Deborah Galyan, "Bloomington, Indiana, in Conrad's Light," in *Townships*, edited by Michael Martone (Iowa City: University of Iowa Press, 1992), 55.

of material wealth. I was a stranger because I already knew these things and had no cause to join in the astonishment. In the long run toward middle age, the estrangement I felt leaving home interests me less than the familiar homeground from which I departed. I write here not as a stranger but as a native guide to the exotic and endangered world of my childhood.

It is not purely nostalgia that compels me to look back. Bill, Deborah, and our kind are not the only ones in this story to have lost something of value. The United States has lost the secure, stable blue-collar communities that made it possible for families like ours to thrive and for children like us to aspire to jobs less harsh or tedious than those our parents performed. The country is spiritually poorer for it, and many of its hard-working citizens are materially poorer than they would have been in the heyday of the meatpacking industry, with a strong, focused union to defend their interests. Yet the so-called family wage wasn't Easy Street. Now we acknowledge "dual-career families," because they have become commonplace in the middle class. Our mothers' devotion to the housewifely ideal of the 1950s made it easy to forget, sometimes, that they worked for pay too—part-time if that sufficed, or temporarily if they could afford the breaks. Bill's mom ran a beauty salon in her home. Mine was a seamstress and salesclerk. Women also worked at the packinghouse, in "female jobs" on a separate wage scale.

Although I have lived in Minneapolis nearly all my adult life, I say that I am "from" Albert Lea, one hundred miles south on Interstate 35 at its junction with Interstate 90. Albert Lea is my hometown. It is a fitting example of Hometown America, not because it conforms to some Norman Rockwell image of placidity, but because it is, like Arlington, Texas, like Wooster, Ohio, a town whose well-being fluctuates with the economic circumstances of its major employers. As Bill Yost discovered when he came "home" for our high school reunion, the meatpacking plant still dominates the townscape. Drive in from Interstate 35 past the hotels and food franchises along East Main Street and, as you pass through the first traffic light and head up a slight incline, the plant appears abruptly on your left, spread over thirty-seven acres. Park in the lot behind the Episcopal Church and look across the bay of Fountain Lake. The tall brick boiler building with its three smokestacks jutting into the sky says "factory town." Cruise along the new scenic drive by Albert Lea Lake and there it is again, across the railroad spurs where beef luggers, hired for their short, muscular stature, once filled car after car with quarters of prime beef bound for New York and other points east.

What you see is a grand illusion. The certainty of a union-scale packinghouse job is no longer available to Albert Lea's young workers. The kills have stood empty since 1994, a spooky monument to their prosperous past. In the years since 1983, when Wilson & Co., one of the Big Four packers, filed bankruptcy, the plant has changed hands several times and even been closed down temporarily while the city sought new owners to bring it back to life. The cars scattered in the parking lot belong to the 500 employees of Farmland Foods, who process pork slaughtered elsewhere and trucked in. On a list of local employers published annually, the packinghouse has been passed up, in sheer numbers of personnel, by the hospital and its clinics and by two nursing homes, occupied no doubt by a goodly number of aging packinghouse workers. A 1997 cartoon-style map of the city distributed by the Albert Lea *Tribune* doesn't even show the packinghouse, but replaces it with a grove of trees.

During the industrial boom of the 1950s, Albert Lea's Wilson plant employed 600 supervisory and office personnel and 1,100 production workers, who slaughtered and processed an average of 2,700 hogs, 500 cattle, and 500 sheep each day. Wilson's paid fifteen percent of the town's payroll to twelve percent of the town's laborers. Packinghouse wages were among the highest in town, thanks to Local 6 of the United Packinghouse Workers of America (UPWA), Albert Lea's largest union, which kept a vigil on pay and working conditions from its new office in the sturdy brick Union Center a few blocks up East Main. Livestock farmers in southern Minnesota and northern Iowa looked to Wilson's consistent slaughtering pace as a reliable source of income.

The Albert Lea of my memory and imagination is an industrial town of 13,545 people surrounded by cornfields and set among lakes and cattail marshes, knolls and oak groves in a landscape that outsiders perceive as flat. That 1950 census figure is stuck in my head alongside outdated telephone numbers and the prices of bread and pastry at Swen's Danish Bakery, where I worked all through high school. In this remembered Albert Lea, the stores are open on Friday nights and the street life "uptown" is thriving. Cars with dual exhaust pipes "drag" Broadway while my best friend Linda and I pace the sidewalk, in search of excitement of a kind we think possible only in distant cities. We pass the dime store where old farmers lean against the plate-glass windows talking Norwegian, glance at the diamond rings in the Deutschmann's Jewelry window, pass the Rivoli Theater where B movies play, and Bisgaard's Shoes with its Buster Brown foot x-ray machine. We wait for the stoplight that lets cross-country traffic through town on Highway 16, then pass Wallace's Clothing Store and Wolf's furniture and clothing, affordable only at clearance time, and cross Broadway from the Broadway Theater to the Hotel Albert, which doubles as the Jefferson Lines bus depot. We stop next door at the Canton Cafe for cherry Cokes and french fries and flirting, then pass Monkey Wards and Stevenson's Dress Shop and head into Skinner's Department Store, site of Albert Lea's only escalator. We take the basement stairs to the women's restroom where we can sit on a bench undisturbed and talk as long as we want without having to buy anything. These memories reel through my mind to a soundtrack of rock and roll music and the reek of animal flesh curing into meat.

There is, of course, a present-day Albert Lea coexisting and often conflicting with my hometown image. Highway 16 is a county road now, and travelers only skirt the town on the Interstates. Cars still "cruise" Broadway, but the shoppers have moved to Wal-Mart or the Northbridge Mall, leaving "downtown" to social service agency offices and low-overhead specialty stores. The population has grown to about 19,000, by annexation and by urbanization, as young adults from nearby farming towns move in for jobs with the small manufacturing companies recruited to fill the gap left by the closing or downsizing of the town's larger industries. They make twine at Bridon Cordage or coffee machines at Fountain Industries or prepare and package deli salads at Mrs. Gerry's Kitchen. The main tenant at the Union Center is Local 6 of the United Food and Commercial Workers, which absorbed the old UPWA and has unionized most, but not all of the smaller food-processing companies. Albert Lea has never had any significant wealth. Its "rich people" are white-collar professionals and business managers. The town is still identifiably working-class in character. As my citified daughters point out, there is no Gap, no Contempo, no J. Crew. Even J. C. Penney's left town when it went upscale.

I have discovered yet another Albert Lea in the microfilm

room at the Minnesota History Center. The farm crises of the 1920s and the Great Depression of the 1930s have worn away the prideful veneer of early local boosterism. Working people—many of them Danish and Norwegian immigrants or their children—are calling attention to low wages and unfair treatment. The Albert Lea *Evening Tribune*, shockingly anti-labor in its news reportage, has a rival in the weekly *Freeborn Patriot*, which refers to the *Tribune* as "the kept press." Here, amid news of the Independent Union of All Workers (IUAW), the Farm Holiday Association, the Farmer-Labor Party, and the cooperative movement, my great-grandfather, a self-taught poet and essayist, waxes Tennyson-like about the beauty of the prairie and its artesian lakes, now despoiled by the forces of greed. This bolder, clear-spoken Albert Lea is a lost legacy, and it is easy to dream my way back to those heady days.

Albert Lea, however, is not a place to be sentimental about. It is a real place I left behind because I did not choose to live the life it offered me. Yet neither can I keep a safe, objective distance from it. Aunts and uncles, former playmates, and untold first and second and third cousins live there. One-third of my graduating class has settled in town or in nearby rural areas, which means, of course, that two-thirds of us left home. Those who stayed were not necessarily less favored with opportunities than those who left. A few have taken over the management of family businesses or followed their fathers into the professions. One packinghouse kid returned home after college to teach and to coach the basketball team that was his springboard to education. Another has retired to Albert Lea after teaching in American schools abroad. One who started his adulthood on the beef kill found his calling as a juvenile officer on the police force. Still, the ambivalent story of escape and displacement that Bill Yost and I can tell is the more common story of UPWArdly mobile children of the postwar working class.

One question presses upon us: How can we show respect for our parents' work—work that others revile and that we would never choose for ourselves or wish upon our children? Our parents stuck with it precisely because they wanted something different and better for us. Their hard labor is why we are where we are, doing what we do. When we talk about the differences in our working lives, we risk mystifying either their work or ours. Processing food is unpleasant but essential work. Being "ah! a published author," as people say, means that I string words into sentences, then delete them and start over. Few people would find that work pleasant, and even we who do it sometimes doubt its value.

Much of the story I tell here focuses on a particular event in 1959, a 109-day meatpacking strike that turned violent and nearly split the town in two. When the governor called in the National Guard to quell the violence, and closed the plant besides, he raised issues of governmental authority that drew national media attention to Albert Lea. Writing about this event is risky. First, I might unearth old hostilities that many Albert Leans would rather leave buried. Second, I might contribute inadvertently to a romantic view of labor history that I would rather argue against. Labor's supreme moment of glory is not the occasional militant strike but, rather, a good day's work rewarded with respect and a livable wage. Third, I was neither a major player in this event nor a *detached* witness, so I am incapable of either a reliable firsthand account or a dispassionate historical analysis. I was only fourteen. My family and my town were caught up in an event of such importance that it even made the TV news. The strike was, for me, a classic loss-of-innocence, a jarring into consciousness of the blurry boundaries of right and wrong. Whose rights should prevail, those who supply the money or those who supply the labor that keeps towns like Albert Lea vital? UNFAIR in block letters on a picket sign carried us kids all too quickly from the "no fair" of a child's argument to weighty questions of justice that may be in dispute forever.

Outside of Albert Lea, the 1959 Wilson strike is long forgotten. Microfilm and memory are where it lives now. Microfilm is the sturdier of the two, but it lacks the passion of memory. I know that the strike was a critical event for me, with lasting consequences, because it lives on in my body, the seat of memory. I remember the strike in the sudden rush of air that passes through my chest when I come upon an old newsphoto of National Guardsmen posted outside the plant, the tension that draws my shoulders forward as I read the company's ads for replacement workers, the flight-or-fight gush of adrenaline when someone makes a crack about labor unions. "Emotional memory," I call this. Steady and fervent and nearly obsessive at times, my emotional memory compels me to tell about the strike, and it animates my face and flutters my hands as I do. But as a source of information, the emotional storehouse is random and unreliable. I have absolutely no memory of 2,500 people marching down Broadway in a solidarity demonstration, yet I can recall the sensation of sliding a marshmallow on the antenna of a National Guard jeep in an act of "girl vandalism" I committed only once. Having little control over the retrieval of these memories, I have turned to microfilm and scrapbooks and file boxes to piece together this fragmented story that will not let me go.

The questions about fairness that the strike aroused in me at fourteen have become, in my fifties, matters of loyalty. Despite moving away from home, getting an academic education, and working at the middle-class occupations of writing and teaching, I find that my deepest allegiance is to those who labor, whether they are indentured children stitching soccer balls in Pakistan or unionized American workers who earn more than I do. Public discussions of class, rare as they are in the United States, reduce it to economic formulas and deprive it of real life. I can't separate my own class consciousness from lakes and corn and cattails, the noon whistle and the smell of the packinghouse, men in bib overalls and women in Penney's housedresses. Memoir, with that eye-opening strike at center, is the best way for me to discover how and why the values of a working-class upbringing refuse to fall away entirely, despite the laws of propulsion.

For a native Albert Lean to write a memoir requires some audacity, a characteristic that the culture does not encourage. A 1990 article in the Minneapolis *Tribune* tells about a free store set up in one of Albert Lea's two half-empty shopping malls. People left unemployed by the temporary closing of the packinghouse were invited to come and choose Christmas presents for their families. "The clothing bins are stuffed full and the toy displays have all the right stuff," the paper notes. Yet a Salvation Army volunteer staffing the store reports that underwear is "the biggest mover." "Some people don't dare take anything nice," she explains. This is as true a depiction of my home culture as any I could come up with on my own. Feelings of entitlement do not come easily, and deprivation is thought to build character. "What makes you think you're so special?" taunts the elementary school moralist who still resides in my conscience. I wouldn't stand out in a Midwestern crowd, nor would I wish to. I have chosen the documentary, collective memoir as my vehicle because it allows for more voices than just my own. I have interviewed other people, some with fuller memories than mine, and I blend their voices in as quotation, paraphrase, or background. Even my own voice is split, alternating between childhood recollection and adult reflection. Still, a collective memoir requires a consistent narrative voice, preferably one that aims to be truthful and unapologetic. If this memoir is to be true to its setting, however, its narrative voice has to make apologies: Why me? How do I dare say these things? Paul Gruchow supplied me with an answer when he spoke of a favorite high school teacher he had run into decades later who asked him, "What are you doing to honor the people who raised you?" Not everyone who writes memoir feels this obligation, but it can weigh heavily on those of us who have left our childhood environment for another. This book, with all its ambivalence, is what I can do.

THE PLANT

The Field Trip

In a town without museums or amusement parks, which Albert Lea still was in the late 1950s, elementary school field trips tend to be excursions in industrial technology. Touring the sites where people do their daily work has to serve as both entertainment and education. My classmates and I clucked at baby chicks still wet and sticky and confused in the electric incubators at the hatchery, and watched a row of women at Kroger's Produce "candle" freshly laid eggs: lighting the eggs with a lamp from behind, they could see inside and check for embryos. We crowded around the printing press that clanked out the Albert Lea Evening Tribune, made our voices echo in the tall stairwell of a grain elevator, and stood entranced as bottles and cans moved along conveyor belts to be automatically filled and sealed at the Morlea Dairy, the Coca-Cola bottling plant, and the National Cooperatives cannery. We never did visit the mysterious, brick-walled Olson Manufacturing Company on South Broadway, so we could still chime in with the local joke, "Why are there so many Olsons in Albert Lea? They make them here."

These field trips rarely bored us. I assumed my classmates were as fascinated as I was with the notion of work and its secret words and special skills. Mom taught me "dart" and "tuck" and "gusset" and showed me how to use a gauge and a tracing wheel. As I helped Dad with his house projects, I learned "dowel," "trowel," "sillcock," and "miter box." I looked forward to the day when I would master something and speak its language with confidence, but until then, I enjoyed peeking in on the work that grown-ups did, and seeing who did what, and where. For the parents of us Lincoln School kids, "where" was likely the Wilson & Co. packinghouse.

We knew that a visit to Wilson's required some degree of maturity, or at least the early signs of adolescence. A hodge-podge of brick buildings and tin and wooden sheds, Wilson's sat in a shallow depression between U.S. Highway 16, our Main Street, and the Chicago–Milwaukee–St. Paul and Pacific railroad line that ran along the weedy shore of Albert Lea Lake, also known as Lower Lake. "The plant," we called it, a name that marked it as the primary local industry. Security fences and a large employee parking lot made it look vast and impenetrable and even a little scary, yet it imposed itself on our lives in ways so familiar and habitual we rarely paid attention. The ceaseless industry of the packinghouse filled the air on the north side of town with a smoky, rancid odor, turned Albert Lea Lake slimy with effluents, alerted us to the passage of time with a steam whistle at noon, blared out livestock prices on our radios, and kept many of us fed and clothed and sheltered. "The Wilson label protects your table" was not only an advertising slogan, but the literal truth. We knew there would be no table to sit at if it weren't for Wilson's.

The closest I had come to the plant was the side gate where we picked Dad up from work on the days Mom needed the car. To reach this gate, we turned down a narrow gravel road that ran alongside another enterprise known as "the foundry" and dead-ended where the railroad tracks crossed the channel connecting Fountain and Albert Lea Lakes. Mom wrestled with the steering wheel of our hulking 1948 Pontiac to pull it over as close as possible to the scraggly willows that hung over the water. We sat silent in the shade, waiting and watching while one man, then a pair of men, and another, most of them swinging barn-shaped, black dinner pails, came streaming out under an arched sign that read Safety First. Some of the men exchanged good-byes with a guard who sat in a booth at the entryway. Finally, we would spot my dad, freshly washed and dressed in khaki pants and a checked shirt. He'd break into a grin as soon as he saw us, and I would climb over the seat into the back.

I had only a vague understanding of how Dad spent his days beyond the Safety First sign. I wasn't sure how to interpret the few clues he carried with him at the end of the day. He might hand Mom a bottle of candy-sweet cough syrup that the nurse in the infirmary had given him, or a jar of drawing salve that pulled stubborn slivers out of your fingers overnight. Some days, he reached into his pocket and tossed me a heavy cylindrical magnet the size of his thumb that had been salvaged from a cow stomach. Farmers shoved these magnets down the animals' throats to catch nails and wires that might otherwise pierce their intestines. A magnet was already an object of mystery, and one that had been inside a cow's stomach was enhanced in value by its association with the grisly and the sacred. Our kitchen drawer at home was filled with butcher knives of thick, discolored metal that Dad bolted between

matching hunks of wood in spare moments at work. He said he
was a "millwright." For all I knew he made knives for a living.

When the phone rang at lunchtime each day, we knew it
would be Dad, yelling above the roar and clatter of machinery,
needing us to yell back. He talked loud when he first came
home, too, until his ears had adjusted to the quiet. Starting out
before dawn and working overtime most days left him tired
and sore enough by late afternoon to stretch out on the living-
room floor and fall asleep, regardless of what went on around
him. We girls stepped over him to turn on TV or to read in the
big chair in the corner where he worked his crossword puzzles
in the evening.

Gradually I understood that animals were "slaughtered" at
the plant, that the cattle and pigs hauled into town in semitrailers, their ears and snouts poking through red wooden
cross-hatching, emerged from Wilson's as steaks and bacon.
Dad seldom talked about how this transformation took place.
Instead he told us stories about people with names like Booger
and Buckshot and the tricks they played on one another. To
celebrate Dad's birthday, they had carried him on their shoulders and sprayed him with the water hose. He didn't tell us
how powerful the stream of water was or what the hose was
normally used for. Once my sister asked him if he had a nickname at work. His face turned beet red and the grin stretched
so tight he couldn't answer at all.

Many of Dad's funny stories had a dangerous edge, like the
one about Buckshot falling into the condemned beef chute.
There was a hole in the floor of the beef kill where anything
that failed the federal inspector's test had to be tossed. One
day Buckshot got too close to the hole, lost his balance, and
fell three stories, headfirst, into a pile of contaminated beef.
Dad saw him disappear and rushed down to find an inspector

who could unlock the door to the chute. Buckshot's glasses had flown off and his face was covered with blood, "but it wasn't his own," Dad explained. He sat up, rolled his eyes, and muttered, "Where am I? Where am I?" "Well, Buck," Dad told him, "you're not in heaven."

Sheer good fortune put Lois Ann Kriesel in charge of our sixth-grade field trip to the packinghouse. A brand-new graduate from Mankato State Teacher's College, she seemed a species apart from the plump old-maid schoolteachers in their crinkly navy blue crepe, who shushed whispering girls and grabbed show-off boys by the shirtcollar. At twenty-one, Miss Kriesel was young enough to be our sister, inquiring enough to understand our morbid curiosity, and wise enough to know that our illusions about hot dogs and the enticing freedoms of adult life could use a reality test.

Turning real-life events into teachable moments was Miss Kriesel's strong suit. When Billy Emstad threw a tennis ball through the open classroom window and hit Miss Kriesel on the shoulder, she arranged a trial with judge and jury, who acquitted him for lack of proof that he intended harm. When we grew tired of the school's meager record collection—Haydn's Surprise Symphony was no longer surprising, and we knew all too well what the *klo-kla-klo-kla-klo* of Ferde Grofé's Grand Canyon Suite was supposed to represent—Miss Kriesel invited us to bring our own music: Elvis Presley and Fats Domino and Albert Lea's own Eddie Cochran. We hummed chords and tapped out rhythms and never imagined we were learning anything. The 1956 presidential campaign was rife with educational possibility, and Miss Kriesel set up rival political conventions. To keep things even, some of the Democrats had to volunteer to be Republicans, a chasm I couldn't cross even for pretend. I beat David Peterson for the Democratic nomination, a serious blow to a boy who was already planning his strategy for the 1980 presidential election. To retaliate, he offered Tootsie Rolls to anyone who promised to vote for my Republican opponent, Kathy O'Neal. I voted for her, too, with no Tootsie Roll reward, because it would have been "conceited," as we labeled any display of confidence, to vote for myself. Kathy had no choice but to be Republican, as I understood it, because her dad was management. But she was a nice girl and a good friend, and she offered us her dad's job title as a tongue twister: "Pickled pigs' feet foreman, pickled pigs' feet foreman, fickle fig peet . . ."

A field trip to Wilson's required a good deal of preparation, for what we might experience there and for how we would need to behave. I knew already, from Dad's stories, that the federal inspectors were very finicky. They discarded whole slabs of meat just for one small dot of impurity. A child bumping up against a skinned carcass would require the sacrifice of potential spareribs, loins, chops, hocks, hams, sausage, bacon. It might also mean nightmares for the child. Meat, at this stage, was still, after all, dead animal. Miss Kriesel prepared us for both contingencies, reminding us to be cautious and follow directions, and warning us that some things we saw might not be pleasant. If we didn't think we could handle it, we could ask our parents to write a note excusing us from school that morning. Once inside, we were committed to finishing the tour. There would be no turning back.

Wilson's office was a brick building about the size of Lincoln School, and the other packinghouse buildings loomed over it much the way the high school next door dwarfed Lincoln. As we gathered out in front, Billy Emstad's dad walked by and greeted us. He was buttoning a white coat, like a doctor's, over his suit. The suit, of course, meant that he had an office job. Before we could go into the plant, we had to listen to headcounts and price figures that only a brain like David Peterson's would still contain by afternoon. There were moans of disappointment from the boys when the guide announced that we would not be allowed to see the kill itself. I had heard my dad say that he spent the day working "up on the beef kill" or "up on the hog kill," and I imagined them up in a tower, like the Tower of London, where the kings of England had their enemies beheaded.

In those days, before cholesterol scares, before pasta and veggies, bankruptcies and buyouts, Wilson's worked to full capacity. Semitrailers lined up outside the stockyards waiting to unload their mooing and grunting freight. Our tour started with that phase of the process, watching the animals get lured up the ramp by the Judas goat, who led them, as literally as we would ever see it, like lambs to slaughter.

From there, we were ushered into the packaged meat division, where bacon was sliced and wrapped, and pork was ground and stuffed into casings or sealed in cellophane to be sold as wieners and bologna. There were women working in this area, a few familiar moms dressed in white coats and head coverings that looked like shower caps. Their hands moved quickly and they could look up only briefly to raise their eyebrows in greeting. It was strange, even a little shocking, to see them this way: hushed, restrained, their movements regulated by the rhythm of the machinery. It made their home behavior—the range of their voices, the rushing up and down basement stairs with baskets of wash—seem like random bursts of energy.

With fresh memories of ham baking in the oven, I expected that walking into the smokeroom and inhaling deeply would be a pleasure. Up close, the aroma gave way to a stench. It was as if the odor that hovered in the air on the Northside and hit the rest of us with a shift in the wind had been bottled, left to stagnate, and then released with a quick twist of the lid. Kids made gagging noises, pinched their noses, and crowded around the door, ready to escape. The smokeroom employees went on working as if they had no sense of smell.

So far, it was only raw and cured meat we saw, not much to remind us of the doomed creatures in the stockyard pens. Then, while we walked two abreast along a passageway, the line abruptly stopped and narrowed as the kids in front pressed their backs to the wall. "Those things are glaring at me," someone cried in a voice pitched so high with fright that it was unrecognizable. More shrieks, some laughter and jostling as we stared into pans piled with eyeballs, brains, hearts, and tongues. Tongues were a delicacy, the guide told us, and parts of the brain were used to make headcheese, a word that reminded me of toe jam, though I knew it was something that Danes ate in the Old Country, along with lard sandwiches. Stomach linings were cooked up and eaten as tripe, and the intestines were shipped down South, where Negroes ate them. Some internal organs were made into medicine to save us from deadly diseases. We might have taken the medicine without even realizing where it came from, the guide conjectured. Miss Kriesel slung her arms around the shoulders of the two rubber-legged kids standing nearest and reminded us of our promise to finish the tour.

We were not in heaven, and there was no turning back. We climbed wooden staircases, wove in and out of large, high-

windowed rooms, some filled with steam from vats of hot water, others damp and cold as the inside of a refrigerator,
where men hacked at red flesh, ground blades against bone,
stripped blue veins still leaking blood, and scraped pale yel-
low globs of fat from foul-smelling hides.

I kept an eye out for my dad the whole time. I knew from
his stories that he was out and about a lot. By this time, I had
learned that he spent his days fixing machines that had broken
down. I watched for his khaki pants and the rust-and-green
checked shirt he wore most often. He found my class before I
spotted him. "Cheri! There's your dad!" someone called, and
I turned and caught the gold-toothed grin on a man wearing
jeans a little too large and a blue shirt gone limp in the moist
air. I had never seen my dad in jeans. His legs looked even
shorter and stubbier than I knew them to be. He looked frail,
in spite of his stocky build, dwarfed by the proportions of the
room and pale in the yellow-green light. But he was free, not
moving to the pace of a machine or rooted to one square-foot
of floor space. Years later I read in a book about the meatpacking industry that the millwrights are an elite among blue-
collar workers, descendants of the skilled artisans who formed
the guilds that preceded the labor union. But at that moment,
against that backdrop, he just looked small.

Our tour indoors, we realized, was moving backward, from
finish toward start, easing us into the reality of animal slaughter. As we climbed higher in the building, slabs of meat became
carcasses, there were fewer women, and the men seemed to get
larger and more muscular. A man I recognized as the father of
a playground bully turned briefly to wink at us as he split one
smooth, pink hog carcass after another in long, powerful, vertical strokes. Another man was cutting the necks at the spinal

cord with a scissors larger and more threatening than a garden shears. Clip, clip, clip, the heads dropped loose so the next man could slice them off.

There was some hubbub in the group as we were routed into the space where newly killed hogs were hung to be drained of blood and then dropped into the dehairing tank. A couple of breathless boys claimed to have seen, through a briefly opened door, the killing itself, or at least the knock on the head that stunned the animal. Miss Kriesel pushed through the crowd to calm them, and we settled into reverential whispers before a sight that felt taboo, as though we were peering in on a secret ritual with the power to transform us. A conveyor mounted on the ceiling brought one huge, dead hog after another past us gawking children. The hog's expressions were not so different from ours—eyes fixed in fear, snouts and lower lips parted by gravity. Each body hung heavy from the chains that bound its legs, swinging slightly, ready to crack the ribs of anyone who got in the way. Blood was running in streams to the floor below. A younger man directed the blood toward the drain with a water hose, the kind they must have sprayed my dad with on his birthday. Still, blood splattered the shirts and soaked the workboots of the dads and uncles who would come home that afternoon deceptively clean.

One of the hogs was still half alive and squealing in agony. A man stabbed it quickly with a large knife and blood gushed from the wound in its throat. "Look at that!" David Peterson burst out. "He got him right in the jugular!" What has preserved this moment in my memory, as much as the gruesome sight itself, is the word "jugular." I had never heard it before. I didn't know what it meant. It was mystery—jargon that belonged to the work we were witnessing. I wondered why David Peterson alone had been let in on the secret.

Back at school, we spent the rest of the day ridding ourselves of the horror by telling one another, over and over, what we had seen and what we only thought we saw. I don't remember Miss Kriesel ever spelling out the message she had planted deep inside us, where fear and desire lie waiting for the spark that welds them into will: *Start planning your escape. Everything you do from now on must help you out of here.*

Dad Talks about His Work

At this telling, Gordy Register is an eighty-five-year-old dynamo, his energy wound down only a bit, and more by the tedium of my mother's Alzheimer's disease than his own physical ailments. He sits on the edge of his easy chair, his hands gripped around the front of the arms as though he's ready to spring up at the first drip of a leaky faucet or an off-tune hum in the refrigerator. He is a man who fixes things. His first day at Wilson's packinghouse, he won the coveted job of millwright. It was wartime and there was a need for skills and quick minds, for gifted Depression youth whose dreams of education and a chosen vocation had been disappointed. This critical work in the food industry even won him a draft deferment. He was thirty-one years old with a background of steady farm labor to recommend him, and, for motivation, a frustrated effort to earn enough as a wholesale grocery salesman to support his growing family. By the time he retired from Wilson's, in 1974, his age had doubled and his body had been molded into the burly shape of the laborer.

On an afternoon in 1943, on impulse, he walked into the Wilson employment office to see Don Carlsen, the hiring boss, who knew the Register family. "Well," Carlsen told him, "you boys have been pretty handy at fixing things. We've got some openings in the machine shop. Common labor is seventy cents an hour, but I'll start you out at seventy-five, give you a little boost." There were jobs available in both the millwrights' and the carpenters' gangs. Dad chose millwright because it offered more hours and more chance for overtime pay.

His first assignment was to fix the dishwasher in the plant restaurant, not much of a trial at all. The job that followed tested his stamina for packinghouse work. It plunged him right into the tankage, the foul, unusable animal parts that are dried into fertilizer:

"They told me to come in at five o'clock and help Larry Parker. He was working in the big dryers that dried all the tankage and stuff. We had to crawl in there and fix paddles. You had a little hole you had to crawl in and you could just barely get in there. The tanks were about thirty feet long and not very big around. They had a big shaft in there with paddles going around, and you had to crawl in between those paddles to work, and you didn't know if some yahoo was going to plug it in or something, so we always grabbed all the fuses out."

It was two years before he got his first raise. "My foreman came to me and he said, 'Well, I put in a raise for you for top pay. You've been doing a good job and you work hard and you always find something to do, so it isn't fair that you have to work for less money.' So I'd been there two years and I got top raise. It went up to ninety-five cents. That was quite a bit then."

Dad's job varied a lot his first years, both in hours and location, sometimes in the shop itself and sometimes "out in the house." He worked relief for the kill mechanics when they took vacations. Those days he went to work at two in the morning: "That wasn't a bad job, but the hours were kind of crazy. The kills started at seven, and we had to have everything ready to go in the morning when they came. Put water in the scalding tub and get it heated. Get all the machinery in shape and all oiled up and everything ready to go. Then we were on standby until noon."

Back in the shop, he made hand trucks for hauling: "I had to weld them and put them together and make up the pieces and figure out the angles on the thing so they'd all work right. I had that job for a long time." A breakdown on the line would rouse everybody out of the shop, as long as their work could be left sitting for a while. "Some of the jobs weren't so nice sometimes. You had to get in the wet and slush and the cold and hot. The coolers were the worst. When they had a big pileup in the cooler, they'd stop the whole kill because they couldn't get the hogs in there. So that was a hurry-up job. Every time we had a breakdown we had to really work hard to get things straightened out. You'd have about four or five foremen down from the office and they'd try to walk around in the way, and our foreman would tell them, 'You get out of the way so our men can work. We can't get anything done when you're standing around here.'"

Working on breakdowns and spelling vacationing members of the shop gang showed Dad the range of jobs done at the plant, as well as who did them. Give him a name and he can still tell you what that person did, plus choice facets of the person's character. Working conditions ranged from relatively clean, for the machinists who spent all day in the shop at their lathes, to grotesquely filthy and hazardous to the health.

"We had one guy that used to crawl in the big lard cars with a steam hose to steam them out. Those are the railroad cars—tank cars—that they ship the lard in. He'd come out of there just soaking wet, even in the wintertime. We had to get him in where it was warm.

"The worst job in the whole plant was working in the tankage room, breathing that tankage all the time when they were processing it. And then the hasher. All the guts and stuff went down in there and they had to grind them all up. Your clothes would just get plastered with that tankage and stuff. Booger would hang them in his locker, and the cockroaches would get in there so thick that anybody next door would get cockroaches, too. He pulled his clothes out and threw them on the floor a couple times and about a thousand cockroaches came out with it. Some of those darn things were about three inches long."

His last twelve years at Wilson's, Dad had a steady assignment as houseman up on the beef kill. He went to work at seven in the morning and stayed until the work was done, about five or six o'clock. "I had to see that everything was put away for the night and taken care of before I went home. I was the mechanic there. I took care of all the machinery. I did all the ordering of parts. We had a lot of air-powered equipment and I had to overhaul all that. They had about twenty air-knives going all the time. I had to grind the blades on those, and all the saws. I had to keep that stuff all in repair."

The three chains on the overhead rail system that carried the beef carcasses through the kill area also were Dad's responsibility. "A lot of times somebody'd foul up and they'd get the chains out of time, so I had to retime the whole thing. One chain would carry the beef on to another chain and that would pick up the beef and take it around. They had to mesh just perfect. Otherwise it wouldn't work."

Dad's relationship with foremen was generally smooth, with an exception or two, but he had a clear favorite:

"Helmer Olson was foreman on the beef kill, and he was the best guy to get along with there ever was. I knew Helmer when I was a kid, 'cause we were on the same threshing crew out by Conger. He'd stick up for you. One time they had a breakdown in the cooler and I looked at the rails and I said to Helmer, 'They need fixing.' So he went down to the shop and the shop foreman said, 'Aw, they don't need fixing.' And he said, 'My mechanic says they do, and you'd better get them fixed.' He would push. Ya, he was good, Old Helmer. He got mad at me one time and he called me a name. He wasn't supposed to do that. If I'd have turned him in, they would have raised heck with him downstairs. I went down to lunch, and Helmer sweat all the time I was gone. Then when I came back, he came over to apologize. He said, 'I hope you didn't say anything.' I said, 'Helmer, I fight my own fights. I don't have to go to anybody else.' After that he was the best friend I ever had."

One thing Dad appreciated about Helmer was that his promotion to foreman hadn't made him high-and-mighty or changed his loyalties.

"Helmer hated the scabs. During that '59 strike, when they wanted the foremen and office help to give rides to all those scabs they brought in, Helmer wouldn't do it. He just told them, 'I'm not hauling any of your damn scabs.' One time one of the scabs that stayed on in the machine shop after the strike was working up on the kill. They had a big chain they used to pull the beef with to put them on the rail, and the darn mechanic welded the chain and it broke and the beef fell. So Helmer called up the shop and he got a hold of Ben Jackson, who was mechanic foreman, and he said, 'How would you like to have a goddamn big log chain wrapped around your goddamn neck? One of your goddamn scabs fouled up and pret'near killed one of my men.' Ben said he wouldn't have had to use the telephone, he could have heard him anyway. The beef fell on the guy, crippled him for the rest of his life. He had to retire on disability."

This was not an unusual occurrence. Meatpacking still has the highest rate of injury of all American industry. If, as is usually the case, one worker in three will be maimed or scarred or disabled or killed on the job, then all three contend daily with the possibility. "Oh, I saw a lot of accidents," Dad recalls. "I saw guys that cut themselves so bad they had to have about ten stitches, or they'd cut the guy next to them. Then we had a guy by the name of Radar that worked there, and he was quite a drinker. He was working with one of those big air-clippers. They clip the legs off the cattle. He couldn't hardly stand up. He was staggering all over the place, and he was trying it out to see if it would work in the morning, and he was feeling of the blade with his hands. I said to Helmer, 'You better get that guy out of there. He's going to cut his arm off.' He looked at me and he said, 'Ya, I think so,' and he put him on another job. He'd have either cut his arm off or somebody else's. That'll snip the hind leg off a cow, just CRACK like that, it'll take it right off.

"One time Bozo Bennett was working on the saw and he sawed the cord. It knocked him off the bench. They said his eyebrows lit up and said 'Tilt.' He walked around and rubbed his head for about a half hour. I got that one time with a welder. I took a transforming welder that was supposed to have two lines hooked on power and one on ground, and the electricians hooked them all on power. I grabbed a hold of the welder and it knocked me on the floor. The handle fell on my leg, and I just stiffened. I couldn't let go of the thing. I still had a hold of the handle. Russ Hoyne was there and he pulled the plug. The electricians sat there and laughed. They thought it was smart. They were the ones that made the mistake. Another five minutes and I'd have been fried."

Like other situations of constant danger, packinghouse work breeds a black humor, a culture of mock violence that helps would-be tough guys live with their fear:

"People used to pull all kinds of stunts. There was a place where the hogs would go around the line, and the inspector stood there, and if the hogs weren't clean, they'd have to push them onto the siderail, see. One guy would always watch to see if he could get me. I had to walk down that aisle quite a bit, and then he'd swing those hogs down there. I was smart enough, I watched him and I'd duck and they'd go over my head. Oh, they'd pull all kinds of stuff. They threw pig toes and kept hitting us on the head. A guy did that to me three times, and I got up on the roof and I had a tub of water and I put a pail of ice in it, and then when he got over under the window I dumped it on him. He didn't do it anymore. Oh, you had to fight for your life out there."

Some packinghouse stories become legendary, told so often you wonder if they ever really happened. This one I've heard from others besides my dad: "One time they had a new guy shackling sheep, and the Judas goat was up there. He always led the sheep up. Well, this guy hit the goat on the head with a hammer and knocked him down and hung him up on the rail. One of the guys on the chain saw it and he stopped the chain and they took the goat down and put it in the pen again, and he laid there for a little while before he come to. And all at once he said, 'Brroww,' like that and he ran over the gate and down the chute. He never come up again. They couldn't get him to come up again. He'd had enough."

In his thirty-one years at Wilson's, Dad saw the wage scale

increase and the number of jobs decrease as the disassembly process became more automated. "When I first went there common labor was seventy cents an hour, and when I left in 1974 I was getting five dollars and a quarter, and that was top pay in the shop. Common labor was about $4.70. The best-paying job in the plant was the skinners, the people that skinned the beef. They got top brackets, probably $5.35. They even got as much or more than the engineers got. (I could have been an engineer one time, but I didn't want to breathe all that coal dust.) The beef were all laying on their back on the floor. They had to bend over to skin them. They had six beds and in each bed they laid six beef, and they'd go from one to the other. When they got them skinned so much, all except the back, they'd pull them up and hook them on the rail, and some guy down the line would drop the hide off. It was a tough job— hard on your back. We had one guy that was eighty-five years old that was skinning beef when I came, Old Frank Jara. But then they put in Can-Pak."

Can-Pak was an automated system introduced in the 1960s that did much of the skinning with circular air-knives and hydraulic hide pullers. It was, of course, both blessing and curse. Doing away with physically strenuous work was good for the workers' health, but it also deprived them of skilled work and reduced their pay to common-labor rates. Eventually it cut the workforce, a troublesome issue for the union. Can-Pak was a temporary boon to the machine-shop gang because installing it and keeping it in repair often required overtime work. A rare eighty-hour week getting Can-Pak up and running produced a whopping paycheck. As a highly skilled and experienced millwright, Dad was even sent to plants in Iowa and Indiana to help install Can-Pak and train the maintenance workers. Though he worked himself to exhaustion on these trips, he was obviously pleased that the company recognized his talent.

Can-Pak also saved Wilson's money by making formerly rigorous jobs accessible to women, who were paid on a separate, lower scale. Dad watched this change take place, too.

"For about three years I took care of the skinning machines on the hog kill. They'd save the hides to use when they made footballs and stuff like that. We were in first place in the whole division on the amount of fat on the hides when we threw them in. Albert Lea had the record for all the time I was on that job. I could set the knives just right. They had about ten or twelve of those skinners going all the time. They had girls on most of them—women. There were other women on the hog kill scraping hogs and saving glands, and things like that. There weren't too many on the kill itself, but a lot of them in casings down below, pulling chitterlings and washing casings. A lot of women worked in the sausage department and in the canned meats. They didn't pay as much. Every job had a different rate. The women couldn't do the heavy work. When those heavy jobs came open, some of the women applied for them. Then they'd have a big tub of meat to lift and they'd say, 'We can't do that, we're women.' Well, then they couldn't have those jobs."

In his twenty-ninth year at the packinghouse, Dad suffered his most serious injury: two broken wrists and permanent damage to his spine. When the call came that he was on his way to the hospital in an ambulance, Mom told us she had expected that call every single day he went to work. Dad describes just how it happened.

"I had to come in on a Saturday and we were in a hurry to get out, and I had to change oil in a machine up on top and so I had to go up a ladder. There was a bench about five feet high

and the ladder went up from that bench. I was taking the can
of oil in one hand and I had a hold of the siderail on the ladder, and the ladder went straight up. The night man had oiled
the rungs the night before. See, they sprayed oil on anything
metal that could rust. If the inspectors saw rust, they'd make
them get rid of it. Well, I had leather soles on my shoes and
they slid off. I came down about five feet and hit that bench on
my back and went off on the floor and caught myself with my
hands. I looked at my wrists and they were awful short. Both
of them were broken. I got up off the floor but the guys made
me lay down again till they come with a stretcher. I was laid up
for six months."

Much of his time and attention during that six months was
spent getting Wilson's legal department to agree that the injury entitled him to workers' compensation. He knew that if he
retired early on disability, Wilson's would also quibble over his
pension. But sticking it out until age sixty-two was also a matter of pride.

"Doc Steiner wanted me to take a retirement. I only had
two years to go, and I know if I'd taken a retirement on disability, why then, anybody'd see you mowing your lawn any-
time, they'd say, 'Look at that guy. He's disabled and he's out
mowing his lawn.' So I worked two more years. I went back on
my ordinary job on beef kill, but I couldn't handle it. It was too
much lifting. They brought a guy up there to do it and he
couldn't do it. So the last two years I just kind of helped him."

In retrospect, Dad's injury looks like a lucky break. After
much contention, he was awarded a $14,000 cash settlement
from Wilson's insurance company. "That's how we started our
nest egg," he says, as he tells how he invested the settlement
and managed it with his usual thriftiness. He also took up a

new career as a county commissioner, an elective office with a small stipend and health and retirement benefits. The fall from the ladder left him much better off financially than he would be on a $244-per-month Wilson & Co. pension. Loans from that nest egg have even helped his upwardly mobile daughters refinance mortgages and buy cars.

A Nod to Vegetarians

You may wonder why I have gone on so long about meatpacking without a word in defense of the slaughtered animals or a plea to readers to eat lower on the food chain. Truth be told, I am a carnivore. I eat meat in moderation, choosing fish and poultry more often than the red variety. But I never pass up an offer of Korean bulgogi, and I drive into Albert Lea with my taste buds set on a pork tenderloin sandwich.

I know that too much animal fat wreaks havoc on the human body. I would like to believe that limits on North American meat consumption will alleviate world hunger by freeing cornfields and rangelands for food crops. Nevertheless, if a vegetarian claims moral high ground in abstaining from meat, I bristle. Who, I want to know, will answer for the fate of towns that depend on the productivity of the packinghouse?

Whether humans are born carnivores or falsely acculturated to eating other species, there is no dishonor on the sliced bacon line. If there is dishonor on the kills, it is not in the basic act of killing for food, but in the grotesque speed and repetitive motions with which it is done. The model for human-animal interdependency is another I know from childhood: the 4-H kids at the county fair who sleep in the pens with the calves they have raised, knowing all along that they are destined for the slaughterhouse. What would become of cattle and pigs if they had no use as food? Would they survive running free in woods and plains or in city streets? Would the trendsetters fancy lapcows and guard hogs? Besides, anyone who recoils at eating living creatures should shudder before plunging a knife into a ripe tomato or tossing into that vile human mouth a handful of freshly picked berries, the most beautiful creatures on earth.

The human body's need for protein and iron has turned the bloody hacking of flesh into both livelihood and life risk. "Food processing" this work is called, a dispassionate term for the nasty transformation of raw material into edible goods. It is necessary labor, worth greater rewards than it earns. When food is detached from this process, and its value enhanced beyond reach of a packinghouse paycheck, my deepest loyalties get tested. Sitting in a linen-enshrouded restaurant, watching the candlelight flicker and gleam in my crystal water glass, I feel like an intruder. When the entrée is set before me, translated into French or Italian and concealed under exotic sauces, I see it for what it is: meat, pork, hog. I think about the people who "processed" it and wonder whether they have tasted it this way.

It isn't only meat that awakens these associations. A fancy salad, a plate of stir-fried tofu and vegetables also give me pause. I will respect your challenge to my carnivorous habits if you agree to honor the people who process your food. Please ask a few silent questions before you lift your fork: Who "walked" these soybeans in the hot sun? Whose back hunched to hoe these onions? Who picked these tomatoes, as the leaves prickled and stung his forearms? Who packed them for shipping, her elbows and finger joints steadily wearing away?

At the End of the Trail

A child of the 1950s, I was as enchanted as any other American kid with the myth of the Wild West. Huddled with my cousins in the darkness of the Rivoli Theater on Saturday afternoons, I slurped my Holloway bar as Roy Rogers or Randolph Scott rescued cattle and women and justice itself from the villainous schemes of Jack Palance or Lee Van Cleef. All week long we hunted each other, aiming cap pistols from behind bur oak trees, or lying in wait on the slope of a dirt mountain while the bad guys crouched in one of the newly excavated basements in our booming frontier neighborhood on the western edge of Albert Lea. Dressed in a hand-me-down fringed skirt, cotton-hide bolero, and red felt hat, I learned to push my well-practiced skip into a gallop. I had holsters, too, but they were usually empty. Girls didn't get guns for Christmas, so I had to borrow my cousins', when they would let me, or use a rock to bang and blacken my ten-cent roll of caps against the concrete steps.

Our landscape was waterlogged black soil that sprouted green even without planting. We played hard to conjure up the red canyons, the parched gullies, the trails packed firm and worn weedless by the hooves of a thousand head of cattle and the palominos and Appaloosas that drove them. "Git along! Gee! Haw!" we hollered as our bike tires spun in the loose gravel of Hillhaven Road and Belair Drive.

Beguiled as we were, we couldn't tell a *real* cowboy from the celluloid imitation. When we sat on the ditch embankment along the highway and waved at the cattle trucks slowing into town, the men who waved back wore feed caps, not Stetsons. Parked in a line along Garfield Avenue and Eberhardt Street, waiting to unload at Wilson's stockyards, they climbed out of their cabs, reached into their pockets, and drew the deadliest weapons they carried: packs of cigarettes and shiny metal lighters that smelled of gas. The cigarettes dangled from their lips as they lowered the gates at the backs of their trucks and let the cattle stumble out. No one hollered, "Git along, little dogie!"

It has taken me all these years of memory to realize that we lived the life we thought we had only imagined. When the cowboy reached the end of the trail, there we were, we Albert Lea kids with our holsters and high hopes. Those thousand cattle that thundered across the movie screen were herded into feedlots in places like Cherokee, Iowa, and Abilene, Kansas, to be "finished," or stuffed to prime weight, then trucked into Albert Lea or Ottumwa or Cedar Rapids to be "processed," finished for good. The point of all that lassoing and branding, the point of the movies' territorial shoot-outs, was to get the beef to market in time for the highest price broadcast on KATE radio's morning livestock reports. Once there, up the chute to the packinghouse kill, it took only two days of shift work and overtime to reduce a thousand head of cattle to meat, hide, and entrails.

Of course there were no wranglers or cowpokes or bucka-roos in Albert Lea. The men in bib overalls or khaki pants we passed on the sidewalks uptown, the men who ushered us into church in their Sunday serge were knockers, shacklers, stick-ers, splitters, neck breakers, gutsnatchers, kidney pullers, skin-ners, flankers, rumpers. Too big-bellied to be called "lean and lanky," they stayed ruddy or pale year-round. Only the farm-ers, who grew corn for cattle feed where the grazing range ought to be, had John Wayne's squint lines and weathered skin.

Dad was a cowboy fan, too. When we finally got a TV, just in time for my tenth birthday, the two of us perched together on the edge of the davenport to watch *Gunsmoke*, *Wagon Train*, *Death Valley Days*, *Wyatt Earp*, *Rawhide*, *The Virginian*. We winced when Doc sawed off a gangrene-infected leg or probed a painful wound to extract a bullet. Dad had learned to dodge the hazards of the cowboy's life: a finger severed by a boning knife, a face scalded in a burst of steam, an ankle twisted and broken in a misstep on a wet and bloody floor.

When Marshal Matt Dillon, caught in the small-town law-man's dilemma of conflicting allegiances, bravely held out for truth and justice, Dad sniffled a bit and poked a finger up un-der his glasses to catch the tear, trying not to look conspicuous. The Wild West myth offered an impassioned escape for our parents, who knew far more than we kids did of the reality it masked. I guessed that Dad envied the cowboy his wide, open spaces, his campfire under a starlit sky, his quiet, clear air.

The year I turned fourteen, we learned that "marshal" could also be spelled "martial." Albert Lea had become as un-ruly as the Wild West, the television news reporters claimed.

The lawman's six-gun was replaced with a rifle and bayonet, his ten-gallon with a riot helmet. As the strike dragged on all winter, I found a deeper attraction in the cowboy romance: its world of clear motives—evil or good—where bad guys never smile and certainly don't have children, and running them out by sundown frees the town of greed and intimidation and requires no sacrifice at all.

The Wild West has long since lost its popular appeal. As our fantasies unreeled across the screen before us, we never guessed that our real life, too, was dying away. During Dad's thirty-one years at Wilson's, employment in the meatpacking industry nationwide declined by one-third, even as production and profits rose. Neither Gene Autry nor Audie Murphy could outdraw that tall, black-hatted stranger, Automation.

The story of the American West is the story of meat, traced back from Stuart Anderson's cowboy-themed steak houses through the telltale smell of smoke-and-flesh that hovers over towns on the prairie to the Plains Indians' pursuit of the buffalo. "More than most other sectors of the nation's economy," historian Jimmy M. Skaggs writes, "the interstate red-meat trade encompasses the national experience, from the taming of a raw, unsettled frontier, which eventually gave rise to a complex agrarian supply base, to the evolution of industrial colossuses as competitive as any other American enterprises."*

Relics and monuments scattered across the country trace the meat industry's westward path of development. On a visit to the United Nations Plaza in New York City, I stopped to read a commemorative plaque. This was the site of the S & S

* Jimmy M. Skaggs, *Prime Cut: Livestock Raising and Meatpacking in the United States, 1607–1983* (College Station: Texas A&M University Press, 1986), 3.

(Schwarzschild and Sulzberger) packinghouse and stockyards, it told me, and I checked to see if it was a phantom, invisible to other tourists. Who else would care to honor meatpacking history? When the railroad and refrigeration moved meatpacking west from the coast, closer to the big cattle ranches on the Great Plains, Chicago became "Hog—and Beef—Butcher to the World." The Union Stockyards were touted as the Eighth Wonder of the World when their 350 acres of livestock pens opened for business on Christmas Day of 1865. A century later, when I moved into my college dormitory three miles away, the large disassembly plants that ringed the stockyards were closing down. All that remains now is the massive stone entrance to the stockyards on Halsted Street. With Chicago out of competition, South St. Paul became the largest livestock market, but it, too, soon declined. The South St. Paul Livestock Exchange, a five-story limestone building with copper cupolas and ornate woodwork that long sat boarded-up, has been refurbished and reopened as the Castle Hotel.

By the 1870s, when they built their Chicago plants, Philip Armour and Gustavus Swift were already fixing prices and dividing markets to protect each other's livelihoods. It is shocking to read that Armour's personal fortune reached $25,000,000 in 1890, a signal that the worst hazard of industrial capitalism, a vast disparity of incomes and interests between owners and workers, had definitely taken hold in meatpacking. When I learned in fifth grade about Jane Addams's good works at Hull House, I had no idea it was families like mine she hoped to save from destitution. The packinghouse workers themselves responded to the owners' greed with the founding of the Amalgamated Meat Cutters and Butcher Workmen (AMCBW) in 1896, and with a walkout of 22,000 employees in 1904. Journalist Upton Sinclair's novel *The Jun-*

gle, published in 1906, brought public scrutiny to the barbaric conditions in the new colossus that the slaughterhouse had become. But it was the mishandling of meat rather than the mistreatment of human beings that horrified influential, well-off readers, who lobbied Congress for food-inspection laws rather than for fair labor standards. *The Jungle*, or at least an excerpt from it, ought to have been required reading in Albert Lea High School's English curriculum. Some of us did learn Upton Sinclair's name at least, attached to the label "muck-raker." For a time, I aspired to be one.

Gilded Age Americans' taste for meat transformed the Great Plains, by the 1910s, into an expanse of cattle ranches, which fed not only stomachs but also the fantasies of those eager to preserve the mystique of rugged frontier life from the urban scourge of industrialization. It wasn't Upton Sinclair who first stirred my dad's boyish imagination, but Zane Grey, an Ohioan who published fifty-four novels about the Wild West. Dad can still recite the titles of his favorites. The cowboy, a laborer with as much actual social standing as a hired hand on a Midwestern farm, had morphed into American pop-culture hero. The image of the freewheeling, solitary cowboy obscured the truth that vast stretches of that wide-open range were owned by wealthy Eastern investors who chose the urban social whirl for themselves.

By the time Dad took a job in meatpacking, in 1943, there were few chaps-clad cowboys left. A national highway system and the refrigerated semitrailer truck had dispersed the industry from the big cattle-trading hubs to small towns in the corn belt where area farmers supplied grain-fed cattle that produced the tastier prime beef consumers now preferred. The booming market in cattle feed had transformed a landscape of prairie and wetland and hardwood groves into endless cornfields, man-size stalks with dark green ribbons waving on to the horizon.

In the meantime, the labor radicalism of the 1930s had launched a new Congress of Industrial Organizations (CIO) union to rival the Amalgamated's increasingly conciliatory policies. The United Packinghouse Workers of America, founded on the principles of democratic industrial unionism and racial equality, expected each of its local affiliates to be active in union governance. The Wild West had settled in my home territory, with packinghouses strung across the southern tier of Minnesota counties like knots on a rope. The true crusader for justice was no longer the Lone Ranger but the union steward, one keeping vigil in each department of the packinghouse.

Albert Lea's meatpacking history begins, in characteristic Minnesota fashion, as a Scandinavian-immigrant success story. I was surprised to learn who gets credit for laying the foundation. Two Swedish-born brothers, Axel and Charles Brundin, opened a retail butcher shop in 1877 in the center of Albert Lea, a city where Swedes were a rarity among Norwegian and Danish immigrants. The two boys were amazingly young to be so enterprising. At eighteen, Axel already had three years' experience as a retail clerk. Charles was just sixteen. They had come to the United States ten years before, along with their parents and siblings. Their father, John Brundin, operated a foundry and machine shop in Albert Lea and presumably offered them financial backing.

Both Brundins established themselves as leading citizens, Axel in local politics and public service, and Charles in music and entertainment. The same year the butcher shop opened, Charles, a cornetist and violinist, organized Brundin's Band, a twenty-piece ensemble of men and boys that played at local dances and festivals. Charles Brundin's violin is a familiar relic from my childhood. It hung on the living-room wall, above the piano, at my friend and classmate Ginny Jacobson's house. I knew it then only as her great-grandfather's violin and didn't know his name. I never heard the Jacobsons, who owned the fading Hotel Albert, boast about being packinghouse heirs.

Twenty miles to the east, in Austin, a contemporary of the Brundin boys, George A. Hormel, had also taken up the meat business. In 1891 he began building onto an old creamery he had converted into a slaughterhouse, redesigning it on the disassembly model of the Chicago stockyard plants. The Austin *Register* of that year reported that he planned to make his packinghouse "one of the leading industries of southern Minnesota . . . Mr. Hormel possesses tireless, persistent enterprise and vim which is bound to bring success." An exacting butcher and ham trimmer, Hormel initially worked alongside his employees, but by 1899, the company's official history records, he "put down the cleaver" and "put his overalls away," to become the dress-suited manager of the company.

The prosperity that the Hormel Company brought to Austin aroused some jealousy in Albert Lea. I've often thought of the Austin–Albert Lea relationship as a sibling rivalry, with Albert Lea as the neglected little sister. This anonymous poem in the Albert Lea *Times-Enterprise* of February 15, 1922, takes the same view:

Albert Lea vs. Austin

There, little girl, don't cry,
They have beaten your census, I know,
And with comment that stings
They have said horrid things

Since the days of long ago.
But time will tell, and you'll pass them by,
There, little girl, don't cry.

There, little girl, don't cry,
They are jealous of you, I know,
And the things they say
In that nasty way
Are to bolster their courage low;
For quality counts, more than gross amounts,
There, little girl, don't cry.

There, little girl, don't cry,
They have got the figures, I know,
And their high school new
And "Hormel's" too,
The plant that made them grow,
But they'll still be a bush when you're sky-high.
There, little girl, don't cry.

The quotes around "Hormel's" require comment. The company name was Frenchified to Hor-*mel* for greater commercial appeal, but the family kept the German pronunciation for private use, and you can identify us locals by our persistence in calling the company *Hor*-mel's. Outsiders who see Austin and Albert Lea as twin towns or, worse, confuse them overlook a decisive piece of their history: While Hormel's remained locally owned and vigilantly managed by George A. and his son Jay, who practiced a benevolent paternalism toward employees and community, the Brundin Packing Company took a very different turn. After rapid early growth, the Brundins opened the company to investment by other local businessmen and gave up controlling interest. Renamed the Albert Lea Packing Company, the slaughterhouse was moved in 1912 to the shore of Albert Lea Lake, its present site. Two years later, it closed down for a time because of an oversupply of meat on the market. Nineteen fourteen seems to have been a troubled year for small packers and a golden opportunity for the big companies. Armour was building a plant just thirty-five miles to the south, outside Mason City, Iowa, and soon Albert Lea, too, was being scoped out. The *Tribune* reported that "several heads of big packing concerns were in the city looking over the Albert Lea Packing Company with something in their heads besides idle curiosity. They stated that Albert Lea was the most logical point for a big packing plant than any other city in northern Iowa or southern Minnesota. The railroads furnish the best shipping facilities and the territory surrounding is a stock raising community which was passed upon very favorably by the big packers."

A Virginia corporation controlled by Sulzberger and Sons, an offshoot of Schwarzschild and Sulzberger, the old New York packers, ended up buying the Albert Lea Packing Company. Two years later, J. P. Morgan's heirs and the Rockefellers bought controlling interest in the corporation, ousted the Sulzbergers, put Thomas E. Wilson in charge of the meat-packing plants, and renamed the enterprise "Wilson & Co." When I first learned about the superwealthy industrial magnates of the Gilded Age, I had no idea their reach was long enough to set the course of daily life in my hometown, a town the Morgans and Rockefellers probably couldn't locate on a map without a gazetteer.

On Labor Day of 1923, the Albert Lea *Tribune* carried a holiday message from Thomas E. Wilson and characterized him as one who "came up through the ranks as a worker with

his hands as well as with his mind. He has retained an appre-
ciation of the viewpoint of the toiler as well as acquiring the
responsibilities of leadership." He did not live among his
workers as George A. Hormel did, however, but in a mansion
in Chicago's Kenwood neighborhood, a wealthy area just far
enough east of the stockyards that Lake Michigan's breezes
pushed the odors away. Thomas Wilson made occasional visits to his company's sites around the country, as did his son
and heir, Edward Foss Wilson. "They were nice people," Dad
recalls.

"Nice" is a relative term here, to be read in contrast to the
Wilsons' successor as company president, "Judge" James A.
Cooney, an Iowa native who had served briefly as a federal district judge. Wilson's hired Cooney away from the bench in
1926. He had already acquired a reputation as antilabor, and
he continued his union-busting as Wilson's company attorney
and vice president for labor relations. While the Hormels worried about how to stay competitive with low-wage packing
companies without skimping on safety and cleanliness, Wilson's management seemed more concerned about keeping labor costs down and curbing dissent. In a speech to the Rotary
in Owatonna, Minnesota, in 1937, Jay Hormel maintained
that if employers really understood labor, they would volun-
tarily recognize basic workers' rights such as self-organization
for collective bargaining, seniority for job security, and
"proper wages with extra earning power by the employer
bringing extra wages or bonuses to employees." "The idea that
an employer is the lord and master of his own business is an
antiquated notion," he continued. "If you are an employer or
if you are the proprietor of a business, you have a job and a
trusteeship." Whether this was spoken from the heart or as a
concession to the Independent Union of All Workers (IUAW),

which was achieving a foothold in both the Hormel and Wilson plants, is beside the point. Judge Cooney would never have uttered such words. That same year, the newly constituted National Labor Relations Board (NLRB) had to intervene to stop Wilson's from setting up its own company union in Albert Lea, a violation of the Wagner Act of 1935.

Judge Cooney's promotion to Wilson's presidency in 1953 was not a good omen for the company's production workers. Management personnel remember him as a stern personality yet a fair-minded employer, but in union households like mine he was a Wild West robber baron who maintained a terroristic control over our town. Rumors flourished that he would punish demands for better working conditions by pulling up stakes and moving the Albert Lea plant down South, where the labor movement was weak. A local story tells of Judge Cooney declaring to the chamber of commerce that if it weren't for Wilson's, grass would grow down the middle of Broadway. He was no more beloved in Chicago. An article in *Forbes* magazine in August 1959 claimed that Cooney "probably qualifies as the most unpopular man in town. . . . Rightly or wrongly it is he who is credited with having touched off the industry's wholesale exodus from the city." He became even more demonized when news spread that he had doubled his share of Wilson stock by trading at an insider price less than one-third the stock market cost. "Cooney stole the company on stock options, you know," my dad reiterates nearly every time his name comes up.

During September and October of 1959, while Wilson's was holding off on a new contract with the UPWA, the Hormel Foundation, established in 1941 to serve "religious, charitable, scientific, literary, or educational purposes," was building a $500,000 research institute in Austin. Wilson's brought no

such benefits to the city of Albert Lea or any other of its plant
locations, despite additional profits from its sporting-goods
company, which used up the animal hides, and its pharmaceutical division, which made medicine from glands and other tis-
sue. Despite its dominant position in Albert Lea's economy,
Wilson's never enjoyed a good reputation as a corporate citizen. "Headquarters" in Chicago, 400 miles distant, was the
point of recalcitrance. The local plant manager, plant superintendent, and other "bosses" blended well enough into the
community, joined churches, fraternal orders, and service
clubs, and sent their kids to school with the rest of us. Some of
them were Albert Lea natives, old pals of the laborers they
oversaw. But in times of conflict, they were the front line of defense for the top management and the owners, who stayed
safely removed from the fray.

The packinghouse sat just outside the city limits, which
meant that Wilson's avoided the tax obligation that would
have helped educate the children of its employees. Nor could
the plant be held subject to the city's public health codes. The
Minnesota Department of Health repeatedly investigated
complaints about the odors in the air and the pollution of local waters and urged that Wilson's cooperate with the city in
building a sewage-treatment plant. Sometimes citizen protests
against the plant's foul emissions took the character of guer-
rilla theater. Dad tells a story that circulated, about a certain
meeting between health officials and Wilson "bigshots" from
Chicago. As the bigshots extolled their excellent sanitary provisions, Owen Johnson, the local parcel-post man and a life-
long conservationist, walked in with a bucket of bloated animal parts he had fished out of Albert Lea Lake and dumped
them on the conference table.

In 1960, after strike violence highlighted the fact that Wilson's had only a limited entitlement to city police protection, a serious, determined effort to annex the packinghouse was finally undertaken. The argument in favor of annexation was simple enough, in Mayor Niles Shoff's view: "If they are going to live on the fruits of the city, they should be a participant in the city and pay taxes in the city." The newspaper coverage of the heated public debate about Wilson's and the city's mutual obligations is colorful and revealing. Twenty-some local businessmen turned up at a city council meeting to ask that annexation efforts be dropped. Even the most vociferous argument on Wilson's behalf was damning. Comparing the $19,000 in additional taxes to the loss of a $165,000 payroll should the company get mad and pull out of town, Chamber of Commerce President Floyd B. Nichols argued, "I feel we need that plant far worse than they need us. . . . We just can't afford to cross Wilson. I'll grant that Wilson is all wrong, but gentlemen, we can't afford to cross them." This fear of a punitive response was, as it long had been, persuasive, and the city council voted to drop the annexation proposal. The next day a political activist identified in the style of the times as Mrs. Keith Quinlivan wrote a long letter to the editor of the *Tribune* charging "pressure tactics," "corruption," and "decadent" behavior. A specially called council meeting one week later was packed with observers. The council immediately rescinded its previous vote and put annexation back on the agenda. Floyd Nichols likened this change of mind to pouring salt into an open, festering sore—a reference, no doubt, to the lingering effects of the strike. Asked why Wilson's hadn't sent a representative to state their own case, Nichols answered, "I have tried to get them up here and they said the town can dry up as far as [they] are concerned."

As it turned out, there had been a gentlemen's agreement

in effect since 1914, the year the plant was sold to Sulzberger & Sons, to sweeten the deal for investors by allowing the company to remain outside the city. This agreement had been renewed as recently as 1950. Once the secret was revealed, the annexation bill passed easily. On April 24, 1961, a banner headline in the *Tribune* proclaimed, WILSON TO ENTER CITY.

I wonder what course the city-packinghouse relationship might have followed had the Brundins held on as firmly as the Hormels did. Might Charles and Axel have become wealthy benefactors, outfitting the hospital with new technology and the high school with labs and books and athletic facilities? Would the kids of my generation have stayed home for job security with a company that seemed to value their labors, rather than fleeing town for cleaner, more highly regarded work? Of course, the Hormel family's beneficence and hometown loyalty did not last forever. Third-generation George II jet-setted away from Austin and married a French movie star, Leslie Caron. I like to imagine my friend Ginny Jacobson as the Geordie Hormel of Albert Lea, married, perhaps, to Alain Delon. Would her mother still have been our Brownie leader? Would she have invited me to her birthday parties in the Brundin mansion, later donated to the city for civic uses? I doubt that she would be writing pension plans and living up the street in an ordinary wooden house in my middle-class Minneapolis neighborhood, as indeed she does now. In spite of her family's humble origins and its reverence for skill and hard work, Ginny would, like the Hormels, be filthy rich, and the rich develop interests at odds with those who serve them. Once the Hormel family was out of the management picture, the company rescinded the extra wages and bonuses that Jay Hormel had instituted, even as profits soared. The Hormel

Foundation, seeking higher and higher returns, now invests its money outside Austin, over the protests of local citizens, who cite Jay Hormel's legacy of stewardship. There is no just and satisfying ending, either in fantasy or reality. But I can make myself smile when I imagine Ginny's daughter, adopted from an orphanage in northern India, as the heiress to a meatpacking fortune.

Smiles are not my usual response to developments in the meatpacking industry. Shock is more likely. I remember Dad telling me, in 1967, that Wilson's was being taken over by Ling-Temco-Vaught, a conglomerate with no particular interest in meatpacking which was, he said, buying up businesses and running them into the ground. He and his coworkers were justifiably nervous at the prospect. In the fourteen years that LTV owned Wilson's, it sold off the sporting-goods and pharmaceutical lines, closed the older, larger plants, and drastically cut beef production. Albert Lea's plant, which was growing obsolete, got little money for updating and repair. When Wilson's was spun off from LTV in 1981 to become an independent corporation again, it was left with sixty million dollars of debt. Conglomerate takeovers left the union scrambling as well. Plant closings and downsizings drastically reduced the UPWA's membership, and in 1968 it merged with its rival union, the Amalgamated Meat Cutters and Butcher Workmen. The AMCBW was suffering losses, too, and the joint union eventually moved in with the Retail Clerks under the umbrella of the United Food and Commercial Workers (UFCW). For a time, the packinghouse locals kept a P in their name as a final mark of identity.

In April 1983, my then husband, a lawyer with a large Minneapolis firm, came home with news he felt compelled to tell me, in violation of his ethic of confidentiality. Wilson's was filing for bankruptcy. Though he was not involved in this case, I felt tainted by the privileged information. He should be warning the Wilson employees, not confiding in me. Don Nielsen, president at the time of Local P-6 and of the "Wilson chain," the assembly of Wilson workers within the United Food and Commercial Workers union, told me recently how he learned of the bankruptcy:

"We had settled a contract in '82, and it was a good contract. We had cut back in some areas, but it was basically a good contract. We went into Chicago for a Wilson chain meeting. We met out at the hotel at the airport, first time we ever met there. The regulars came in a night ahead of time, and everybody's just wandering around and having a few drinks, and everybody's talking to each other from the different plants. I was sitting down in the bar having a beer and here starts dribbling in all of the bigshots from Wilson's, along with the plant manager from Albert Lea, and the personnel manager from Albert Lea and all the other plants. I went up to the room and called our gang together and I said, 'I don't know what's going on here, but we got more than just us here. I see the whole company's here.' The next morning we started our meeting about nine o'clock. We were meeting in a big conference room—just the Wilson chain—and the telephone rang. Lewie Anderson was at that time director of the packinghouse division and he answered the phone and said that Don Davis, who was head of Wilson's personnel, wanted Lewie and I to meet him downstairs and talk to him. So we went down. And he said, 'As of now, we have just filed bankruptcy. You no longer have a contract.' And he gave us another contract and he says, 'That's it.' He dropped the rates down to $6.50 an hour from $10.69. It went down to *$6.50 an hour.*"

The union tried to avoid a strike by asking workers to put in forty percent less work for forty percent less pay while the officers pursued negotiations. But it did take a strike five weeks later to bring the base wage up to $8.50, a twenty percent cut. Though the bankruptcy was unexpected, Nielsen had reason to suspect that the company was in financial trouble. There were rumors that Wilson's president had risked and lost a good deal of money in the futures market. A man from Wilson's headquarters had come by the Union Center one afternoon to ask if the union had any interest in buying the plant, as the Rath workers in Waterloo, Iowa, had done. It was a rare instance of labor and capital appreciating their uneasy dependence on each other. Nielsen shook his head in dismay as he recalled this conversation, "You've got to have money to run a plant."

Bankruptcy reorganization did not help Wilson's recover. The Albert Lea plant was closed the next year, then reopened as Cornbelt Meats, by local investors who struggled to keep it alive through temporary shutdowns and reorganizations. Renamed Farmstead Foods, it finally gained solid footing, it seemed, when Seaboard Farms, based in Merriam, Kansas, took it over in December 1990. The city had courted Seaboard with loans and grants to improve the facility, including a new hog kill and low utility rates. A massive, new, $34,000,000 wastewater treatment plant had already been built to accommodate the packinghouse's constant water flow. Seaboard, for its part, reduced wages even below Wilson's post-bankruptcy level, leaving its workers unable to afford housing and in need of public services. "It's what we had to do at the time," City Manager Paul Sparks later explained to *Time* reporters investigating Seaboard's reliance on corporate welfare. "I don't know what else we would have done to get people back to work."

On my daughter's eleventh birthday, January 19, 1994, we went out to celebrate at a neighborhood pizza parlor. The loudspeaker just above our booth was broadcasting radio music at low volume, and I strained to hear as the music was interrupted by a news item: "Seaboard Farms has announced that it is closing its hog and lamb slaughtering operation in Albert Lea, a loss of 650 jobs." Impending death again. This time, a $720,000 dislocated-workers' grant from the State of Minnesota offered job retraining and tuition assistance to those left unemployed. For some, like my cousin Michelle's husband Bruce and my high school classmate Steve, layoff was a way out of taxing labor and a new start in boilermaking or mechanical drafting. That following May I talked with six Albert Lea High School seniors whose parents had worked at the plant. There were rumors, they said, that Seaboard planned to move what was left of the processing operation to Oklahoma. Unemployment, or the fear of it, was causing tensions at home, and they hardly dared talk too eagerly about their plans for college, which could be scratched at any time.

The meatpacking industry has become unrecognizable to those who knew it in the days of the UPWA. In a development known as the "IBP Revolution" after Iowa Beef Packers' quick rise to the top, packing companies have broken down skilled jobs into a series of repetitive motions on a faster-paced disassembly line, and dispersed the work to small slaughterhouses and processing plants that employ nonunion workers at wages as low as one-third the buying power that kept my family afloat in the 1950s. The pay scale doesn't appeal to the long-term residents of the small towns and rural areas where the plants are located, nor does it secure adequate housing for the Latino, Laotian, Somali and Balkan immigrants who are brought in, sometimes with the support of refugee resettlement programs, to take these undesirable jobs. Unorganized, unable to converse with many of their fellow workers, and eager to move on to more tolerable work, the new packinghouse workers have little bargaining power with IBP (now owned by Occidental Petroleum), Excel (owned by Cargill), or ConAgra, which bought up Armour, Monfort, and Swift in the 1980s. "The New Breed Meatpackers" is the name that industry observers apply to these agribusinesses. "The New Jungle" is investigative journalists' term for the modern packinghouse.

Albert Lea is experiencing the best, maybe, of drastically limited possibilities. Farmland Foods, the largest farmer-owned cooperative, with half a million members in the United States, Canada, and Mexico, owns the plant these days and employs nearly 500 people in the final processing of convenience foods made of meat slaughtered elsewhere. Freeborn County residents describe Farmland as a "decent" employer, and UFCW Local 6 helps keep it that way. Chuck Lee, the former president of Local 6, calls Farmland "pretty good, smart operators. I think if there's money to be made, they'll be able to make it, and if there's any salvation for this plant, they're the ones that can probably do it." A classified ad in February 1998 announced openings in production at a starting wage of $7.90 an hour, but by the end of 1999, thanks to a labor shortage, it was up to $8.85. New hires who survived probation could expect $9.60 in a year, plus life insurance, medical and dental coverage, a 401-K retirement plan, and paid holidays and vacation. A new ham operation doubled the workforce in 1999, and there are hopes that Farmland might continue to expand, even reopen the kills, but that may be nostalgia speaking. In the meantime, the old Land O'Lakes poultry plant has evolved into Schweigert, with nearly 400 employees, and the union is optimistic about its future.

Albert Lea has weathered an uneasy century-long co-existence with the meatpacking industry and opted to re-distribute its eggs among several baskets. Civic, business, and labor leaders have worked hard to diversify the town's econ-omy. The effort began at the end of World War II when the U.S. Department of Commerce offered to aid selected cities that would serve as models in providing jobs and housing to re-turning servicemen. Jay Hormel, in a neighborly gesture, nominated Albert Lea, and the city geared up to accept the of-fer. Jobs, Inc., was created to recruit new industries and situ-ate them in newly built industrial parks with water, sewer, elec-tricity, and a labor force imbued with the work ethic. Its initial successes were featured in national business magazines, and the momentum has persisted. As Albert Lea's other large manufacturers have closed or downsized, small workshops of less than one hundred employees rise up to ease the loss. Four hundred new jobs were created in 1997 alone. The town boasts virtually full employment, yet thirty percent of its ele-mentary students come from families with incomes low enough to qualify for the federally subsidized school lunch program. These are the "working poor," a category made up of common, ordinary people such as my family was in the 1950s. Among laboring people, there is suspicion that local business interests have turned away high-wage, unionized in-dustries. "It's hard to put a finger on any specific situation," Chuck Lee says. "We know for a fact that there were business people that had strong feelings about keeping affiliated union companies out of here. I don't think it's a personal thing as far as us guys that were involved. It's just the idea that they didn't want their place of business organized, and they felt that if the town became too well organized, then they would be on the list. And of course some of them were."

It is no longer the cattle drive that ties Albert Lea to the myth of the ever-expanding American frontier but other Wild West images that prod it to keep struggling for survival as a laboring town: The cowboy riding off into the sunset. The ghost town—mined out, cutover, decaying. I see the signs of prosperity: the sprawling, highly mortgaged new housing north of town, which masks the shortage of low-cost housing for unskilled workers; the new high school under construction; the chain hotels along the freeway exits. Yet when I drive by the old plant, I feel a hot, dry gust of desert wind. I miss that putrid, yet comforting, slaughterhouse smell. There's no grass growing on Broadway, as Judge Cooney predicted, but it's so quiet at times I wouldn't be surprised to feel a tumbleweed nestling against my leg. My kids are convinced that no one under sixty lives in Albert Lea, and I'm told it's because the teenagers are at home watching videos—no cowboy shows for this era, but equally escapist action thrillers. Big Bad Wal-Mart is making off with the cash that used to be spent at the locally owned Skinner's Department Store, now long gone. As I recall how bustling Broadway used to be, I'm struck for the first time by the irony of "Skinner," one of those old occupational names. Even Albert Lea's leading merchant family was branded with an ancestral memory of the slaughterhouse.

LEGENDS AND LOST HISTORIES

How We Became Working Class

My entire family failed at farming in one of the richest
stretches of the corn belt, where water was so plentiful it had
to be drained away and the soil was so thick that geologists
could find no exposed rock. I used to make this claim with a
perverse pride. At Albert Lea High School in the 1960s, the
quickest teasing insult one town kid could flip at another was
"You farmer." The reasons for this town–farm antagonism
were never quite clear to us, except when Wilson's recruited its
strikebreakers from the farms that produced its livestock.

Four distinct kinds of Freeborn County farmers live on in
my memory—categories derived from biased observation and
local stereotype rather than any clearheaded survey of census
records. The dominant group was the Norwegians and Ger-
mans—lanky and slow of speech—whose wealth was obscured
by Old Country frugality. Lutheran churches thrived under
their beneficence, and their sons, recognizable by their blue
Future Farmers of America jackets, could count on farming

their own share of the family's land someday. Then there were the big sugar-beet and vegetable growers around Hollandale, Dutch masters of the peatlands whose daughters wore matching sweater sets and Capezio flats and referred to migrant workers as "our Mexicans." I see now, by the county plat books, that there were few of these, and that most Hollandale farmers had relatively little acreage. The third group was also smaller in reality than I remember it: those who owned choice land that others farmed while they worked at professions in town. These land speculators' names matched city streets and buildings, suggesting an early and long-held claim to the land. The speculators' work was done by the fourth group: renters, with houses and pickups in need of paint and kids at risk of getting "sent up" to reform school.

Against these stereotypes I posed my own heroic family image: my great-grandfather Elbert Ostrander, whose eighty acres produced raspberries and watermelon more readily than the lucrative grain crops. Stories told by his children, the oldest my Grandma Grace Register, portrayed him as more passionate about politics and the natural landscape than about agriculture. He would stop plowing in midfield to follow a flock of Canada geese to Bear Lake or to write one of the long and rather florid, yet incisive poems and essays he published in local magazines under the name Elbert H. Ostrander, Freeborn County Pioneer. ("Pioneer" was a boast better suited to his parents, who had come out from New York via Wisconsin in 1859.) My favorite poem is dedicated to Farmer-Labor Party Governor Floyd B. Olson and the Minnesota Legislature in honor of the 1933 moratorium on farm mortgage foreclosures.

Grandpa Ostrander was too splendidly eccentric a character to fit my lackluster image of farmers. He trusted newly released felons from the state prison to work alongside his chil-

dren; he kept a pet bear; he learned Danish so he could speak
to the immigrants. He read Shakespeare aloud at the supper
table and encouraged his daughters to study medicine or law.
(None of them took his advice.) Only lately have I learned,
from my youngest great-aunt, just who paid the price of his in-
difference to farming. His tiny, frail wife Bertha, who bore
eleven children in twenty-four years, hauled water from an
outdoor pump long after neighboring farms had generators
and kitchen spigots.

My pride has been tempered by adult understanding and
accumulated knowledge. I can see now the loss, the humiliation, the sorrow in my family's unsuccessful efforts to live off
the land. It was loss that consigned my dad and many other
farm kids of his generation to the factory instead: to turning
farm products into food, for an hourly wage, at a pace determined by cost-effectiveness rather than the rising of the sun
and the cycle of the seasons.

It's no mystery why my mother's parents, Francis and Alma
Petersen, were washouts as farmers. They had not grown up
on the land. Friends and distant cousins, they emigrated to the
United States from the urbanizing east shore of Denmark as
working-class teenagers. Francis, who had begun his work life
at twelve in a Copenhagen cigar factory, left at eighteen to join
his wandering father in Alden, just west of Albert Lea. Like
Clarks Grove to the north of Albert Lea, Alden was already a
well-established Danish community. Back in Denmark five
years later, in 1911, he persuaded nineteen-year-old Alma
Jensen, his sister's friend, that America was her safest escape
from a romantic triangle that had set two lovesick brothers at
each other's throats. She, too, had gone to work at twelve,
picking fruit in an orchard, and had since found a job to her
liking as a cook in a Roskilde boardinghouse. Relocated in

Alden, she was hired on at fellow Dane Peter Lauritsen's restaurant. Francis had worked as a farmhand on his first so-journ in the United States, even after surrendering all four fingers of his left hand to a corn sheller. This time, he found a job driving a wagon for Hemmingsen Transfer Company.

After six years of marriage and three children, the first of whom died in infancy, the Petersens opted to try the area's most common path to financial security. In the sixteen years they spent farming, however, they never earned enough to buy their own land. They moved from the Melander farm to the Carl Nelson farm to the Walker farm, routed once by a fire that destroyed their house and all its contents. In 1934, with three of their six children still at home, they gave up farming altogether and took over a vacant building on Alden's single commercial street. An auction of farm machinery and live-stock yielded $1,000, the same amount they had invested in their first farm in 1918.

Their final enterprise, which lasted twenty years, suited their talents much better. Petersen's Cafe, a simple white storefront with a banging screen door, was, for my sisters and me and our baby-boom cousins, a land of enchantment, where grandmotherly love was dished out in double-dip ice-cream cones topped with malted milk powder. "The restaurant," we called it, without meaning to exaggerate. It was a narrow, linoleum-floored room with a bar along one wall, four or five booths along the other, and a short lunch-counter in back. It smelled of beer, sweeping compound, and boiled potatoes, and was so thick with cigarette and cigar smoke that our eyes still stung as we closed them for sleep in the car on the ten miles home to Albert Lea. Beer flowed from the taps behind the bar, soothing the pains of the old Danish farmhands who nodded off in the dark, varnished booths, heads falling forward and fingers relaxing their grip on the beer glasses. Grandpa, "Lille Frankie," as Grandma called him, stood behind the bar—skinny, subdued, and a bit pickled himself much of the time. He seemed an odd match for Grandma, a heavy woman with a resounding laugh and generous disposition who limped from kitchen to serving counter on a misshapen ankle. Her leg had nearly been severed when a house trucked in to replace theirs, which had burned down, slipped off its jack. The jolt tore a crack in the porch floor and her foot was caught in it. She held the foot in place with her hands all the way to the hospital.

Roomers from the Hazel Hotel across the street, mostly single men, boarded at the restaurant. They turned up at noon each day for a sixty-cent meat-and-potatoes dinner and returned in the evening for the "sanvits" Grandma made from the leftovers. Alden had a busy street life in those days, and Petersen's Cafe was its throbbing center. The door banged often as people stopped by to report good news and bad, seek Grandma's counsel on problems of home or heart, share a ribald joke, or confide secrets in Danish, the adult code that let us kids know this conversation wasn't for us. The restaurant welcomed every quirky character in town: Herman High, who slept in a car full of boxes behind the hotel and drained any beer glasses left standing on the bar; Jack Beach, who walked on tiptoe, with head down, to avoid stepping on cracks; and Wobbly Pete, whose name says it all. On the sidewalk across the street, Bena Bearhide sat wrapped in a blanket on a wooden chair and watched nothing much happen. "Misfit" was the word I first thought to use for these people, but they actually fit just fine in a town of less than 700 that seemed to have a place for everyone.

We kids had the run of the restaurant. In the kitchen, we

eavesdropped on the women who sat at the round oak table pouring out their troubles while Grandma sliced and stirred and sighed "Gud bevare oss," God preserve us, which we repeated as "Goopevass." Out in front, we were privileged to flip the switch of the jukebox and punch tunes for free: "The Blue Skirt Waltz," "I'm Looking over a Four Leaf Clover," and "Too Fat Polka." The regular customers slipped us nickels for twirling and tap dancing across the linoleum or doing arithmetic in our heads, while the occasional strangers who chanced by the place at lunchtime looked puzzled. Jensy Boy, a tall, lean Dane with a mottled red face and a wool tweed sports cap (known in our family as a Jensy Boy cap), dipped into his pocket and pulled out silver dollars.

Behind the childhood idyll was a harsh adult world of alcoholism, fist fights to break up, wayward husbands to hunt down and drag on home, shell-shocked veterans to pity and comfort, and, I learned much later, outcast homosexual men to mother. Proprietorship, entrepreneurship, whatever you might call the good fortune of owning a small-town business, was sheer hard work: hauling beer cases up from the damp basement, scrubbing counters and floors, washing and scalding dishes and pots, vanquishing rats and cockroaches. I have never entertained any fantasies of getting rich quick on a trendy restaurant idea.

Grandpa and Grandma and my bachelor uncle Kenny lived in an apartment above the restaurant, and Mom and Dad and my two sisters and I squeezed in with them for several months in 1948. Dad had been using his weekends and vacation time to build us a new house on the outskirts of Albert Lea when a strike at the plant depleted our funds and made the rent on the duplex we lived in unaffordable. We would just camp out in Alden until the weather warmed up enough to let us move into the shelter of our unfinished house. Nancy, at thirteen, was greatly embarrassed by our temporary uprootedness and feared being expelled from school if anyone learned that we no longer lived in the district. There was plenty of opportunity to get caught. Uncle Kenny, a young, fun-loving veteran who dropped Nancy and Joey at school on his way to work, was often running late, and Nancy had to conjure up yet another excuse for the attendance monitor. "Hangover" was a word we learned not to repeat to just anyone. Yet Mrs. Brenneman, whose name Nancy remembers with gratitude, evidently saw her distress and always excused her. Toddlerhood protected me from such humiliation. I celebrated my third birthday above the restaurant, and the few incidents I remember—my tumble down the stairs, tailing Kenny across the street to the pool hall—are preserved like glossy photographs with a fog of thin white cracks from affectionate handling. Return trips to Petersen's Cafe, a Sunday ritual, felt like homecomings.

Late each Sunday afternoon, we said our lengthy Minnesota good-byes at the restaurant, packed ourselves back into our 1940 Ford, and headed out to my dad's parents', Leslie and Grace Register's place, just three-quarters of a mile away at the edge of town. Walnuts pinged the roof of the car as we pulled into the driveway, the yard lit up, and Grandpa's "Hellooooo" resonated in the cooling air as he hurried out to welcome us. "Place" was the only suitable word for this not-quite-farm, a nine-acre oasis of fruit and weeds in the monoculture desert of corn. Across the road, a wealthy farmer's fattening herd of steers kept a steely-eyed watch on our comings and goings, unaware of their own imminent departure to Wilson's packinghouse.

As I prepare to describe the Register place, the word that comes to mind is "déclassé," a contemptuous term I imagine hearing from those who have no intimacies outside the educated middle class. It does fit the signs of ruin all around, but I feel no contempt—only a nostalgic fondness. A tumbledown coop at the back of the yard held nothing but rusty machinery, moldy feathers, and the lingering smell of chickens. It would have been a great place to play if it hadn't stunk so badly. Beyond it lay a field of strawberries that Grandpa and Grandma sold in pint and quart baskets or on a pick-your-own basis. What we kids picked went, of course, directly from hand to mouth. Gradually, the strawberries gave way to junked cars owned by—or at least in the doubtful possession of—a hustler cousin. Imaginary driving trips became our favorite outdoor game.

Grandma tended a small orchard at the side of the house, a tangle of apple trees, grapevines, and prairie flowers, known in those days as weeds. A proliferation of cats crawled out from under rotten boards, furniture, or up the musty basement steps. Grandma was a delightfully messy housekeeper, and her house was a respite from Mom's constant vacuuming and scrubbing, which turned our postwar rambler into a model of propriety. Once when she was helping Grandma clean up, Mom found the doughnut maker soaking in the sink. "Oh, did you make doughnuts this morning?" she asked. "No," Grandma said, "that was a couple days ago." Mom sucked her nostrils shut, gave the inside of the doughnut maker a good swipe with the dishrag, and let out a shriek. Clinging to the dishrag were two black snails. "So *that's* where they went," Grandma said, unfazed. "I knew they'd crawled out of the aquarium."

From the evidence on the dining-room table, you could never quite tell if a meal was coming or going. Mostly, meals were *on*going, as relatives, neighbors, hunters, and campaigning DFL politicians dropped in expecting to be fed. Visitors rarely rang the doorbell but just tromped up the short flight of stairs from the back door, announcing themselves on the way. The front door was usually blocked with furniture, so the kitchen was the point of entry, whether the guest was a reform school parolee with no home to go to or Billy Williams, long-time aide to Minnesota's governors, who came down every year for pheasant season.

Grandma Grace was a precious pewter spoon in a silver-plate world, a small, round woman with twinkly blue-green eyes that squeezed shut when she laughed, which she did readily, often at her own jokes and follies. A valedictorian at Alden High School, she spoke with grammatical precision, said 'tis and 'twas in normal conversation, and could still recite her Latin lessons. She had graduated from Normal School before marriage and went back to teaching in a one-room country school after her six children were grown. A boy in my Sunday school class—a Norwegian FFA-type named Luther—asked me once if I was related to Mrs. Register. "She's your *Grandma?*" he said, his eyes wide with awe. "She's your *teacher?*" I sighed, equally jealous. Grandpa, who died when I was twelve and comes back to me as an off-pitch voice and a flannel-shirted bear hug with bushy eyebrows, had no discernible occupation but plenty of skills. He had helped build the movie screen at the Starlight Drive-In and had worked on the Alcan Highway to Alaska. I can picture him straddling the roof of our new house, laying tarpaper over the boards that he and Dad had hammered in place.

Despite appearances, there was something "cultured" about Grandpa and Grandma. They could talk intelligently about any subject that came up and they had firm opinions on current issues. There were reproductions of real art on the walls: a dark-toned painting of a doctor leaning over a dying girl, which gave me the creeps, and Millet's *The Angelus*, named for a bell that was rung, Grandma explained, to allow the workers in the field to pause for a moment of silent prayer. Shortly after Grandma died, I was browsing at an estate sale and found myself drawn again and again to a picture I couldn't imagine myself liking. The dominant color was a pale orange and it depicted sailing barges on a river, not my favorite motif. I tried leaving without it, but came back and shelled out my two dollars. Later I had a chance to walk through Grandma and Grandpa's house one last time before it was all cleared out for the new buyers. There on the living-room wall was that painting.

I thought of Grandpa and Grandma as carefree vagabonds, and the image fit well with the canvas-covered pickup they slept in on trips to northern Minnesota, the Black Hills, the Pacific Northwest, and the deserts of Arizona and New Mexico. The house was littered with souvenirs of those trips: rocks and seashells and dried-up hunks of cactus, bottles and cartons too pretty or potentially useful to be thrown out, dried flowers and cobs of Indian corn. Everything could be touched freely, even though my boy cousins were heavy-handed. I was drawn to the *National Geographic*s stacked halfway up one wall of the living room, and the largest collection of View-Master reels I've seen yet. The whole world was contained in that crowded little room, which was powdered with dust stirred up by passing cars on the busy gravel road out front. Brush the dust off a magazine, open it across your knees, and you were in the Swiss Alps.

Grandpa and Grandma had no material wealth to boast of, nor were they the sort to boast. When Grandma died at eighty-seven, the most valuable items at the estate sale were the oatmeal tins and wooden cheese boxes that the antique hunters scrambled for. Yet I remember their place as lush and rich—rich with ripening fruit and steaming pies, with slithering cats that left hair on your clothes and green-husked walnuts that left stains on your hands, with the chatter of unexpected but welcome company, with personal loyalties and political allegiances that mattered more than money and modern comforts. I thought they had chosen this life with the same enthusiasm we grandchildren brought to the pleasures it offered us. I never imagined financial disaster as a part of their story.

It wasn't for lack of clues. Dad had a favorite boyhood story he told over and over, which began, "I drove the team of horses when we moved from Moscow to Alden when I was ten." It came more alive on each telling, like an outline slowly coming into focus on a movie screen. Though the year was 1922 and the West was long since "won," I envisioned the scene as an epic westward journey like the pioneer wagon trains. Two horse-drawn wagons poked along against the northern horizon loaded with furniture and household goods that lurched and strained against the ropes that held them in place. On the first I could make out Grandpa's strong profile, and on the second, lagging a bit behind, young Gordy with his dark hair standing straight up in front the way it did in family photographs. One retelling of the story transformed the first team of horses into a Fordson tractor, Henry Ford's new, steel-wheeled promise of agricultural prosperity. Another added an old silver Airedale named Duke to the scene, then placed him in the wagon, "pretty well banged up" but still alive after getting hit by a car. The tractor sputtered and died just past Hayward, and the caravan had to wait for a part to be delivered from Albert Lea. I imagined restless Gordy skipping stones on the narrow arm of Albert Lea Lake or running up and down the esker, the ridge of glacial debris that snakes alongside. It took ten hours to travel the twenty-five miles across the county, a fifteen-minute trip these days on Interstate 90.

I assumed it was a welling up of boyish pride that prompted Dad to tell the story, and I smiled at the thought of him clucking at the horses and slapping the reins a bit more than necessary, for the novelty of this manly chore. Seventy years after the fact, I finally asked the reason for the move, and I feel foolish that it took me so long. What, after all, would compel a family of seven to leave behind a grand farmstead on 393 acres of rich, black loam for nine scrubby acres and a four-room house in need of quick expansion? Dad had the answer ready all along: Grandpa had bought out his parents during the economic boom that followed the Allied victory in World War I. Three years later, land and crop prices plummeted. American history books label the farm crisis of the early 1920s a foreshadowing of the stock market crash of 1929. By 1932, farm income had declined to one-third of what it had been in 1920. Dad describes these trends in more personal, concrete terms: One day his dad went to Austin and bought three hundred-pound bags of sugar on sale for $100. The next week sugar was selling at $10 a bag. The bank gave him one year's grace on the mortgage he had taken to buy his parents their freedom to move to the Twin Cities, but finally the payments were impossible. The eighty head of cattle he had bought on a special trip to Omaha had to be sold off at less than the purchase price. He couldn't even recover the cost of their feed.

That epic westward journey I had projected onto my mind's movie screen was no eager frontier adventure, but the slow march of the dispossessed. The corrected image is straight out of a John Ford movie: the Cheyenne trudging out of Oklahoma territory to make way for the Sooners, the Okies in rattletrap pickups, fleeing the dustbowl for the false promise of California. My grandparents were certainly not the only ones in jeopardy in 1922. Speakers at a national agricultural conference attended by President Harding all reported a general depression in agriculture that was seriously affecting related industries, such as meatpacking. A January report to the Albert Lea *Times-Enterprise* by C. T. Helgeson, the Freeborn County register of deeds, expresses "pleasure" that relatively few mortgages were foreclosed during the preceding year, but then opines,

> The farmer who has invested his few hard-earned thousands in a farm home and heavily encumbered it for the balance of the purchase price is entitled to every possible consideration in his honest efforts to lift this heavy load from off his property, his wife and children.
>
> Much of the discouragement to children on the farm comes from the hopeless outlook into their future occasioned by the cloud of a heavy indebtedness and the heartless and utterly unsympathetic attitude of the money lender or mortgagor.

I should have caught on sooner to Dad's message of loss, just from the circumstances in which he told the story. It unfolded along Highway 16, on our periodic drives to Moscow to look over the old homestead where our ancestors, Robert and Mary Speer, settled in 1855. Dad's fondness for the Moscow farm was palpable. He was born there in 1912, the oldest son and heir, in the tall white farmhouse his grandfather had built. Dad's father, Leslie, was born in 1889 in the original log cabin, also the birthplace of Leslie's mother, Amanda, the youngest of the Speer children and the one who stayed home to inherit the farm, along with her husband John Register.

We drove through the village of Moscow first, past the old

creamery and the town hall and the school. The farm was just to the west, those fields there and there, all that land along the drainage ditch. The slough that Dad's granddad had vowed to preserve for whatever purpose God intended had since been drained away, but the natural spring was still working, last Dad had heard. I have no memory of stopping, driving up the drive-way, or knocking on the door of the house, except for one dim sensation of standing on the lawn, which I could as likely have dreamed. Usually, we just made a slow pass on the county road, restaking our claim, I understand now, on land that had been ours for sixty-seven years.

Dad reminded me each time how the Speers came by ox-team from Wisconsin even before Minnesota was a state, making them almost the first white people in Freeborn County. To begin with, they settled eighty acres along Turtle Creek. Robert Speer had to walk to Chatfield, sixty miles away, to file a claim at the territorial land office. As other settlers came and went, or died of smallpox, the family bought up adjoining farms.

Despite my love of history, I had put surprisingly little stock in my connection to these people. I was already past forty when it occurred to me that I am a fifth-generation Min-nesotan. Few European Americans of my age are so deeply rooted here. I am, indeed, a fifth-generation Freeborn County native who broke the continuity by living and raising my chil-dren in Minneapolis. This realization was prompted by a magazine article about a prominent fifth-generation Min-nesotan, the scion of a family that had steadily prospered, each generation building on the wealth of the last. That is, of course, the expected pattern. The early bird not only gets the worm, but lords over the juicy spots where worms emerge. Un-til that strange awakening, I had always identified myself as a third-generation Danish American, preferring the drama of my maternal grandparents' trans-Atlantic migration, which I could hear about firsthand, and in an endearing Danish accent. My Petersen ties linked me to an exotic motherland of thatched roofs, storks, and fairy tales. The Speers, Midwestern farmers, were less glamorous and too long dead: too dusty and musty to excite my imagination.

Now I hang on Dad's stories, wondering why the West's rule of first come, first served didn't quite hold up for us, why our family names aren't attached to parks or streets or spelled out in concrete on city buildings like those of other early arrivals. Our roots in North American soil reach deeper even than the Cedar Valley limestone that lies underneath Moscow's loam. One alleged ancestor was a British lord who shipped his house over in pieces and reassembled it in Virginia, rather than face disfavor or even death at the hands of King James. If the risk was so great, I wonder, how could he take the time for all that dismantling? While some families painstakingly trace their genealogies, ours seems content with hearsay and conjecture: tales of descent from William Bradford of the *Mayflower*, or a family name on a Revolutionary War memorial at Valley Forge.

My great-great-grandmother Mary Hutchinson Speer was a midwife, Dad says, who rode horseback twenty miles to deliver babies. One of many unsung women who managed frontier farms while their husbands were off fighting the Civil War, she went blind when a milkcow that had wandered into the "smartweed," the nettles, switched its tail across her eyes. A crumbling newspaper memoir by her daughter Marrietta, then ninety years old, identifies Mary as "the community doctor," equipped with medicine for fever and snakebite. Their most frequent visitors in the early years were Indians who came to ask Robert Speer, a blacksmith, to fix their traps. "Mother was never afraid of the Indians," Marrietta testifies, "for they were always pretty friendly." "She was half Indian, you know," Dad reminded me from time to time. "Canuck and Indian, from Canada." I had grown wise to this phenomenon: an Indian ancestor allows run-of-the-mill European Americans a share in the mystique of the ancient, as well as absolution from the guilt of genocide. "How is it," my Dutch mother-in-law asked me once, "that every American I meet is descended from an Indian princess? How many princesses could there be?" So I dismissed any real likelihood of Native ancestry, until I saw a photograph of Mary's daughter Amanda, my great-grandmother. Now I relish the way our slightly mixed blood complicates an already zigzagged story of progress and failure, and I am not immune to the romanticism either.

As descendants of Minnesota Territorial pioneers, we hardly fit the midcentury stereotype of the American working class: urban "white ethnics" whose Old Country habits and faulty English violated middle-class etiquette, and Appalachian hillbillies supposedly condemned by isolation and inbreeding to the white trash heap. "White ethnics" had names ending in -ski and -ini, never -son or -rup or -quist, and the hillbillies' longevity on U.S. soil didn't entitle them to the American Dream. Clearly, the image needs revising. A roll call of Albert Lea's packinghouse workers in the 1950s would turn up other casualties of the post–World War I farm crisis, and certainly of the Great Depression that tossed Dad into long, weary dollar-a-days of farm labor rather than the chemistry studies he had hoped for. In Albert Lea's Chamber of Commerce and in Local 6 of the UPWA, the names were Scandinavian and German and English and Irish. The union also listed names like Acosta, Duenes, and Zamora.

The Moscow farm was the Register family's Garden of

Eden, the 1920s recession our Fall from Paradise. Golden Age myths feed the human psyche's hopes for better times. Former glory makes future glory thinkable. Once daring pioneers, sturdy farmers, we didn't have to be satisfied with wage labor. Contentiously proud as we could be of our working-class status, especially when it was demeaned by others, we were not bound to the time clock forever. I knew this much, without knowing the full story, and never took "working-class" to mean inferior or unintelligent or unambitious. Sure, the packinghouse had its share of the down-and-out, but most of the people who worked there were just like us, and this "us" was a mighty cluster of proud humanity.

For Dad, the Moscow farm is both symbol and gripping reality. He lived in that paradise for the first ten years of his life. Turtle Creek, the corn and oats and stands of oak, the wetland that has since been ditched away, the silos and elevators along the road through Moscow village were his first home landscape, the one that shaped his notions of comfort and beauty. Aunts and uncles and grandparents were frequent company. He can still recall the names of the teachers at Moscow School. Not all the memories are pleasant, however. "See that silo over there?" he gestured to me on an afternoon drive. "We were playing there one day when one of the Ruble boys fell into the feed chute and smothered under the grain. I was a pallbearer at the funeral. I was seven years old." A stand of cedar trees prompted another story, this one told in a bolder voice. "We had fourteen acres of woods on our place. There was a bounty on crows back then. I'd climb up those trees and take the eggs out of the nest, and put them in my cap and carry it down in my teeth. I got fifteen cents apiece for those eggs. That's how I earned my spending money."

How does a boy who knows the danger of a feed chute, who steals eggs from crows, who calls the clucking of 500 laying hens "singing," who cups his hands under a natural spring to catch drinking water, envision the course of his life? He stands up, turns slowly around with his eyes on the horizon, and breathes in home. And what becomes of that life course when home is abruptly and irrevocably altered? The few memories Dad recounts from his adolescence in Alden are brief and stark. He wore his uncle's cast-off pants to school, cut down to fit him. "I hope you're as smart as the last guy who wore those pants," he reports his teacher chiding him. For a time, he even moved in with his granddad Ostrander to keep out of reach of his dad's short-fused temper. "It was like the spirit went out of him," Dad says now of Grandpa's reaction to losing the family homestead. Even on summer days, he sat inside the house with no heart to go out and work his diminished land.

The "News from the County" page in the Albert Lea *Times-Enterprise* has given me an unexpected glimpse into the Register family's comfortable life in Moscow that highlights the contrast with their poverty in Alden. Among the daily accounts of who visited whom, I read such items as:

"L. A. Register had a 'hauling bee' last Monday, when six neighbors with teams and John D. Ruble with his truck hauled the straw which he sold to the Clover Leaf Farm near Austin.

"Mr. and Mrs. Leslie Register gave an oyster supper to a number of friends at their home Saturday evening.

"Florence Anderson is assisting Mrs. L. A. Register with the housework this week.

"Leslie Register is driving a brand new Ford sedan, purchased at Blooming Prairie.

"L. A. Register and Mr. Dickman each have a new Fordson tractor, delivered last week.

"L. A. Register and E. Hubbard families motored to Clear Lake, Ia., Sunday."

The more puzzling surprise was that these signs of prosperity were published throughout 1922, the year of the big move. When I brought this to Dad's attention, his usual abiding trust in memory remained unshaken. "They must have gotten it wrong," he said, meaning the newspaper had the wrong date printed on its masthead for three years running. I, on the other hand, can't dismiss hard evidence quite so readily. I guess I'll have to amend the story and tell it to my daughters again: "Grandpa drove the team of horses when they moved to Alden when he was eleven."

Work—hard, physically taxing work—has been the hallmark of Dad's determination not to fail. He approached his work at the packinghouse with a pioneering farmer's independence of mind, physical fortitude, and tolerance of hardship. Leisure hours were spent on household repairs or in his abundant backyard garden, which supplied Mom with enough vegetables for canning to last the winter. From early loss, they both learned to make do, to find satisfaction in a life full of disappointments but remarkably free of rancor.

Dad's first paid work, in the summers of his teenage years and again after graduating from high school, was farm labor. Graduation was a privilege for a rural Minnesota boy. Only six of the fourteen boys who began high school with Alden's Class of 1929 made it through, along with twenty girls. Dad's two brothers were not so lucky. Even with a diploma, Gordy plowed, threshed, hauled bundles of grain, dug potatoes, for pay when he could get it, but sometimes only for room-and-board and potatoes to take home to his folks. At twenty-two he married Ardis Petersen, a brand-new high school graduate who in different circumstances might have been a teacher. When my sister Nancy was born in 1935, Dad was still earning only a dollar a day. Though they lived with Mom's parents the first years, family life required steadier, better-paying work, which Dad found as a carpenter with Ivar Ofstun, an independent Albert Lea contractor who paid him a healthy fifty-five cents an hour. Ivar's most lucrative source of work, ironically, was erecting new buildings on farms repossessed by Prudential Insurance Company.

Carpentry was seasonal and required weeks away from home, a hardship for my mother. Before my sister Joey was born, the family moved to Albert Lea and Dad found a promising commissioned job as a wholesale grocery salesman for Western Grocer, stocking stores from a truck he drove to Austin and to smaller towns in the area. Gregarious by nature, he thrived on conversation with regular customers he saw at least weekly. But after six years, the work week had lengthened, and mysterious accounting practices deprived him of money he felt he had earned. The promise of a streamlined route with a higher level of decision-making and better pay turned out to be a ruse to keep him from straying elsewhere. The day it was exposed, he left the wholesale warehouse at lunchtime and headed out to the Wilson plant, where the war had shortened the daily lines of job seekers. It was 1943, the same year that the Packinghouse Workers' Organizing Committee of the CIO won representation at Wilson's and reconstituted itself as the United Packinghouse Workers of America. As a packinghouse worker and a union man, Dad acquired new loyalties.

Until that day, my sisters, eight and six, felt comfortably placed in the world. They lived in a small but adequate rented house on a Southside block well populated with children. My mother's sewing skills sent them to school well dressed, and Dad went to work in a suit and a hat. They had a new car, the 1940 Ford we were still driving fourteen years later, when we bought Grandpa Petersen's 1948 Pontiac. Nancy remembers Dad's change in jobs as an abrupt change of life: no more dropping by "the office" on weekends, no more Sunday drives to Northside Drug for ice cream. It was also her first aware-ness of social class. When the landlady reclaimed the house for her son, who would soon be home from the war, the family left behind the furniture that came with the house and moved to a duplex in a run-down neighborhood across the street from warehouses and factories. Only a curtain shielded their door-way from the common entry, and they had to tromp upstairs to use the shared bathroom. Moving again, to a nicer duplex, was a mercy, except that it placed the girls in the same school as the richest kids in town. For Nancy, whose new friends were mostly from white-collar families, the lack of furniture and other material niceties and of money for movies and snacks was an embarrassment she worked hard to conceal. She baby-sat as often as she could, began sewing her own clothes, and avoided bringing friends home.

By the time we moved into our newly built house west of town, when I was three and my sisters thirteen and nearly eleven, we were on somewhat better footing. Dad had moon-lighted as a cabdriver through the war years and beyond, and Mom worked whenever necessary as a salesclerk at Wallace's department store, as a distributor of Madame Dulcey Cos-metics, and as a seamstress at Munsingwear. With two daugh-ters well into elementary school, the family seemed complete by the time of my unplanned conception. My caboose-baby childhood was shaped by rising expectations, buoyed by a post-war economic boom. Yet I feel as though I were born with a sensitivity to class. I understood, from Mom's fretful look, that bedsheets dyed chartreuse and hung over the living-room win-dows were a poor substitute for drapes. School confirmed my hunches about our social status. In the real world of the *Dick and Jane* readers, "Father" went off to work in a suit and a hat.

Writing my family's history as the tectonic shift of economic fortunes is satisfying in its simplicity and its absence of blame, but it is not the whole truth. Dad never tells the truth whole, all at once. Why did Grandpa have to buy the farm if it was already in the family? I finally asked him. Because his parents wanted to get out of farming, Dad explained. Maybe they could see the hard times coming. Couldn't they have helped him out with the money they got from the mortgage? Dad supposed they could have, but there were other problems involved. "You know, my dad and my granddad were both pretty stubborn. They didn't always see eye to eye." I know that family trait well from my feuding aunts and uncles. Dad didn't always see eye to eye with Grandpa, either. A few years after the loss of the farm, Great-Grandpa Register did offer up a loan to buy back a piece of it, but he made the offer to his second son. Maybe my sensation of standing on the lawn is a long-ago memory of a rare visit to the farmer relatives I never got to know.

It is strange to think that better luck or more wisdom might have made us a long entrenched farm family. Certainly my childhood and teen years would have been different: 4-H projects, country school in Moscow and high school in Austin rather than Albert Lea, a gilt or a heifer to groom for the Freeborn County Fair, firsthand experience at walking soybeans and detasseling corn. Had our nearly 400 acres yielded well, I might have enjoyed more popularity at school, thanks to my proud bearing and my nicely matched sweaters, bought at the Sterling Shopping Center in Austin or even at Dayton's in Rochester. In December of 1959, I would not have felt righteous anger at Wilson & Co. for daring to replace my dad with a scab. I would have been whispering nasty words instead about those union roughnecks who were keeping my dad from delivering his livestock to the plant—unless we followed Great-Grandpa Ostrander's predilection for Farmer-Labor Party politics. I can't help but assume that we would have. Imagining my family as Republican is too long a stretch.

There is, however, little cause for idle dreaming about what might have been. As a practical matter, the burden would have fallen to my sisters or me, in a later crisis, to farm more efficiently or forfeit the land. In recent years the farm has been subdivided and some of the buildings leveled. It has not remained the secure family estate that Robert and Mary Speer may have envisioned. Even many of those frugal Norwegian FFA boys have moved on to other endeavors; perhaps some work now for the agribusiness corporations that today hold the rights to their family's land.

Sometimes I daydream about getting rich on my writing (fantasy for sure!) and buying back the Moscow farm, the way my favorite Swedish novelist, Selma Lagerlöf, reclaimed Mårbacka, the country estate where she lived as a child. What would it be like to look out across those fields with the pride of ownership? My city backyard is daunting enough, demanding not pride but constant maintenance. And my edge-of-town childhood taught me that I could love a prairie sky or an oak savanna just as much from outside the barbed-wire fence. The old homestead has already given me enough, entitling me to a deep and tenacious hold on Freeborn County, whether or not I live there still, reminding me that prosperity is always precarious—unless you tighten your grip till the greedy squeeze of your fist is all you can feel.

Besides, the role of reclamation fell not to me but to my cousin Alan, one of those heavy-handed boys wrestling around in Grandma Register's overstuffed living room. A well digger's son who grew up in a converted storefront on Alden's main street, he took up farming and has prospered, with hard work and an intelligent command of agriculture and economics, on 200 acres just five miles, as Freeborn County's still too numerous crows fly, from the old homestead. But thriving as a farmer is no sure thing these days either. Alan also is an electrician.

It is not, after all, the storied Moscow farm that draws me back to ancestral roots or to the fundamental values of my childhood. The landscape of the farm was never stamped on my consciousness the way that more familiar, intimately known surroundings were. On crisp fall evenings, as I stand in my yard and look up through the leafless branches into the moonlit sky, I'm suddenly awash in a feeling of contentment. I recognize immediately where I have seen the sky in exactly that way through the branches of a walnut tree. I have been transported in memory to the yard of that run-down Register place where I first felt certain I was happy and secure. It was a fine enough place from which to take wing.

A Dream of Joe Hill

"I dreamed I saw Joe Hill last night alive as you or me," a popular labor song begins. I don't literally dream about Joe Hill, but the IWW troubadour has haunted my waking hours since I first read about him in novelist John Dos Passos's *U.S.A.* My discovery of Dos Passos while still in high school endures as a literary and political epiphany. Joe Hill, a Swedish immigrant allegedly framed on a murder charge by antilabor schemers and executed in 1915, seemed a perfect hero for a Scandinavian-American girl from a working-class family, especially one with literary aspirations and a passion for history. As a martyred songwriter, he stirred my imagination, and as an itinerant laborer born Joel Hägglund in a country next door to my ancestral Denmark, he could help push my roots a little deeper.

That's what I reminded myself when Swedish director Bo Widerberg's film *Joe Hill* arrived at the Varsity Theater in Minneapolis's Dinkytown neighborhood in 1971. I had recently moved away from the campus of the University of Chicago, where I often felt displaced among fellow intellectuals unfamiliar with factory whistles and the tense uncertainty of a long-lasting strike. Yet I felt no more at home in my new life. My husband, fresh out of law school, had been hired by a prestigious Minneapolis law firm that paid its new associates nearly twice as much as my dad was earning after twenty-eight years of skilled labor. We were flush enough to be homeowners already, which had taken my parents fourteen years of married life, carpentry skills, and a mail-order catalog of house blueprints. A dose of Joe Hill promised both a familiar anchor and the excitement of the new: a rare chance to listen to Swedish dialogue. I had made one last attachment to home by pursuing a Ph.D. in Scandinavian languages and literatures.

Walking from the car to the theater alongside my wary husband, who preferred James Bond to Joe Hill, I replayed Grandma Petersen's boastful stories about hiding in the fruit trees at age twelve when she heard the *tap-tap* of the cane her employer, the orchard owner, used on his inspection and disciplinary rounds. I wondered what stories Grandpa might have told about the cigar factory, had I taken time to ask him. Joe Hill had left Sweden just five years before my grandpa arrived in America, perhaps with similar dreams of "scraping gold off the streets."

The movie was a disappointment, and I soon chimed in with my husband's whispered cynical commentary. Actor Thommy Berggren was too sleek and fine-featured to be a convincing laborer. I had expected a body type I recognized, one that showed the effects of hefting sheaves of wheat and prying copper loose from walls of rock. I wanted him to be an average Joe, a man-on-*my*-street. (Now, having seen photographs of

Joe Hill, I realize that casting Thommy Berggren was not far-fetched. Joe Hill was just a bit lankier and more craggy-faced, a familiar type of Swedish physiognomy.)

The film's story of capitalist cruelty versus worker idealism was too simplistic to engage my intellect or to further my budding understanding of the factional disputes in labor organizing. Despite their plea for "one big union" and their creativity and vitality, the Industrial Workers of the World—the "Wobblies"—captured only the fringe of the labor movement. They were certainly not the whole of it, as the movie would have us believe. Worst of the disappointments, the movie's dialogue wasn't even in Swedish. Of course, the setting was America and Joe Hill had presumably left the oppressive narrowness of Swedish culture behind. Never mind the historical record, which, though meager, shows that he frequently sought shelter with other Swedish immigrants as he roamed the country.

Hard as I tried to keep pace with my husband's cynicism, however, I was soon blinded by the hazy wash of light that bathed Joe/Thommy's lovely face in glory. I sniffed. I dabbed at my eyes. I mocked myself for being undone, once again, by the manipulative sentimentality of a dumb tearjerker. Finally, at the end of the movie, nostalgia for his homeland overtakes poor doomed Joe Hill and he utters a bit of Swedish. As he stands blindfolded before the firing squad, a bird chirps and sings beyond the prison wall. Joe cocks his head to listen. *"Fågel"*—"bird"—he whispers just before the guns go off. I left the theater red-eyed, clutching my saturated Kleenex, with my disgruntled husband clucking at my side.

I wasn't at all prepared for what happened next. As we headed toward Bridgeman's Ice Cream, where we would likely rehash and pan the movie, three young men, dressed like the student radicals at the nearby University of Minnesota, came striding by, singing Joe Hill songs at full voice in a triumphant camaraderie. Their joy should have been contagious. What better high could there be than to leave a movie singing? A surge of emotion nearly lifted me from the sidewalk, but instead of joining in the chorus, I burst into sobs. This was not the sentimental sorrow the movie had evoked, but the righteous anger of the deprived, the disinherited.

The realization struck hard: I had never sung a Joe Hill song, had never even heard one sung until college introduced me to Folkways records. We didn't sing Joe Hill at Christmas parties in Albert Lea's Union Center. I don't remember hearing a single labor song during the Wilson strike of 1959, when silence was prudence. There was no Joe Hill sheet music on our battered, out-of-tune basement piano, no renditions of Joe Hill songs in our collection of 78-RPM records. I wondered if Grandma and Grandpa Petersen even knew of him, if his execution had been reported in the Danish-American newspapers, assuming they even subscribed. The year of his death was the year they lost their first little girl to brain fever. Private sorrows always overwhelm public tragedy. That seemed to be the case even now, for me.

I cried out of grief for my lost heritage, but the hurt ran deeper than that. I was jealous and angry over these boys' gleeful appropriation of what was rightfully mine, over their acceptance of moviedom's mythologized Joe Hill as a symbol for the grueling work, the curtailed aspirations, the arbitrary decisions, the physical dangers that shaped the lives of blue-collar families. And now they were carrying him back to campus, where his songs would nourish their self-styled, unthreatened radicalism on the University's grassy mall. I had a sudden inclination

to throw the man out with the myth. Joe Hill may be worth
dreaming about, but neither his song lyrics nor his martyrdom
told the truth as I knew it. He was a hero for those privileged to
rally around the glorious margins of labor-movement history
without ever wading into its turbid mainstream. And yet I
wanted him so badly to be an icon for me, torn as I was between
pragmatism and poetry.

"*Fågel, fågel,*" whispered in my brain the following week.
Where was that bird? How did it manage to fly away? Where
were the songs that ought to have fed my dad's spirit as he
packed up his dinner pail and drove off to the packinghouse
before dawn, just as the birds began tuning up for the day?
Where was the songbird that could have parried the accusations cast at the strikers, turned them into satire, let us laugh
and sing and feel radical as we drowned out the opposition
with Joe Hill's own "pie in the sky"? When I pronounced the
word "bird" in Danish—*fugl*—I thought I had hit on an answer.
Fugl to an English speaker sounds like "fool." "Fool," I
guessed, is how Dad would characterize the young, naive Joe
Hill, so carried away by idealism that he'd forget to watch his
back, so convinced of his righteousness that he'd put others in
jeopardy for the sake of an unattainable vision. Dad wouldn't
say all this. "Foolish" would be enough—as foolish as the Wilson strikers who threw rocks at scabs' cars, thinking this could
stop the company's efforts at union-busting. As foolish as the
nightriders who broke windows and burned down corncribs in
unrestrained surges of bitterness. They risked losing their jobs
forever and forgot to think twice about jeopardizing their fellow workers with families to support and dwindling possibilities at forty, forty-five, fifty. Our family's hero was not the
songbird with the wild fantasies but the plodding drafthorse,

organizing, negotiating, attention riveted on the point-by-point compromise. I hadn't known Joe Hill, but the face of CIO President John L. Lewis, bushy eyebrows drawn inward for his signature scowl, had been etched in my memory since early childhood.

The labor songs I never learned to sing still stir me to tears and incite me to an anger that has no clear object. Sometimes I want to bite the singer, but that's no consolation. Pete Seeger, for example, is so benign, so gentle. How can I begrudge him his genuine sympathy for the miner's plight, just because his musical talent and cultured Manhattan upbringing spared him from descending into the dark stagnation of the mine day after day? Often, I glare at the stomping, cheering audience, whooping in scornful glee at the singer's lampoon of the boss's greed. "What do *you* know?" I want to demand. Sometimes I just look away in shame, silenced by a gnawing suspicion that if these songs truly represent working-class culture, then what I have lived is not the real thing.

Why not just accept the Joe Hill legend as romanticized history, as innocently distorted as Johnny Appleseed or as Davy Crockett killing a b'ar when he was only three? Why not just enjoy the sing-along, as though it were "Oh, Susanna" or "Yankee Doodle," melodic ditties whose original meaning has been left behind in a past irrelevant to present needs? Why not refuse to listen altogether, ignore the rowdy chorus and hide away in the tiny niche I've earned among the intelligentsia? I am welcome to drown my sorrows in Vivaldi and Mahler on public-radio broadcasts. As I consider these obvious, reasonable questions, each song I add to the repertoire becomes another provocation.

"That's the Rebel Girl, that's the Rebel Girl, to the working class she's a precious pearl." I'd like to pretend we sang this

song around the kitchen table, that my parents taught me Elizabeth Gurley Flynn's defiant courage. But it was not the Rebel Girl I longed to be. It was the Clearasil Personality of the Month, her smooth, blemish-free face spread across the shiny pages of *Teen* magazine, which also listed her supergirl accomplishments: straight As, first chair violin, hospital candy-striper, homecoming queen. Joe Hill, even as Thommy Berggren, was no match for Frankie Avalon and Fabian, true working-class troubadours—urban ethnic greasers—who crooned about teenage romance, the most pressing problem in my little world. Would Joe Hill, reimagined as an outlaw hero-of-the-people for a TV western, have torn me away from *Gunsmoke*? We working-class kids were subject to the same empty but persuasive commercial culture that seduced most American children of the 1950s and 1960s. Without a television set, it might have been different. Or maybe not. My sisters, who listened to swing bands and the strange harmonies of the Four Lads and the Four Freshmen on the radio, were even less acquainted with Joe Hill. We did learn to sing one labor song, I remember now: *"Look for the union label."* It was performed as a radio and television jingle promoting the International Ladies' Garment Workers Union. We took the message to heart, too. Turning clothes inside out at Penney's to find the union "bug" sewn into the seam became my family's ritual of solidarity. No, that's badly overstated. We just did because it was right.

Dream of Joe Hill alive as you or me? I was more likely to dream that I walked the picket line in my Maidenform bra. Maybe that silly magazine advertisement holds the key to my tangled maze of emotions. Why would a fantasy of being exposed in public in my underwear induce me to buy Maidenform? Why would a self-conscious teenager, obsessed with the

competitive pace of anatomic development, give in to such
perversion? I wouldn't be caught dead in my Maidenform bra,
with or without a union label. To be caught in public stumbling
over the lyrics to "The Preacher and the Slave" is equally humiliating. Better to avoid the risk altogether, or to impute dishonest motives to the people who sing along easily. Consider
this actual dream:

*I am teaching a class, sitting at a table before rows of college
students at desks with writing arms. The music of "The Internationale" begins playing outside the classroom windows. A few students immediately stand up, reverently, at attention. Gradually,
others join them, though these students look either confused or
apprehensive. I rise up partway, unsure whether this song is indeed "The Internationale." I'm afraid I might have it mixed up
with "La Marseillaise," and I don't need to stand for that, since
I'm not French. Uncertainty keeps me in an awkward crouch until the very last verse, when I decide it has to be "The Internationale" and lurch upright, unnaturally stiff. I'm greatly embarrassed, having exposed my ignorance to my students.*

The day after I awoke from that dream, snatches of the
melody kept playing in my mind. I wanted to sing along, but of
course I didn't know the words. The dream, I concluded, smug
in my reading of its symbolism, was about "taking a stand,"
which is not as easy as it might seem.

"Which side are you on? Which side are you on?" Never has
this song struck my ears so discordantly as it did in 1985, in the
turmoil of the Hormel strike in Austin, Minnesota. The lyrics
presuppose a clear choice, and told to check a box for labor or
management, I would not hesitate. My loyalties are firm. I do
not cross picket lines. But when the complexities of survival in
a declining economy degenerate into a simplistic either/or

choice, a "with us or against us" ultimatum, I balk. Witnessing the support of Twin Cities intellectuals for Austin's Local P-9, which was conducting a strike of its own despite negotiations underway by the United Food and Commercial Workers international union, I felt shamefully ambivalent, as if I were being asked to choose between bread and roses, between slow, persistent, behind-the-scenes argument and a showy gamble for total justice. Friends and acquaintances spoke with enthusiasm about the rallies and fund-raisers they were attending on behalf of the Hormel workers. They expected I'd be there, or at least be impressed by their allegiance to my people. They thought they were speaking my native tongue. Some even thought I was from Austin, a common but annoying error. I seldom felt that I could explain my dampened enthusiasm intelligibly, or as succinctly as the occasion required. Nor could I talk about the awful vulnerability I felt when my ambivalence was exposed. Which side *was* I on?

Nothing about Austin is simple for an Albert Lea girl. Like a favored sister, Austin, in my teenage years, had everything we wanted: a strip-mall shopping center, a junior college, specialist doctors, a Frank Lloyd Wright house, the Terp ballroom with live rock and roll, well-equipped athletic teams that consistently beat ours, Scholastic Aptitude Tests (college-bound Albert Lea kids had to drive to Austin to take the SAT), easy girls who stole away our boyfriends, smooth-talking boys who seduced our best friends. Our parents, too, had much to envy: a benevolent hometown meatpacking company that paid well, offered bonuses when profits were up, treated its employees respectfully, and never threatened to pull out of town at contract time. Hormel's hadn't had a strike since the organizing days of the 1930s, thanks to the company's "me too" policy: af-

ter the workers at Armour, Cudahy, Swift, and Wilson had bat-
tled out a master agreement, Hormel's went with the terms,
and then some.

Even after the tide turned at Hormel's and the reward system was trimmed back, the Austin workers had the best pay
scale in the meatpacking industry. The company's withdrawal
of profit-sharing incentives still left them better off, in plain
wages, than their counterparts in Albert Lea. Wilson workers,
remember, cut back from a base wage of $10.69 to $6.50 by
the company's bankruptcy, had gone on strike and renegoti-
ated pay at $8.50. Though this was a drastic cut in income,
most people realized that no more could be pumped from a
drying well. With fears of the plant closing altogether, it was
not easy to work up sympathy for dissatisfied but better-off
neighbors. Bucking the national union and refusing the con-
cessions called for in the industry-wide contract might put the
long-term job security of packinghouse workers across the
country at risk. The Hormel strike was, on its face, a coura-
geous stand, a simple insistence on what's right, but, considering the trend toward bankruptcies, downsizing, and plant closings, it looked self-destructive.

I was eager to know where Dad stood, but he, normally gar-
rulous and opinionated, seemed to be avoiding conversation. It
hurts a great deal to admit that your strongest loyalties are suffering strain. At the mention of Ray Rogers, the charismatic
showman brought in to lead a "corporate campaign" directed
at Hormel's stockholders and business investments, Dad's
hackles rose a bit. He shook his head and muttered, "Leading
them down the primrose path." A songbird, a *fugl*, I suspected,
who might even fly low enough to eat the bread crumbs that
could show the lost souls their way back home. Years later,

someone offered, as a semi-apology for Rogers, that his most valuable contribution was the creation of a "strike culture" that the local leadership could never have inspired. It was fun to hang around the union hall. There was real spirit there. A rousing chorus of Joe Hill songs, I imagined, to ease the bitterness of lost jobs and long-lasting animosities.

This time a movie affirmed rather than provoked my sensitivities. Barbara Kopple's Academy Award–winning *American Dream*, a documentary about the Hormel strike, debuted in Austin on a weekend when I was visiting my parents in Albert Lea. I mentioned it to Dad but got no response. When it turned up at my neighborhood theater several weeks later, I determined to go, but not alone and certainly not with a cynic. I called my old Albert Lea friend Linda. Our junior high friendship had survived the Wilson strike, even though her dad, a salesman, had to report for work across the picket line. Linda's husband Dick, a therapist who works with teenage lawbreakers, had made regular weekly visits to a group home in Austin all through the strike. He could see beyond the rebellious fervor to the toll it took on families. Tears dribbled down our faces as we watched the strike come to life on-screen and relived the ache of ambivalence. Kopple had left the complexities unresolved and had let the players speak for themselves, though of course she kept the privilege of editing their words. There were no romantic heroes, no happy tunes to hum. Some members of the audience clearly wanted it otherwise. They laughed knowingly with Ray Rogers whenever he said something clever. They booed at Lewie Anderson, the dogged negotiator for the UFCW. Afterward, Linda, Dick, and I took refuge in a restaurant down the street, where we spent an hour in intense but sober conversation. Had someone dared to burst into labor songs in that charged atmosphere, I might have burst into bits.

I really do long to sing. I'd love to send my quaking, middle-aged voice soaring in a chorus of *"Oh, you can't scare me, I'm stickin' to the union. I'm stickin' to the union till the day I die."* Most labor songs are feel-good songs, meant to charge up the crowd and pare away any hint of pessimism, any factional differences, any subtleties that dim belief in the common vision: society will reward work fairly. They are meant to be sung heartily the way Welsh church congregations sing, not like the old joke about Unitarians, who can't sing with gusto because they are too busy reading ahead to see if they agree with what comes next. But these are difficult times for singing. Can music stem the disappearance of blue-collar jobs from the U.S. economy? I still look for the union label whenever I shop for clothes, but I rarely see one. "Made in El Salvador," "Made in Macao," the labels say. What songs do the garment workers sing while they work for pennies an hour in the maquiladoras, turning out clothing that produces megadollars for big-name fashion designers? Perhaps because the labor situation has deteriorated so badly, casting greed and poverty in such stark, unambiguous relief, I am feeling the necessity for song, for a swooping flock of noisy birds to keep the chorus going. I have even begun to sing along.

One Saturday night I had arranged to go out with my friend Sara for a rare evening without our kids. Dinner and a movie was the original plan, but thumbing through the newspaper, I had come upon a feature article about Joe Glaser, a seventy-five-year-old man billed as "labor's troubadour" who was performing that evening as the finale of a conference on "Arts in Solidarity." I was curious, intrigued, and wary. Sara is one friend I can trust with my mistrust of romanticism about the working class. A history professor who teaches and writes about American women's history, she is exceedingly sane and fair on the subject of labor history, which overlaps her own field in ways other scholars often ignore. My dad has bestowed his highest mark of approval on Sara. "Real common and ordinary," he called her once, and she and I laughed at how those words would sound to her proper, Carolina-bred mother, to whom they mean crass and unmannered.

"There's a concert of labor songs," I began. "Oh, let's go!" Sara urged. She needed to learn a few new ones, she said, for her undergraduate survey course in U.S. history. In sessions billed as "history karaoke," she flashes lyrics on the overhead projector and invites the class to sing songs commemorating the events they are studying. "I don't know," I balked. "If it's a bunch of intellectuals playing at working-class radicalism, I may wish I hadn't come." When I checked to see where it was being held, my fears eased a little. The Machinists' Union local on the industrial edge of Sara's middle-class neighborhood certainly wouldn't tolerate sham labor-symps.

Sara had been taking a course on stress relief that required her to spend forty-five minutes a day listening to a taped "body scan" exercise. She had saved it for my arrival, so we spent the start of the evening stretched out on our backs in a near-hypnotic state, though the monotone voice on the tape kept assuring us that we were "fully aware." When I finally peeled myself off the carpet and stood on rubber legs, I felt resilient enough for any provocation, like one of those weighted children's toys that refuses to be knocked over.

Still, I lingered over our dinner at a neighborhood café, not wanting to be among the first to arrive for the concert. Like a secular Jew or a lapsed Catholic at holy day services, I wanted to slip in unnoticed and not risk betraying myself by responding shyly to a hearty greeting or bumbling a new ritual I hadn't learned. There were just a few parking spaces left when we pulled into the lot alongside the Machinists' Hall. Inside, folding chairs were arranged in rows, already three-quarters filled with elderly couples, families with children, and a few political activists. We recognized at least one other history professor.

I don't know if it was the residue of the relaxation tape or the comfort of home that settled over me as Sara and I draped our jackets over two chairs at the end of the second row. The setting was so familiar, the union hall just as utilitarian and unadorned—all Sheetrock and linoleum, just as permeated with cigarette smoke as the meeting room in Albert Lea's Union Center where I had recently spent hours looking through strike memorabilia. A labor-history exhibit brought in for the occasion lined one long wall of the room. Just to my right stood a panel headed "Minnesota National Guard vs. Packinghouse Workers" with a subheading "Albert Lea 1959." I stepped over, took off my glasses, and leaned in close to check out the three newspaper pages displayed, then smiled to myself when I spotted Chuck Lee, the retired president of Local 6, whom I had recently interviewed. He had told me that the iww was the first union to try to organize the packinghouse. The "Independent" Workers of the World, he called them. Wobblies in Albert Lea? Humming on the hog kill? Why hadn't I known? (Actually, it was the Independent Union of All Workers, no direct relation to the iww, though its chief organizer, Frank Ellis of Austin, had been a Wobbly.)

The emcee for the evening, a man about forty years old named Mike, stepped up onto the low platform that functioned as a stage and called us all to attention. He had the muscular, foreshortened arms, the barrel chest, and squat neck of a man whose job demands body strength. "My kind of guy," I whispered to Sara, recalling the adult men of my family and my old neighborhood, a different species from Cary Grant and Gregory Peck. Mike introduced Joe Glaser, an elderly man I had noticed wandering around the room, in and out of conversations with the crowd, seemingly unconcerned about turning his personality "on" for a performance. He ambled up to the stage, chatted a bit with Mike, opened the conversation to us, his audience, then sang a couple of rousing songs. This was no star from the Coast flown in first-class for the show. The lights never dimmed, no spotlight set him apart from the rest of us. "Labor's troubadour" was hardly a death-defying, righteousness-exuding romantic hero; he was just an old guy with a clear voice and a good heart, whose vocation is to make songs of a truck driver's weekly routine and the grievances of hospital employees out on strike. Pragmatic poetry, you might call it.

With a generosity most audiences would neither expect nor tolerate, he quickly invited up some of the locals who were leaning around the edges of the room with guitars slung over their shoulders or resting on their laps. Larry Long, an institution on the Twin Cities folk-and-protest-music scene, sang a song he wrote not just about but *with* seven women who walked out of the American Linen Company in Hibbing, an Iron Range city with a vigorous history of labor conflict. There was not a "union maid" or a "rebel girl" among them—just Ruth and Bev and their coworkers. A UPS driver from the Teamsters' Union put in a pitch for part-time workers like herself, a mom who wanted time to pass on her union legacy to her children. Her contribution was a Marvin Gaye song done a cappella because no one in the group could provide the instrumentation to match. Except for the guitars, the instruments were make-do. An ensemble of AFSCME members—clerical employees from the university—and their children played bongos, homemade drums, and plastic ice-cream pails, to accompany a rap they had written on newsprint and taped to the wall.

I was glad it was Sara sitting next to me. I could be sure that she would find this event fun and even a bit silly. She'd make no effort to exalt it as the prelude to a proletarian revolution. On the other hand, there would be no eye-rolling to contend with, no belittling chuckles, not even the puzzled silence and polite applause of the respectful outsider. I could think of other friends who might have relished the amateur performances as kitsch. My limbs still humming with stress-free pleasure, I was content to set my misgivings aside and let the event be what it was. We, the audience, had been invited to witness a proud display of shared values and renewed hopes, and we were welcome to sing along. I sang in full voice.

As I reviewed the evening, later, its historical meaning became clear. This was not a celebration of burly stevedores tossing cargo into the bay, nor a lament for miners trapped in the shaft while their wives weep at the gate. The New American Worker is a mom in her thirties risking carpal tunnel syndrome, eyestrain, and the unexamined dangers of electromagnetism in order to boost her kids a little higher on the social scale.

Joe Hill did make his requisite appearance. A local folksinger, Barb Tilsen, interwove the lyrics of "Joe Hill" with a poem by Meridel Le Sueur which makes reference to Joe Hill's death and the legendary distribution of his ashes to IWW locals around the country. She didn't tell us, but surely many of us knew that Barb Tilsen is Meridel Le Sueur's granddaughter, one of a family of politically engaged Tilsens noted for their support of labor and human-rights issues. I felt a twinge of envy—oh, to be the heir of this inspired family line—and then came sorrow about all that isn't said and isn't passed from one generation to the next in "common and ordinary" families. Had I been born a Tilsen, I would surely be teaching labor songs to my children. Of course the Tilsens are not laborers. The family matriarch was a poet with labor sympathies and radical politics that got her blacklisted and kept her literary career muffled for decades. Her son-in-law is a lawyer who represents the underdog—sometimes a political activist prosecuted on a possibly concocted felony charge, the modern-day Joe Hill. The Tilsens are troubadours, songbirds. Let them sing.

As I drove home from the concert, with two of Joe Glaser's tapes tucked in my purse, I finally came to terms with my attraction and resistance to Joe Hill. I am not a songbird, neither *fågel* nor *fugl*. Nor am I the all-suffering drafthorse. A troubadour in prose is the best I can be. I will learn to sing out in my own dry, critical voice, lightened by a touch of whimsy, my saving grace in this divisive world:

I Dreamed I Saw Joe Hill Last Night . . . in My Maidenform Bra

I dreamed I saw Joe Hill last night, alive as you or me. Well, not quite that alive. He was looking thin and ashen-faced. The smell of his musty black coat nearly bowled me over.

"*Hej* Joe," I said. "*Det är 80 långa år sen du gick bort.*" You're eighty years dead!

"*Jag har aldrig dött,*" *sade han.* "I never died," said he.

As I shook his bony hand, the skin of his palm flaked onto mine. He saw me wipe my hand against my skirt, and he gave me a wistful look.

"It takes more than guns to kill a man," he sighed.

"You're a martyr to the cause you loved," I said. "It's a great honor."

"Don't you know it!" he said. "I fell hard for this martyr business. I just didn't expect to end up as a *gengångare*."

"What's that, Joe?" I interrupted.

"*Gengångare*, a ghost, one of those restless souls doomed to wander until their mission is accomplished."

"Or vengeance is done," I caught on. "Like Elsalill in Selma Lagerlöf's story.

"Right. It's just wander and wander endlessly," he complained. "*From San Diego up to Maine, in every mine and mill, where workers strike and organize, it's there you'll find Joe Hill.* That's a whole lot more traveling than I bargained for."

"Sounds like you need some rest," I said, as I gave him a comforting pat on the shoulder. A puff of dust and mold rose up out of his coat and I turned away to stifle a cough.

"*Ja,*" he nodded. "The working class needs a new troubadour, one with a little more energy than I've got left."

"There's Joe Glaser," I suggested, "though he's getting a bit old. We have Larry Long right here in Minnesota, and of course Pete Seeger's been trying for years. Would Bruce Springsteen do?"

"Naw," he protested. "Gotta pay your dues. It's gotta be somebody who can still feel the work in his muscles."

"You're not looking at me then," I said with some relief.

"No, no. You're too prosy . . . and you think too much."

But he *was* looking at me, and it was getting very disconcerting. I found it harder and harder to make contact with his glazed eyes. He kept looking at my chest. I should have known; another hero unmasked. Elizabeth Gurley Flynn's good friend was just an everyday male with a boob fixation.

I dropped my eyes, dejected, and immediately felt the blood

course up my neck and into my cheeks. I was talking to Joe Hill in my Maidenform bra!

"What is that thing?" he asked, after a long silence. *"Vad är det för något?"*

"A bra . . ." I began.

"Bra, ja," he laughed. "You can say that again." Of course. *Bra* means "good" in Swedish.

"The bra—the brassiere—took over for corsets and camisoles about a decade after you died, or didn't die as the case may be. I'm not sure it's an improvement."

He stepped closer, hunched his pointed shoulders, and jutted his long Swedish jaw toward my chest. "Look at that workmanship," he mused. "How do they shape that fabric and keep those tiny seams flat? Must be some skilled sewers in that Garment Union."

"I hate to tell you this, Joe, but the union label is deader than you are. There's hardly even a garment factory left in the United States."

"So who made this, uh, bra then?"

"I don't know," I said as I spun around. "If you flip that band in the back over, you'll find a label right near the hooks. Tell me what it says."

He kept a tight grip on the elastic as he leaned back to focus his vision on the tiny printing. "Made in Hon-du-ras," he sounded out. "Where's that?"

"It's a country in Central America," I said, "where union organizers disappear mysteriously and people work for next to nothing. I wouldn't be surprised if this bra was cut and stitched by a line of fifteen-year-old girls."

"Central America?" he moaned. "Way down south of Mexico? I thought my territory was San Diego to Maine."

"It's called the globalization of the economy," I scoffed,

"just a fancy term for drawing higher profits out of low-wage workers in impoverished parts of the world."

"Well, I'm off to Honduras then," he sighed. "No rest for the *gengångare*."

"Not unless we find you a replacement," I suggested.

"Or an avenger," he added. He was staring off into the horizon with a forlorn expression. Suddenly his head cocked to one side and he held up his hand to shush me.

"*Fågel,*" he whispered.

I listened, and I began to hear it too: a sweet melody far off in the distance. I strained to tune it in. The song was in Spanish. I could pick up only scattered words: *Trabajadoras. Libertad.*

I wound my arm gently around his fragile waist. "*Kom, Julle Hägglund,*" I said, addressing him by his childhood name. "We'll find her. She's going to give Joe Hill a long-deserved rest."

Hearsay

"Oral tradition" is an overstatement for what I am about to tell. The phrase conjures a false, sentimental image of the working-class family gathered around the kitchen table for an after-supper heritage lesson. Stories get told in spottier fashion than that, and they are as often veiled references as detailed narratives. A child who wants to learn where she fits in the social scheme has to listen and watch carefully. Class divisions in a town with no major wealth are subtle, barely evident to outsiders, and may be more apparent from the bottom than from the top. I caught on gradually to the clues. Rich kids studied piano with Sadie Bliss Cox, a professional pianist who rewarded them with plastic busts of composers. The rest of us, if we were lucky enough to own an old upright, took lessons from a Mrs. Nelson or a Mrs. Johnson who pasted stickers of cardinals or Christmas wreaths on the songs we had mastered. Rich people belonged to the Elks or the Lions. Ordinary people like us joined the Eagles. Rich people went to the Twin

Cities to shop at Dayton's and see Cinerama movies. We whizzed right through on our way up north to some musty little resort cabin to fish in a rented boat.

Even before I was old enough to wander out of my neighborhood by myself, I knew Albert Lea's socioeconomic layout. I learned it through a family ritual known simply as "going for a ride" or, its summer variant, "going for a root beer." These excursions also showed me that Albert Lea's sometimes woefully quiet atmosphere was fraught with tensions that hadn't always been so carefully contained. On muggy summer evenings or crystalline weekend afternoons in midwinter, Mom, Dad, and I would climb into the car to cruise the town. Nancy was already grown and gone, and Joey was either out with her friends or working as a carhop at the Dairy Bar, praying we wouldn't stop by and embarrass her. Our route into town crossed over two "vidocks," our word for the kind of overpass that Chico of the Marx Brothers heard as "Why a duck?" I imagined the viaduct, with its lofty view of railyards and industrial sprawl, as every inhabited landscape's highest vantage point. I hadn't yet traveled outside Minnesota, except to smuggle colored oleomargarine from nearby Iowa into our protectionist dairy state, where this cheap fake butter was outlawed.

We drove down-at-the-heels Charles Street to its muddy end at Lower Lake, visibly polluted in those years by sewage and bloated slaughterhouse waste. Thanks to the movement of the glaciers, artesian springs, and white settlers' predilection for "cleaning up" bogs and marshlands, Albert Lea has an abundance of lakes—so many that even working-class families can own lakeshore property. I quickly learned the socially meaningful difference between the house with the sloping lawn and a dock—the powerboat thumping against it in the wake of passing water-skiers—and the house with the spongy yard and flooded basement.

Sometimes we detoured off Main Street to survey Morningside Addition, a neighborhood of small asbestos-sided cabins and Quonset huts nestled in the smoky odor of the packinghouse next door. Mom might exclaim at a tangle of rusty car parts in a yard, and Dad would say something like, "That's Bug Jensen's place. Works down in the hide cellar. Great big guy with a beer belly. Came to work the other day steweder than a billy goat." This was presented as fact rather than moral judgment. Our scorn was reserved for the rich.

The true destination of our rides was Shoreland Heights, the knolls above Fountain Lake where the rich people lived. Across the stone bridge where two bays of the lake came together, we headed uphill on an oak-shaded street called The Fairway, then turned into Lanes as narrow as driveways and Circles that took us back where we started, until we found our way to the gravel road along the lake that showed us the terraced backyards of the biggest "homes," as Mom called them (a bit reverently, I thought). Poking along at gawkers' pace, we noted the double garages, the full second stories, the bay windows. Flagstone trim was a sure sign of excess money. Dad kept tabs on the new construction and was ready to tell us which bank officer or car dealer had joined the "*ee*-lite." When the sunlight faded and the lights switched on, we peered inside the houses as best we could. Mom gasped and clucked over fireplaces, glass patio doors, grand pianos, color televisions—items we might like but certainly had the virtue to do without.

Heading back home along Lakeview Boulevard, the shoreline drive around Fountain Lake, we passed the only house in Albert Lea that might qualify as a mansion. A large Tudor with two stuccoed and half-timbered gables, it sat well back from the street in an expanse of evenly mowed lawn. A row of arborvitae stood guard over the house, and a brick-walled garden stretched off to the side. In the summer, we might catch a glimpse of a patio umbrella peeping over the top of the wall, and there were rumors of a swimming pool. The people who lived in this house enjoyed the rare luxury of double-lakeshore—both front and back. Secluded though the back lawn was, it stretched, we knew, to Dane Lake, a drainage basin that, during rainstorms, lapped over the yards of the small houses on its opposite shore. Across Lakeview Boulevard, in front of the mansion, a footbridge led to a tiny private island, then just a scraggle of weeds and stones and fallen branches ineffectively protected by No Trespassing signs. I had prowled the island with my Girl Scout troop, and I coveted the house and yard. The setting reminded me of an English storybook, and I could imagine myself under a parasol strolling down flower-trimmed paths or, in winter, reading huddled up on a sunny window-seat.

The house, the lawn, and the island all belonged to an aged woman I never saw and knew only as "Mrs. Gas Hans." Her late husband was the ogre, the greedy troll in a long ago event that I heard about bit by bit, in the manner of old-time stories. Dad might tell parts of it as we passed Gas Hans's house or the big brick building uptown on Clark Street that had been his place of business, the American Gas Machine Company, where they made gasoline lamps and stoves. Occasionally I'd catch some brief reference in the conversations I waited out while Dad passed the time with an acquaintance.

"The American Gas Strike of 1937" was the name of this historic event, and its elements were violent and scary, but also thrilling. I understood that it was a heroic story, and that our side had won. Gas Hans, a Dane like my mother's family, only rich, was, as his name implies, the company's owner. It took some strenuous imagining to conjure up the scenes I heard about:

- Tear gas fills the intersection of Clark and Newton as the sheriff's deputies chase the strikers with clubs.
- The strikers retaliate by smashing out all the windows in the factory building with porcelain balls. (I imagined them looking like the china shade on my mom's fake-antique lamp, even painted with pink roses, but these balls were solid, made of the stuff used to enamel stoves.)
- A police car is shoved down Newton—past the Danish Brotherhood building—and into the lake.
- Hundreds of people yell as they march to the county jail to demand that the fifty-some strikers imprisoned there be released.
- Sheriff Helmer Myre waits on the steps of the jail with rifle poised (or is it a machine gun?).
- And, the crowning moment, Governor Floyd B. Olson sweeps into town just in time to disarm the sheriff and let the righteous workingmen out of jail!

This picture certainly didn't fit the quiet, eventless Albert Lea in which I lived. I knew there had been strikes; I had heard Dad refer to "those walkouts we had right after the war when Truman took over the packinghouses." I knew that "'48 was rough." One piece of the American Gas story especially baffled me. If Helmer Myre had been such a villain as sheriff, why was the nature preserve we all called Big Island renamed Helmer Myre State Park in his memory? More troubling still was the fact that his granddaughter was my schoolmate and friend. She was a sweet, trustworthy girl who lived in a house no fancier than ours, even though she was a Republican. She certainly meant me no harm. I assumed that Donna knew the story of the American Gas strike, and though I was curious about how she might tell it, I knew the local code of silence well enough not to ask.

In the safety of distance, the American Gas Strike has become legend, and in the manner of legends, the story as I heard it is not entirely true. Only recently have I attempted to sift objective fact from the wishful thinking of memory. The first rift in the story was Floyd B. Olson's short life span. One day I happened to read that he died in office in 1936, the year before the strike took place. It was Olson's successor, Governor Elmer Benson, who released the prisoners. This was disappointing news. The flamboyant, self-proclaimed radical Floyd B. Olson, Minnesota's first Farmer-Labor Party governor, makes such a fine hero. Dad liked to boast that Governor Olson was a personal friend of his granddad Ostrander. Furthermore, on-the-scene newspaper accounts of the strike say nothing about Benson wrestling Myre for the gun, a move that would have been ill-advised. Years before his election as sheriff, Myre had won the title of national light heavyweight wrestling champion of the world, at Sheridan, Wyoming. There is no mention of Gas Hans, officially Hans Christian Hanson, but only his son Russell, who had already taken over management of the company and acquired the nickname Gas Hanson.

I had assumed that "strike" meant that the workers voted to stay away from their jobs until the company agreed to some new contract provision. Instead, this strike was a "sit-down," an occupation of the plant by those workers intent on establishing a union there, namely southern Minnesota's homegrown Independent Union of All Workers, which was already making headway at the packinghouse. Nineteen thirty-seven was *the* year of the sit-down strike, a new strategy used across the country against employers who resisted union organizing. This strike was set off by the firing of four production employees—Chet Yocum, Ole Bjorklund, Oscar Christianson, and Peter Sorenson, for reasons that vary depending on who reports the story. Was it an ordinary layoff due to a reduced demand for gas machines, as the company maintained? Were these four men "troublemakers" who refused to do their work or did it ineptly, as the Albert Lea *Evening Tribune* reported? Or were they singled out for their union activism, as the IUAW claimed?

It is not the point-by-point researched truth of the American Gas strike that concerns me as much as what the story means to those who pass it on, and just who gets to hear it. Is it a piece of oral history, of working-class lore that preserves Albert Lea's identity as a militant laboring town? Is it an instructive tale, meant to clue the listener to class divisions that are seldom openly discussed? Is there another version of the story recounted in Shoreland Heights? Who among my classmates, I wonder, knew this story, and which version? How many porcelain balls have been preserved as family heirlooms—or thrown out as white elephants?

Why is the story not more public, told more accurately as a history lesson for local children? Why did I have to piece it together myself, when there were so many resources still at hand? Among my grandpa and grandma Petersen's acquaintances was an old man named Chris Nelson who, as a young man, had survived a shipwreck on his way from Denmark to America. I persuaded Nelson to tell a bit of the ordeal on tape one time, in Danish, and though the voice on the cassette has long since worn away, I still remember the drama that imbued his memory. As he listed the survivors of the shipwreck by

number and nationality, he paused before the final beat . . .
"og een Dansker, Chris Nelson." Twenty years later at the Freeborn County Historical Society, I ran across an audiocassette
of an oral-history interview with Chris Nelson. It was the shipwreck story I expected to hear, not a fervid account of Albert
Lea's early labor struggles. Chris, it turns out, had organized
the Carpenters' Union, even though he was an independent
contractor. Since he hired himself and his employees out on a
contract that he had to negotiate, he figured he was really just
working for wages, too. Austin was a better labor town than
Albert Lea, he believed, because Albert Lea had Gas Hans.
Gas Hans may have been a Dane, he allowed, but he treated
people like slaves. Indeed, Chris's sharpest words were reserved for fellow Danes who fought wage increases. "They
were stinkers," he said. "They wouldn't pay nothin'." The
American Gas strike was the critical turning point in Chris
Nelson's account of Albert Lea's labor history: "We got organized and then they had to pay."

Don Nielsen, president of the packinghouse local from
1974 to 1984, was a fourteen-year-old boy with a paper route
in 1937. Sixty years later, sitting in his kitchen across Dane
Lake from Gas Hans's house, he reminisced about selling extra papers to the pickets, who were eager to see what the reporters from Minneapolis had to say about their cause. He had
a friend whose father owned an automobile garage across the
street from American Gas, so Don got to watch much of the
action from the rooftop of that building. He remembers the
event of the porcelain balls: "How they got those balls out of
there I don't know, but they just busted every window out of
the front of that whole building. One other time the sheriff
and his deputies got all of the scabs out of the plant, and we
were sitting up there when they marched them all by that line

of strikers. I don't know how the scabs got by that crowd, but they did. That was a rough strike. I was there the day they rolled the police car down the hill by the Danish Brotherhood and down right into the lake. So I seen quite a little of it, and I was young then." The shattering of windows, the "one other time," and "the day they rolled the police car"—stretched out in dramatic sequence in Nielsen's memory—all share the same date: Friday, April 2, 1937.

I have to admit that Don Nielsen's eyewitness account, told with both relish and headshaking concern, aroused the same mix of emotions in me. Not one to espouse violence, I nevertheless seize upon the American Gas Strike legend as a clear and simple tale of class rivalry, the extreme but logical conclusion of all that I learned growing up about the differences between us and the rich people. Everyone material to this conflict is present; there are no absentee owners with hired managers to do their dirty work. Lines are drawn purely by labor or business allegiance: Dane against Dane, the Norwegian Republican sheriff versus the Norwegian-Swedish Farmer-Labor Party governor. As handed down, it is a story of pure labor unity. There is clearly some cathartic value in casting Gas Hans as the industrial tycoon and Helmer Myre and his deputies as the Pinkerton goon squad in our own little intra-ethnic class war.

In truth, the American Gas strike is a complicated piece of labor history, muddled by factional disputes, secret committees, and outside agitators on both sides. Ferreting out the facts means lining one partisan newspaper account beside another of a different persuasion, to sort where they agree and where they don't. This is a lengthy pursuit that I gladly leave to the labor historians. It's the *legend* that interests me, a never-ending story that morphs as memory fades or returns and imagination intrudes. When I told Dad I was reading old newspaper accounts of the American Gas strike, he immediately volunteered story lines I hadn't heard him tell before. "I was over in Austin that day," he began, "delivering groceries for Western Grocer. I drove by Hormel's just as the whistle blew, and nobody come out. They were all over in Albert Lea, fighting. All the labor-haters were uptown with clubs, and old man Church, I think his name was, an old retired Army sergeant the company hired, was sitting up at the jail with a machine gun." Old man Church? What about Helmer Myre, whom I have envisioned all these years aiming that gun at the approaching crowd?

I thought I might check these discrepancies with my sister Nancy, who was only two years old in 1937 but had at least heard the story closer to its source. *What story?* she asked. She didn't know anything about the American Gas strike until she was older. The dad she remembers from childhood was exhausted and edgy after working at a detestable job all day and hauling drunks home in a taxicab at night just to afford a subsistence living. He never took her to the union hall or out leafleting for the DFL. They didn't go for rides and couldn't afford root beer. Any time Dad had off work he spent building our house, which was still unfinished and barely furnished when Nancy left for Mankato State Teachers' College. When was there time for stories? Oral history, I should have known, takes time to shape itself. It needs some leisure and some prosperity to flourish. As the latecomer child of the postwar economic boom, the heyday of the labor union, I was my family's lucky recipient of this legend from the rough, unruly days of labor organizing.

Enough time has passed now to air the legend safely, in all its variant forms. The city owns Gas Hans's private island and has replaced the tangled undergrowth with a grassy lawn and park benches. The county jail was torn down to make way for courthouse parking. A new Union Center was built in the 1950s, and the Danish Brotherhood building is home to the Veterans of Foreign Wars. The American Gas Machine Company is long gone, done in by rural electrification and a trusted employee who used company secrets to set up a rival business. In its place stand a forum for gassy arguments (City Hall), and a populist hotbed of explosive stories (the public library).

Who knows what other stories remain half-told? At the same time that the American Gas Machine Company was occupied, there was another smaller and less contentious sit-down strike in town. With the support of the IUAW and many sympathetic Albert Leans, eleven dime-store clerks seeking higher wages and better working conditions ate and slept in the Woolworth store on Broadway. Theirs is not a victory story but one of valor nonetheless, though it is hard to tell that from the *Evening Tribune*'s trivializing coverage. The newspaper chided the "girls" who foolishly forswore their chance to parade in their Easter finery and instead displayed their shameful misbehavior in the Woolworth show windows. Here are their names, for all those great-great-grandchildren in need of a heroic legend: Mary Siverling, Dorothy Jensen, Nelberta Gunderson, Mayme Oliphant, Petra Halvorsen, Marion Conway, Virginia Nelson, Genevieve Larson, Viola Heggelund, Charlotte Hovland, and Mabel Christiansen.

The *Tribune* disingenuously refused to publish these names and the names of the American Gas sit-down strikers, to preserve peace in the community, but then, on another page, ran the text of an injunction that included a list of defendants.

Charged with bias in their labor reporting, the *Tribune* retorted, "When some agitator whispers in your ear that the *Tribune* is working against the laboring class of people, tell him to quit 'kidding.'" When I mentioned this to Dad, he said, "I don't know how a paper like that ever survived in a town like Albert Lea." "A town like Albert Lea" means not the quiet, subdued town of my childhood memory, but a laboring town, a town of strong union sentiment, a town where working people insist on decent wages and fair treatment. Those two visions of Albert Lea coexist, sometimes peacefully, sometimes not.

The *Evening Tribune* did, indeed, have a rival for a time, the *Freeborn Patriot*, published weekly from 1934 through 1937. I had known of its existence from a single page stored among family photos and clippings. Beneath my great-grandfather's obituary is a news story headlined EVEN HENRY FORD / TO OBEY LAW. This certainly piqued my curiosity. Reading microfilms of the *Freeborn Patriot* is like watching, from behind the drapes, while familiar dolls come alive after midnight and dance. Here is old Chris Hvolboll, who used to nod off over his whist hand at my grandma Petersen's kitchen table while the ash on his cigar grew dangerously long. He is advertising his grocery store to "Fellow Workers" and is listed among the sponsors of a "mammoth" meeting of the cooperative movement. The Leslie Registers, who disappeared from the county gossip columns after losing their Moscow farm, are hosting Sunday visitors in Alden in the pages of the rabble-rousing *Patriot*, alongside news of the Independent Union of All Workers, the Farm Holiday Association, and the Farmer-Labor Party. In his editorials, Roger Ostby reinterprets news reports from the unnamed local daily, which he calls "the kept press."

The lead front-page article in the *Freeborn Patriot* of Friday, July 19, 1935, is headlined CONNIVINGS OF DISHONEST MEN /

CHEAT NATURE AS WELL AS / FELLOW BEINGS, WRITER
AVERS. It opens with a rather flowery poem, an homage to
"The Land of the Sky Blue Water," then goes on to detail before and after scenes from the writer's beloved Geneva Lake.
A large agricultural drainage project conducted by milling and
refining interests from Minneapolis and Illinois has drastically
altered the lake and its surrounding landscape. "Turn, ye student, to the history of Freeborn county," the writer urges.
"Read of the consignment of all of the objectors to outer darkness, which is the final destiny of all dissenters by the powers
that be."

Returning the dissenters to the light of day is the burden
I bear, I'm afraid. The article's byline reads "Elbert H.
Ostrander." Great-Grandpa Ostrander died a week after the
American Gas strike, and I have long hoped for an afterlife
so that I can meet him. Now I realize he's been here all
along, hounding me, goading me on. *Go ahead and unsettle
that deceptive calm*, he says. *Tell those disquieting stories*.

UNFAIR

1959

One of life's splendid ironies is that times of great uncertainty tend to show us how firmly grounded we are. Nineteen fifty-nine, the end of eighth grade and the start of ninth, was such a time for me. My sense of self, which had begun to falter under the stresses of puberty, was bolstered by a dawning conscious-ness of the world. It's not that I was ignorant of the world be-fore that. I had been reading maps for years and imagining trips through the landscapes they represented. I'd watched Communism bleed across the map of Europe in *The Weekly Reader*, which I not only read in school but ordered for the summer and scooped out of the mailbox with genuine excite-ment. Dad had initiated me into political door-knocking in Adlai Stevenson's first presidential campaign, when I was only seven, and Miss Kriesel had taught us so well in sixth grade that I could describe the federal system of checks and bal-ances, tell you just how a bill passes through Congress, and name all the current Cabinet secretaries. But this was all fairly passive knowledge. I had little sense yet of my own place in this world or my potential as an actor in it. Caught in a new adolescent malaise, I felt isolated and powerless even to set the course of my daily life.

Being fourteen in a town the size and location of Albert Lea was like making a long, tedious turn around the desolate outer rim of American culture. Philadelphia was the whirling center of teenage dreams, the heart of rock and roll, the home of the television show *American Bandstand*. Every weekday after school, unless play tryouts or a school newspaper meeting called louder, I ran home from Southwest Junior High to catch all ninety minutes of *Bandstand*. I typed out the names of all the regular dancers I could identify on Nancy's clattery old manual typewriter, and Mom sewed me a jumper cut to look like the Catholic school uniforms some of the *Bandstand* girls wore. We even found fabric the same shade as the uniforms appeared on our Emerson Easy-Vision TV, which turned everything a pale gray-green.

Underneath this urban, Italian-Catholic disguise, a girdle I dared not go without, even at a scrawny ninety-six pounds, held up the nylons I now wore to school every day. To hear the words "growing up" and "developing" made me cringe with embarrassment, although I had secretly felt impatient for the changes that were finally taking place. Yet I was hardly swept up, as I had expected to be, in the rush of excitement that was supposed to mark the teenage years. My only dance partners were the living-room doorjamb, which stood patiently erect while I spun around it, and my neighbor Judy, who generously agreed to lead while I practiced the girl's obligation to follow. The first time a boy asked me to "go to the show," a Friday-night movie, my mother slapped my stomach butterflies dead with her practical question, "What Hansen does he belong to?" A run-of-the-mill Hansen didn't exactly fit my notion of teenage romance. In my fantasies, I was courted with gentle passion by a swarthy guy named Nick Laurino, whose name appeared to me in a dream.

Fantasy was where I lived much of the time. My real life, to judge from the diary I kept from May 9 to August 24 of 1959, was rather dreary: "Today was about the most boring I've had in a long time. I'm going to start a new game. When I haven't got anything to do I'm going to sit uptown and watch people go by, and try to figure out what they are like." This was a desperate time-passing habit for a teenager to resort to, not the valuable preparation for literary character sketches it might appear to be in retrospect. The diary reads like a formulaic lament for all that is lacking in my paltry life: I wish I were popular. I wish I had a boyfriend. I wish I were a normal teenager—the kind who hangs out at the soda shop after school. I wish I lived in Philadelphia. I wish I had a personality. It was, I believe, adherence to formula that makes the diary such morose reading now. I was writing about the subjects I believed a teenager ought to be recording in her diary. Lacking proper diary material, I could only decry its absence.

Despite the depressive effects of rushing hormones and faulty advice from teen magazines, I had, in fact, a healthy adolescence. I did well in school, where everything except science and gym came easily and home economics set off a stubborn resistance to domestication. I felt confident about my intelligence, which I hoped would someday compensate for my lack of beauty, and I had already decided to go to college. My parents didn't drink to excess, never beat me, and did only a normal amount of hollering. They painted my bedroom the deep shade of purple I picked out, praised my report cards, and welcomed my friends into our house. Those friends, whose names appear in enough entries to suggest a busy social life, were no more aswarm with boyfriends than I was. It just didn't occur to me to write about what really mattered, the experiences that have kept hold in memory without any written record.

In April of 1959, my sister Joey married her junior high boyfriend, Rodger, my favorite of all the boys our family's beauty queen had dated. The wedding was a private, low-budget family affair at the Little Brown Church in the Vale in Nashua, Iowa, the church we had sung about in school, the boys' cracked voices pushing for depth on "Oh come, come, come, come . . ." Music at this church came courtesy of an elderly woman, her legs wound in bandages, who pounded out the wedding march as though Joey and Rodger were headed for war rather than matrimony. Nancy, the maid of honor, sobbed all through the exchange of vows. Not yet attuned to wedding sentiment, I assumed she was crying because her own marriage plans kept getting foiled by the Reformation, which still raged in Albert Lea 440 years after Luther nailed up his Ninety-five Theses in Wittenberg. Hers was to be a mixed marriage, Lutheran and Catholic, as unthinkable as a blending of species. A month later, however, we were back at the non-denominational Little Brown Church to watch Nancy marry *her* Roger without sanction from either of the warring religions.

It only dawned on me later, after Joey had gone "home" to Mankato and Nancy moved away to a new teaching job in Battle Creek, Michigan, what these weddings meant for me. Though Nancy had left for teacher's college when I was eight and Joey for nurse's training when I was eleven, marriage took them permanently from home. I was left behind, an only child in a queerly empty house. Little sister "Beanie" was no longer a viable identity. It was time to figure out who and what I might become.

That question did get occasional attention in my diary. Judging myself totally without personality—more nebbish than tabula rasa—I resolved to get one. As I watched my grade school friends fall away into identities I wouldn't choose for myself, my own core came clearer. "We were parked up by the dime store tonight after the show," I wrote. "There were so many rowdies running around. I don't see why they would want to be rowdies. They're getting worse all the time. If only there was something I could do to stop the rowdy population from growing. It's as if all the people in the world were standing around a hole in the ground and one by one each person was either yanked or fell in until there were only a few 'fairies' left." ("Fairy" was not the epithet for a homosexual but the rowdy word for rule-abiding teenager.) "I know I do many, many bad things, but I wouldn't even consider showing all my bad on the outside, tho' sometimes I've been tempted to rebel."

I was barely beginning to see the difference that social class made in sorting rowdies from fairies. Rich kids could smoke, drink, and make out promiscuously without retribution, but working-class kids who broke the rules risked their reputations, their liberty, and their futures. A girl judged "incorrigible" could be sent to the reform school in Sauk Centre for running away from an abusive home or having a child out of wedlock. "Delinquent" boys were shipped off to Red Wing or else offered "the military option" at seventeen, to be shaped into dutiful citizens at Fort Leonard Wood in Missouri or the Great Lakes Naval Training Center in Illinois. I quickly learned that if I hoped to get away and make something of myself, I had better be "good," and staying good meant, above all, not risking pregnancy. First off, I decided, I would say "hi" to everybody I passed in the school hallways and run for Student Council.

In Saturday morning Confirmation classes that met weekly through eighth and ninth grades, the pastors of First Lutheran Church struggled to hold an impressive ninety-two of us to their vision of the straight and narrow. And narrow it was. Although most of us had known each other since babyhood in the church nursery, and were contending with the same complex matters of morality and faith, there was no room for honest talk about our confusion. Instead, we memorized *Luther's Small Catechism* and listened to the Reverend Melford S. Knutson's warnings about false beliefs: The Methodists believe that the bread and wine are nothing but symbols of the body and blood, but that's wrong; it is *truly* the body and blood, *within* the bread and wine, that are offered for our salvation at Communion. But the Catholics take that too far. They believe the bread and wine are magically changed into actual flesh and blood, so Communion is like cannibalism. And instead of sharing the wine with the congregation, the priest drinks all of it, which is why so many priests are alcoholics. To sort my own instincts about what was right from what seemed to me like bigotry, I took the glow-in-the-dark plastic cross I had won for well-prepared Sunday school lessons into my closet and prayed on my knees for divine truth, crossing myself afterward like those exotic, and thus alluring, Catholics.

Grandpa and Grandma Register's *National Geographic*s and View-Master scenes had long since aroused my curiosity about other cultures and other faiths, and hearing snatches of Danish, Norwegian, and Spanish around town had made me eager to learn a foreign language. I bought a French pocket

dictionary in the basement bookstore at Sanders' Drug and ig-
norantly strung words together in sentences just the way I
would in English. When I enrolled in Beginning French in the
fall of ninth grade, I had at least the advantage of a small vocabulary; learning to pronounce the tight vowels, the dental *l*s,
and the nasal sounds correctly was a joy like singing. Even verb
conjugations were a newfound entertainment, as much fun as
crossword puzzles. The biggest thrill, though, was the news
that French was a unique system of thought, a distinct pattern
of sounds linked with meanings, a special way of seeing and organizing bits of life. I felt as though I had switched on a light
that allowed me to see into new rooms and passages in the
human mind I had never imagined were there. And one room
opened into yet another: Spanish, German, Swahili, Chinese,
Urdu.

My enthusiasm put me in danger of becoming teacher's pet,
but who could resist Mme. Pulliam's good graces? She was our
beautiful emissary from the outside world, a native of Phil-
adelphia(!) who had actually studied at the Sorbonne. She
wore her dark hair long like a beatnik, but her bright red lip-
stick broke the pattern. One day she shocked us all breathless
by showing up for class in red tights and a skirt above her
knees—a woman her age, probably thirty! While other kids
mocked her outlandish dress, a few of us scoured the stores
uptown for Danskin tights and wore them by secret agreement
on Fridays, with our pleated skirts rolled several times at the
waist.

The fall of 1959 brought yet another life-changing development. I made a new friend in English class, a best friendship
that put many of my laments to rest. Linda Melting was six
inches taller than me and had the long, thick eyelashes I had
to fake with Maybelline, but her soft voice and kind manner

soothed the timidity I felt at first. Her dad, a salesman at Wilson's, had been transferred back to Albert Lea after six years in Los Angeles. Linda was not only easy to pass the time with, but she liked to talk about serious things, to sort out puzzling events and make sense of perplexing behavior. I liked the basic me that was reflected back in conversations with Linda, and I guessed that she could help me polish the raw edges I exposed to the world. I could even trust Linda with my heretical attraction to Catholicism and my anger at injustice, though we mostly fretted about boys. Just as our friendship settled into a comfortable daily pattern, however, it was put to a difficult test of loyalties—by a strike that placed our families in opposing camps and brought into view all the subtle differences our parents' jobs made in our own hopes and possibilities.

My new consciousness of the world and of my right to a self-defined place in it was not an automatic result of surviving puberty and growing up a bit. Instead, I felt my family, my hometown, and myself being pulled into the vortex of human history by a series of Momentous Events. The first of these is still commemorated every year on February 3 in Clear Lake, Iowa. WDGY, the top hits radio station from the Cities, brought us the startling news: a small plane carrying singing stars Buddy Holly, Richie Valens, and the Big Bopper from a performance at the Surf Ballroom in Clear Lake had crashed in a field fifteen miles northwest of Mason City—barely twenty miles south of Albert Lea, just across the Iowa border. The following days passed in numb disbelief and mourning; instead of practicing our dance steps, my friend Judy and I sat quietly in front of the TV during *American Bandstand*, worried that our usual giddiness would bring on other disasters. I often caught myself trying to peer over the horizon, to see the awful image my brain kept conjuring up: those revered bodies lying in a field of frozen corn stubble, just like the fields that bordered my neighborhood and our modern, glass-walled, turquoise-tinted junior high. Along with the sorrow came a macabre sense of satisfaction. I had longed so much for rock and roll to come to Albert Lea. Now even the kids on *Bandstand* had to turn their attention to my cold and barren homeground.

The television news those early, wintry months was dominated by reports from Cuba. The bearded Fidel Castro, dressed in military fatigues, was a classic personification of revolutionary chaos, a threat to the orderly democracy we Americans cherished. Dad, who often talked back to the TV, surprised me by defending Castro: if American Big Business hadn't propped up the dictator Batista all those years while he starved out the Cuban people, Castro would be on our side, a good democratic leader, not a Communist. Newspapers, magazines, TV, all were to be taken with a healthy dose of salt. Only the gullible parroted back what they heard. The rest of us had opinions. Besides, the news was funded by Big (I heard "Bad") Business.

My shy and reserved mom had little patience for politics, which she treated as Dad's strange hobby, but there was one subject on the news that always drew her attention. Anything to do with racial desegregation would bring her out from the kitchen, her dishtowel or broom still in hand. I had first noticed this two years before, when she'd shush us up for the latest report from Little Rock, Arkansas. It was not only scandalous but sinful, she let me know, that Governor Orval Faubus, whose face revealed a heartless, mocking hate, would break the law to keep Negro children out of school. There were no black people in Albert Lea and I wasn't sure Mom had ever met any, yet it was clear to her where human decency stood on this issue. Sometimes tears pooled in her eyes as she talked about the courage it must take to face such hatred day after day.

I drew a connection between what we were seeing on TV and the symbol that identified Dad's union. On the front page of *The Packinghouse Worker* and on the union's letterhead was a black hand clasping a white hand in brotherhood. There were lots of Negroes working in the packinghouses in Chicago, he told me, and when I thumbed through *Wilson Certified News*, the company's glossy little magazine, I saw more in Memphis and Kansas City. It was simply right for us to side with people of another race, I understood, and to accept everyone's common humanity. Yet it was hard to reconcile this sentiment with local feelings toward Mexicans, the migrant laborers who had settled into jobs in Albert Lea. It was fine to hang out with my pretty Mexican friend with the long black ponytail, but dating her brother would tip me for sure into the rowdy hole.

One day in the spring, our social studies teacher, Mr. Denzene, showed us a 1945 newsreel about the concentration camps in Germany. We clamped our hands over our mouths as bulldozers pushed heaps of skeletal white bodies into pits the size of excavated basements. Terrible scenes like this had been playing-out in the world just as my classmates and I were being born fresh and innocent. As we struggled to squeeze that knowledge of evil into minds crammed with Sunday school lessons of love and charity, the mushroom cloud above Hiroshima took hold as the emblem for the year of our birth, the beginning of the Atomic Age. So this is what our childhood games of war, our imaginary shoot-outs with Nazis and Japs, had been all about.

We must learn to be wary, we were taught, of dictators who

threatened our American ideal of democracy. We already knew the dangers of Communism from watching *I Led Three Lives*, a show we tuned in with special interest because Richard Carlson, who starred as secret agent Herb Philbrick, was an Albert Lea boy. The major dictator on the scene was Nikita Khrushchev, the leader of Communist Russia who had threatened to bury us. But there on the TV news in September was the very same Khrushchev chatting amiably with a farmer in Iowa, our neighboring state. How were we to tell a monster apart from a smiling, bald-headed fat man?

The human capacity for cruelty had become an unavoidable truth. My friends all seemed to be reading Anne Frank's diary, spurred by the newly released movie starring Millie Perkins and Richard Beymer. I read it with the same pity and horror that strike most teenage readers, yet I couldn't imagine any trait, like Anne's Jewishness, that would subject me to genocide. Instead, I wondered if I could be as brave as the good Dutch people who hid her family, and I had my doubts. It upset me to think I might be too concerned for my own safety to do what I knew was right. My copy of the book has Millie Perkins's mascara-lashed, pouty-lipped face on the cover rather than Anne Frank's natural, openmouthed smile. I can tell by the condition of the pages that I didn't finish it, but relied on the movie for the dreaded ending. The sound of the claxons drawing closer resonated long afterward, and my expectations for normal teenage life began to waver. Was hanging out at a soda shop a proper end for an embattled day at a school where you were shoved and spat upon? Did popularity matter to kids whose lives were in danger? I wondered, too, whether my own life might be more "real," more important, than the glossy fictions I had fallen for. But there was no comfort to be found in *The Diary* for my adolescent uncertainties.

In fact, Anne's deep intelligence put my trivial blatherings to shame. In August I buried my diary in a dresser drawer and didn't write in it again for more than a year.

My world was not as simple and dull as I had judged it to be. My sense of order was, indeed, turning topsy-turvy. By fall, even the television shows to which I had hooked my hopes and passions were suspect. Nobody was really as smart as the single-topic geniuses on *Twenty-One* and *The $64,000 Question*. The quiz shows were rigged. Alan Freed, the disc jockey who had made rock and roll popular enough to vie with oompah bands and Patti Page for playing-time on KATE radio, had been caught accepting payola from record companies, and even *American Bandstand*'s brotherly host, Dick Clark, was under investigation.

In a rush of summer naïveté, I had recorded a glimmer of excitement in my diary. Judy Olson, Joey's successor as Miss Albert Lea, had won the Miss Minnesota title and had a crack at becoming Miss America. "I'm so happy," I wrote. "Maybe Albert Lea will be famous someday. I hate it the way it is now." By mid-December, Albert Lea was famous enough to be swarming with television and newspaper reporters, but not because of its beauty queens.

At 6:30 P.M. on Tuesday, November 3, 1959, the United Packinghouse Workers of America called a nationwide strike against Wilson & Co. Fifty-six hundred production employees in Albert Lea, Omaha, Cedar Rapids, Kansas City, Los Angeles, and Memphis stayed away from work for the next 109 days. Two days into the strike, three inches of snow fell on Albert Lea and the temperature plummeted, over the next two weeks, to six degrees below zero, an unusual pre-January low, even in southern Minnesota's blizzard belt. Although I think of my native landscape as a vibrant green dotted with blue lakes, the entire strike took place in the white and shadow of winter.

I know these facts exactly because I read them in the newspaper clippings that striking sausage worker Hazel Gudvangen pasted each day in her scrapbook, now stored in a cupboard at the Albert Lea Union Center. What I remember on my own from November 1959 is an overcast sky and a group of men standing at the main plant gate, in zippered parkas and caps with the earlappers down, shifting back and forth on frozen, rubber-booted feet. The overcast sky may be a figment of my mood, however. In below-zero weather, the sky is typically a brilliant Arctic blue. The placards resting against the pickets' shoulders stated the problem as clearly as I understood it: UNFAIR.

A month later, "Albert Lea" took on new meaning, even beyond Minnesota: "a spineless, leaderless city" that tolerated "mob rule" by "labor goons." Those goons, I realized, were us. To my mind, Albert Lea had become an honorable labor town where common, ordinary working people sought the fairest measure of justice I could imagine—a right to the rewards of their own hard work. I was no longer just a lovelorn teenager. I was a proud and angry packinghouse kid living, if only momentarily, at the center of the world.

Now I regret that I left my diary blank for so long. I know it would never have matched the eloquence of Anne Frank's, but would more likely read: "Linda and I went uptown after school. A real cute National Guard guy outside the dime store winked at us. Ronnie called and we talked for two hours. He said Tom's brother and some other guys were the ones that burned that scab's car." I would be satisfied even with that measly firsthand addition to the public documents and memory fragments from which I must piece together the most momentous event of my teenage years: the strike that spun me into a frenzy, then planted me back on my own surprisingly sturdy feet.

On Strike

Words—especially strange, new words—fasten my memories in place. A new word cropping up in my parents' vocabulary was reason to stay alert. "Mandatory overtime," I heard Dad intone as he perched on the stool at the end of the kitchen counter, absorbed in one of his ever more frequent evening phone calls. "Mandatory overtime," he said to Mom when he came home earlier than usual one Monday in late October. Somebody in sausage had refused to stay and work overtime. He'd come in early to begin with, and when he'd put in eight hours, he told the foreman he was going home. The foreman told him ok, but don't come back tomorrow then. He was suspended right then and there. When the rest of sausage heard that, they stopped working, too, and they, too, got suspended. Wilson's finally sent the whole plant home on suspension, but now they were trying to call it a sit-down strike.

"Overtime" I had known since I was little. It was the extra time you worked for better pay, "time 'n' a half," double time on Sundays. It was time you didn't have to work, but you stayed on anyway to keep from running up bills, to have cash up front so you didn't have to buy on credit. Dad worked lots of overtime and we usually paid up front or bought on layaway. "You don't want to end up paying for a dead horse," Dad reasoned. Every other Thursday when the orthodontist came over from Austin and Mom dropped me off uptown after school to have my braces tightened, I carried the $12.50 payment in my white bucket purse. Without overtime, I'd be stuck with my crooked Ostrander teeth.

Mandatory overtime was a different matter, Dad explained over supper. He was in a serious mood, with none of his usual suppertime goofiness. Mom didn't have to say "no singing at the table," our only mealtime rule. They couldn't force you to work overtime, Dad insisted; it was supposed to be voluntary. There were laws that limited work to an eight-hour day, a forty-hour week. That much I knew. We had been learning about the eight-hour day in social studies, along with vertical and horizontal labor unions. I had to think hard to keep straight which was vertical and which was horizontal, but in Albert Lea it no longer seemed to matter. Dad's union was CIO, but I had climbed the steep stairs of the old union hall for AF of L Christmas parties well before the AFL-CIO merger and the opening of the brand-new Union Center. Union was union, and Samuel Gompers's ribbon candy and filled raspberries were just as sweet as John L. Lewis's. The only union people we didn't care to side with were the shysters and crooks like Dave Beck and Jimmy Hoffa from the Teamsters, who gave the rest of us a bad name.

Mom jumped up to dish more green beans from the pan on the stove. She was quiet, but she hadn't tuned out of the con-

versation as she often seemed to do. She sucked her lips inward, drew her eyebrows together, and watched the words vol-
ley back and forth across the table as I pelted Dad with questions. She was uncomfortable with all this talk, I could tell, and
with the ominous tone Dad's voice had taken. She liked things
nice and normal. Dad squished the last bit of hamburger
goulash through the tines of his fork and finished it off in
plenty of time to make the emergency rank-and-file meeting
at the Union Center. Even in a hurry, Dad always belonged to
the Clean Plate Club.

After Dad left, Mom sat at the table, finishing her supper in
solitude as she usually did, while I watched *Name That Tune*.
Rather than try to talk to her through her worry, I shut myself
in my room to do my homework. I had preoccupations of my
own, anyway. The day before, I had seen *South Pacific*, and the
doomed interracial love affair between John Kerr and France
Nuyen had left me with an ache at the bottom of my chest.
Even as I worked through algebra problems and tried to fac-
tor out the consequences of a suspension at the plant,
"Younger than Springtime" played on in my head like a dirge,
as though I, too, had lost my only chance at blissful love.

When I came out to watch *Peter Gunn*, Mom was wiping up
the floor in her already immaculate kitchen. The tiny flowers
on her housedress moved in and out of my side vision as she
picked up the living room and straightened coffee-table magazines that hadn't moved all day. I stared at the ten o'clock
news without really listening, then let it flow into Jack Paar.
Mom didn't protest that I was up too late, but sighed her habitual "Oh boy" as she watched for headlights in the driveway.

Dad came home without the puckered look he'd worn
through supper. Eight hundred people had turned out for the

meeting, and they'd voted to go back to work the next day. Wilson's wasn't going to get away with calling this a strike, though they might try the same stunts they pulled in June, when they stopped buying livestock and shut most of the plant down for nearly a week, then blamed the union for a "slowdown." The situation was riskier this time, Dad explained, because the plant had been working without a contract for over a month. If you slipped up somehow, or refused to do what you were asked, no matter how outrageous, they could throw you out on the spot.

Dad was so riled over the next few days that I made a point of tuning in whenever he talked, whether the words were addressed to Mom or to me or tossed into the air at some invisible opponent. The only way to keep someone's job safe was for everybody else to risk theirs, too. The old contract had run out September 1 and the union could have gone out on strike then, the way they did at Swift, but instead they'd gotten Wilson's to extend the contract while they negotiated a new one. But when the old contract expired again, Judge Cooney "unilaterally"— another new word—replaced it with a company proposal that the union had already rejected. The old coot figured he could make all the rules himself and just ignore the working people, Dad charged. Cooney never even showed up for negotiations, but sent his henchman, John Cockrill, to handle it all.

Nobody ever really wanted a strike. The last one, in '48, had been real rough and nothing much had come of it. A bunch of guys—the union officers and others—had even been fired in retaliation. A strike was always a last resort, because of the hardship it caused. The steelworkers had been out for three months already, and the mines up on the Iron Range were shut down for the time being, because there was nowhere to ship the ore. General Motors was out, too. As for Eisenhower, Dad added, he was probably playing golf or at a free feed somewhere, too busy hobnobbing with the big money Republicans to give a damn about us working people.

Hardship was what we would prepare for, and I tried to imagine what that could mean: fried bologna for supper and no Sunday roast beef, no french fries and soy sauce to go with my Friday-night Coke at the Canton Cafe, no more Ship'n'Shore blouses but just homemade ones in end-of-the-bolt material, no gas to practice driving the Pontiac on my learner's permit, a skimpy Christmas. I could make those sacrifices for a valiant cause, I thought, and it might even be fun for a while. Dad's voice on the phone, when he talked to my uncle Ted or called the Union Center for the latest news, was not always solemn. It could be agitated and angry, too, and it rose to a slightly higher pitch as he recited the litany of injustices that Wilson's was imposing on its loyal workers. I tried to read that change in pitch for its secret meaning, which I took to be excitement. We might be buckling down for hardship, but I began to look forward to a glorious rebellion.

Fifteen minutes before the end of their shift on Thursday, when everybody on sliced bacon was looking forward to going home, Wilson's posted an overtime notice calling for another two hours' work. Instead of giving in to it, the women and guys on bacon just quit for the day and started off to clean up. The foreman warned that he'd have to report them if they left the plant, and they might not be welcome to come back Friday morning. So they sat back down, refused to leave and refused to work. By the end of the day more than two hundred people had been suspended and told to get out.

Friday morning, the phone rang while I was still getting

ready for school. As I picked it up, I could hear several loud voices, and then over those was Dad asking for Mom. I hung around to eavesdrop, since a call before Dad's dinner break could only mean something was wrong. His voice, shouting over other conversations, was loud enough to hear if I just leaned in close, and Mom didn't mind. The management was asking people to sign a paper saying that you would agree to work whatever hours were posted and obey all the rules, or be fired. If you didn't sign, they wouldn't let you stay and work. Everybody was down at the Union Center now, figuring out what to do next. That afternoon he had more to say: Signing a pledge like that amounted to a "yellow-dog contract," and the NLRB had outlawed yellow-dog contracts. The company couldn't make people sign their lives away one by one. And they couldn't make you agree to rules if the union hadn't had any say in them. How low-down could Wilson's get, anyway, trying to hoodwink individual people as they showed up for work in the morning, rather than bargaining honestly with the union? And to do it while Chuck Lee and the other Local 6 officers were down in Chicago for negotiations was really chickenshit. Wilson's was going to call it a "walkout" or a "wildcat strike" for sure, but it was really a "lockout." Judge Cooney probably wanted a strike as part of some scheme to kill the union, but the union was going to file a grievance with the NLRB.

I took my new vocabulary to Confirmation the next morning and tested it in conversation until the pastor shushed us up to start the class: *It was a lockout, not a walkout*, I insisted, and *it all had to do with mandatory overtime*. Though they were no doubt bad words in church, "yellow dog," "NLRB" and "grievance" resounded, in my ears, with the same godly sonority as *Luther's Small Catechism*: "We should fear and love God so that we do not rob our neighbor of his money or property, nor bring them into our possession by unfair dealing or fraud, but help him to improve and protect his property and living."

It was Halloween that night, a frustrating holiday for a ninth grader. I was too old for tricks-or-treats and still too young and timid for the pranks the high school kids played: soaping windows, drive-by tomato pelting, dumping onions where cars would run over them and release their stinging fumes into the darkness. But it was a truly eerie Halloween nevertheless, with real specters to fear. Jobs might be lost. Wilson's might make good on its threats to leave town. The prospect of no work, or at best unsteady, low-paid work, was an ugly ghost from our parents' younger days. It both scared and thrilled me, a mixed feeling something like Luther's *fear and love*, I supposed.

The Sunday *Tribune* reported that Wilson's had broken off negotiations after one thousand "strikers" walked away from the plant on Friday. One word, "strikers," was the tip-off that the story was told from Wilson's angle. I felt a surge of pride as I read that "work stoppages" had started in Albert Lea and then spread to other plants. The article claimed that "the nub of the strike was refusal by employees to work scheduled hours in excess of eight hours a day pending signing of a new contract." It failed to mention that Wilson's had given the union its word a week before that there would be no mandatory overtime while negotiations were on. Now, of course, negotiations were off, and Cooney was calling all the shots again.

Dad was off to the Union Center again Sunday night for another emergency meeting. To pass the time, I called Linda and we tried to talk about everything but this threat to our new friendship. It wasn't hard to find other topics. *Blue Denim* with Carol Lynley and Brandon de Wilde was coming to town, and we weren't sure whether we wanted to see it or not. We were curious, of course. "A must for teenagers and their parents," the ad read. We could easily guess what it was about: *When they gave into their feelings, they put themselves in a straitjacket for the rest of their lives . . .* The mystery was what happened after that— whether they got married or she went away to have the baby in secret or just went crazy from the sinfulness of it all. Linda and I tried to figure out how to ask my mom if I could go to the show. Would she expect me to talk about it? I didn't even want her to hear my half of this conversation, and had dragged the phone from the kitchen into the hallway, shutting the door on the cord. Even then I let Linda do most of the talking and answered her with mmm-hmms and code words.

Mom wanted me off the phone before long, in case Dad called with news; but he didn't. She and I both sat down in front of *Alfred Hitchcock*, as primed for suspense as we would ever be, but still easily distracted. The rumble of the garage door and Dad's heavy footsteps in the breezeway propelled us both off the davenport and into the kitchen. There was no strike yet, Dad said. Everybody was reporting for work in the morning, but no one was going to sign a yellow-dog contract.

"Locked out again!" was how he put it when he turned up at home the next morning as I was hurrying through breakfast to make the school bus. This time they had chained off the entrances and made you line up single file to show your badges. When you got inside you had to report to the employment office one at a time to have that paper shoved in your face. The kitchen light fixture rattled as Dad thundered down the basement steps to his workbench, eager for a problem that could be fixed with a wrench or a screwdriver.

The following day, November 3, the union took what was clearly the only honorable, self-respecting action possible: it put Wilson's rejected proposal, the one Cooney was treating as a contract, to a second membership vote. Only fourteen members of Local 6 voted to accept it. Six hundred and forty chose to hold out for further negotiations. Another 400 must have abstained or not come to the meeting. This was not in the strictest sense a vote to strike. As the workers saw it, Wilson's lockout—the company's refusal to let them work unless they agreed in writing to accept its terms—had forced a strike upon them. Wilson's responded with a $250,000 lawsuit against the Albert Lea local. Picketing would start at 6:30 P.M. and run through the night, and Chuck Lee reminded the crowd, "We want no incidents on the picket line." Orrin Bye, the vice president, called for volunteers to banner the plant gates, and Dad signed on for a shift. The signs would say UNFAIR LOCKOUT and WE WANT TO WORK.

Dad reported for picket duty at the main gate, along with Marion Toot, who lived down the street and across the highway from our house. He had brought a thermos of coffee and he offered a cup to Marion, who was standing at his post on the other side of the entrance. As they met in the driveway to pass the coffee, a pickup truck pulled in and the driver called them over. Dad knew the guy, a livestock buyer and therefore a management employee. They exchanged greetings, none too enthusiastically, since they were now on opposing sides. Then the pickup turned around, drove out, and headed down Garfield toward the stockyard entrance. That was the one and only time Dad stood duty on the picket line. After that, he was assigned to drive the scout car that ferried pickets between the Union Center and their posts outside the plant, and he brought them lunch. He wouldn't learn until months later how

fateful that single day of picketing had been and how steep a
price he and Marion Toot would pay for that hot cup of coffee
in the November chill.

Mandatory overtime, I have since learned, was the last straw
laid across labor's camelback. It was also the straw drawn out
of the pile, snapped in half, and held out for the choosing, yes
or no, do we continue to work overtime or not? Rather than
simply bear its accustomed burden, the union paused to weigh
it. Overtime was an unwritten expectation usually met by
workers with mortgages to pay, rusty junkers to replace, fever-
ish children to take to the doctor, or dreams of a fishing boat
and an outboard motor. Wilson's was in the practice of gear-
ing its workload to the supply of livestock on the market and
pushing for peak production. Before the union, they had hired
people short-term and let them go when the need shifted.
Now, with a contract that guaranteed steady employment, the
workers were accustomed to seeing the length of their work-
days fluctuate with the seasons. The fall of 1959 had brought
a glut of hogs and a consequent drop in the price paid to farmers, a near disastrous eleven cents a pound. The company was
eager to crank up the work pace and lengthen the days to get
that abundance of pork into meat markets and grocery stores
under the Wilson label.

This peak supply of hogs offered the union an opportunity
to pressure the company into negotiating a fair new contract.
Wilson's would certainly want to avoid a strike at a profitable
time like this. All it would take, the union leaders believed, was
a refusal to work longer days than the laws governing labor
standards had established as fair. This move could alienate the
already troubled hog farmers, but the UPWA was primed to

speak to farmers' organizations and try to make common cause with them. Like Rosa Parks's refusal to surrender her seat on the bus, the protests in sausage and bacon were not, as I had assumed, the sudden whim of exhausted workers longing for rest. Both actions were strategy. And this strategy was held in reserve throughout September and early October so that the international union could focus on its strike against Swift. The Swift strike was settled on October 25. The very next day, Albert Lea's sausage department refused to work overtime.

This information, which turned up in the UPWA archives in Madison, Wisconsin, caught me by surprise and made me question my childhood memories of how the strike came to be. I would have to see it as a partisan conflict, with reason and passion vying for control on both sides, rather than the one-sided moral struggle I thought I had experienced. I had come through the strike with a couple of gut-level convictions, born of instinct, it seemed, and appropriate to a true-believing teenager: (1) true justice is nearly always on the side of the worker, whom I perceived as powerless, and (2) employers are constant adversaries, driven by greed and deserving of little trust. This knee-jerk response was not worthy of a mature, liberally educated adult, I felt, and would not, I suspected, bear up to an objective test. A more complex understanding of whatever was at issue in the 1959 strike would calm my tremulous knees and engage my judicious brain instead. My plan was to "suspend disbelief" while considering the company's point of view, and to apply skepticism instead to the union's position.

However, a review of documents and newspaper articles showed me why I had come away from this particular strike with those two beliefs so deeply ingrained.

The list of issues on the table was long and tedious, offering occasional curious insights into the conditions of work at the plant. Among the union's demands:

- a raise in the "bracket points" that set the pay scale of each job and measured either its worth to the company or its severity and danger;
- time to sharpen knives in addition to clothes-changing time;
- notification of starting times and overtime at the beginning of each week;
- the right to negotiate new gang speeds and gang lineups, which determined how heavy a workload each person on the line had to bear;
- aprons, rubber boots, raincoats, shin guards, and gloves for those required to wear them. (I didn't know, until he sold them twenty years after retirement, that Dad had furnished his own mechanic's tools.)

Other items on the list were meant to firm up job security:

- protection from discipline for workers whose production did not exceed the standard set for their particular jobs;
- an automation fund, to which the company would contribute one cent per hundred pounds of shipped product, to assist those displaced from their jobs by machines;
- the right for employees affected by plant closings to transfer to another plant with their pension, vacation, and sick-leave credits intact, but without departmental seniority.

Still others would improve fringe benefits:

- insurance coverage for diagnostic testing;
- a right for pensioners to continue their health insurance by paying their own premiums at the company rate;

- pension payments for employees discharged between ages sixty and sixty-five because the company deemed them physically unfit for their jobs.

And then there was mandatory overtime. The union asked that overtime be voluntary after ten hours of work.

Wilson's counterproposal, released to the press at the same time it was offered to the union negotiators, did not speak point-by-point to these demands, but focused mainly on wages. In addition to the basic wage increase sought by the union, the company proposed to pay a bonus of two cents per hour each year for two years "as a compensatory payment in lieu of any and all other demands." "Compensatory payment" translated into union language is "bribe": Give up your pursuit of job security and better working conditions and we'll pay you an extra pittance. The union reduced its list of demands somewhat to maintain negotiations, but Wilson's kept banking on its four pennies to win, if not the union's acquiescence, at least public support.

Nonlaboring newspaper readers are easily persuaded that strikes are chiefly about wages. *Don't they make enough already?* they ask about those whose temporary refusal to work disrupts their travel or their eating habits or their garbage pick up. In 1959, $1.90 to start and an average of $2.60 an hour looked like a decent wage for a job that required no education, not even a high school diploma. To struggling small-business owners, to farmers who had seen both crop and livestock prices bottom out, and to public school teachers (whose annual salaries ranged from $4,200 to nearly $7,000), the Wilson workers looked greedy and disgruntled, with no real cause for complaint.

To union members and their families, the long, drawn-out, stop-and-start negotiations trailed off into one puzzling question: Why should Wilson employees make do with less than other packinghouse workers? The UPWA and the meatpacking industry engaged in one-size-fits-all "pattern bargaining." A master contract had been carefully hammered out by the union and representatives of all the major packing companies, just as in previous years. Armour and Cudahy had signed right away, as had all the smaller packers. Swift had settled its strike and signed. Hormel's followed along as usual and even sweetened the contract a bit with incentives and bonus pay. Only Wilson's was stalled at an impasse.

Nine days into the strike, both Ralph Helstein, president of the UPWA, and Wilson's John Cockrill turned up in Albert Lea to explain their positions to leading citizens of the town, in two separate meetings. Helstein tried to shift the public focus from wages to "so-called fringes," which he defined as "matters of real and substantial substance to the individual worker." "More important to us than wages," he explained, "is job security." There are no reports of whom Cockrill met or what he had to say.

The following day, Cooney sent a letter to Helstein laying out two conditions that must be met before Wilson's would resume negotiations: (1) "Binding assurance" that the "lawless acts" of late October would not be repeated, and (2) "Reasonable proposals" eliminating those demands that "usurp management prerogatives." The impasse was obvious: Wilson's would not even talk to union negotiators unless the employees returned to work and promised to do whatever was asked of them on whatever schedule the management set. In other words, the content of the yellow-dog contracts would be binding for everyone. Even then, negotiations would cover only wages and a few fringes considered reasonable by the company. Working conditions and job security were to be left entirely to the management's discretion. So was overtime.

I see now why my understanding of the strike is more visceral than intellectual, and why I cast it in the form of broader questions of justice, with powerless workers up against a heartless adversary. It was not only teenage ignorance that reduced the issues at stake to mandatory overtime or kept me from seeing labor negotiations as a balanced give-and-take process. Here were two incompatible worldviews, two warring faiths, two different perceptions of what work means and what is owed to or expected of the worker. The long list of issues resolved into two irreconcilable claims, workers' rights versus management prerogatives. The company saw the union as insubordinate, encroaching on its fundamental property rights, which included not only the plant itself but workers' time and physical exertion. The union, founded on the democratic principle of collective bargaining, read the company's refusal to negotiate as a violation of fundamental freedoms, a rejection of democracy itself. This was as adversarial as work could get, and Wilson & Co. during James Cooney's presidency is remembered now as the most hostile adversary the UPWA ever encountered in its twenty-five-year existence. One union officer called Wilson's the most "vicious, lawless, arrogant, and inhuman" of all the meatpackers. But just as Cooney was demonized in my house, we unsatisfied union folk were probably gangsters and goons in his.

Ordinarily, I like paradoxes. Dialectical reasoning appeals to me, and I prefer to leave complexities unresolved, to allow for the existence of multiple truths. In this case, however, one truth too easily deteriorates into plain meanness. Maybe it's because I know the other truth too well, having lived it. Letters addressed "To all Production and Maintenance Employes" before and throughout the strike made clear what authority was contained in the term "management prerogatives." The union called these "Dear John letters," because they usually brought bad news. The pickets were barely in place when Wilson & Co. sent a letter warning that employees who failed to return to work would have their medical benefits suspended. I was a sickly kid, and this threat would no doubt soon be tested in my family. The union quickly arranged to collect a month's premium of $13.57 from each member and submitted a check for the total to the company. The check was refused. This was a low blow, but hardly a surprise.

Fellow Adversaries

If you saw Chuck Lee and Leo O'Neal in a news photograph, you could only guess which is the plant superintendent and which the union president. Both wear hats, Chuck a porkpie and Leo a fedora. Listen to them talk, and apart from the sentiments expressed, their speech patterns are much the same. Chuck's, however, is measured and deliberate, while Leo is more voluble and quicker to launch into a story. This may be the first clue to distinguishing the practiced negotiator from the man used to giving orders. They address their wives, Beatrice and Bernice, by the nicknames "Tootie" and "Beans." Step inside their houses, and neither is decorated more fashionably or with more expensive tastes than the other. Both look like home to me.

Leo and Chuck are Albert Lea boys of Scandinavian heritage, born a dozen years apart yet both introduced to packing-house common labor at an early age. From that first experience of grueling work, their paths diverged. Their upbringing played some role in where they chose to direct themselves, but chance and opportunity figured, too. They are intelligent, thoughtful, and decent men who could have succeeded at anything. They have comported themselves well in what they have done.

Leo was the point man for Wilson & Co. in Albert Lea, the plant superintendent. He was answerable to the plant manager, the highest company official on site, but as far as the production workers were concerned, Leo O'Neal was the boss. His was the personal face of company authority, the one who smiled or frowned upon your work. Ask anyone who worked under him during his twenty-five years as superintendent, and they will probably say something like, "Leo was hot-tempered, but he was fair." As my dad tells it, "Leo'd get mad at some guy and bawl him out, and then he'd go back an hour later and put his arm around the guy." Leo himself owns up to his reputation: "I had a pretty . . . let's say 'warm' temperature. When they'd get me going, I didn't hold back much. And I never held a grudge in my life. It's a waste of time."

He came to Wilson's in 1937, not quite twenty-one, with a few years' work already behind him. His job at a local nursery had just run out, and he and a friend made plans to hitchhike to International Falls where the paper and lumber companies were hiring:

"We got as far as Minneapolis and we decided we were going back and give Wilson's one more chance to hire us. On a Tuesday morning I went out there all alone—and I was a little late getting out there—and I met about a hundred guys coming away who said, 'There's no use going there, because they're not hiring today.' 'Well,' I said, 'I've walked this far, so I'm going to go ahead and go out there and have them tell it to me themselves.' Just as I came up to the step of the employment office, a fellow came out on the step, and I said, 'Good morning.' He said, 'Good morning,' and I says, 'Are you hiring anybody today?' 'Nope.' I said, 'You mean a place as big as this doesn't have a job for me?' And his exact words was, 'Well, if you're so damn ambitious, there's a coal pile over there. You can start moving it.'"

Two days shoveling coal earned him more day labor shoveling salt in the hide cellar, until he was hired on in fresh pork: "There I did the very best I knew how, and in about six months I got a job as the branch house checker. And then in 1942, in February, they made me assistant foreman of the fresh pork department." After ten years as head of the curing department at the Faribault plant fifty miles north of Albert Lea, he came back home as pork division superintendent and was named plant superintendent in 1955.

Now long retired, he looks back on his work with fondness. "There were certain things that were pretty nearly the same every day, but there was always something new and different—more challenges, more problems that needed solving. I never got tired of it. And I never . . . I *never* . . . hated to go to work. It was because the people made it so interesting. I retired. A year later I couldn't figure out what it was I missed so much. It finally dawned on me it was that trip through the plant every morning, when around every corner in every department I came in, somebody had something to brighten my day with, most all the time. There were jokes they would throw at me, especially on the beef kill and the hog cut and what we call the gutdeck. Well, pret'near every place I went. I just kind of lived off of that. It made my day."

His ultimate responsibility as superintendent, the reason for the close watch on the work done in the plant, was to find new ways "to improve the results for the company." He speaks as a company loyalist: "I have nothing but the highest regard for Wilson's. I thought they were very fair. The only thing I can say in retrospect that I didn't appreciate is that they held on to their money too much and didn't want to spend it where it would do some good. I'm talking now about modernized equipment, or a variety of smaller projects that sometimes I had to connive to get." Leo is a superb storyteller, and many of his stories describe his finagling with the Chicago office to acquire that equipment, or, when that failed, the creative rigging he and the mechanical department had to do to make the old equipment work more efficiently. Leo's inventiveness not only got him promoted but kept his job exciting. Competitive by nature, he enjoyed pushing Albert Lea's production figures to the top: "I didn't want to be last on anything."

For the most part, the workers in the plant accepted his suggestions, as well as his challenge to offer improvements of their own. Being a homegrown boss who had come up from the coal pile undoubtedly helped. "The long and short of it was that Leo talked to the people," his wife believes. "He got to know the people and was in the plant *with* the people." "Well," Leo adds, "I could do some of them jobs, too, and they knew I could."

His relationship with the union was generally good, he claims, and he credits the union leadership with helping to maintain a strong, stable, cooperative workforce. He tells stories about grievances and negotiations that stalemated at higher levels, to the frustration of the folks in Albert Lea. Sometimes he and Chuck Lee, or later Don Nielsen, would just sit down and work the problems out themselves. When he talks about the 1959 strike, though, his face gets somber and his eyes cloud up. "It was bad. There's no other way to describe it. The hardest thing about it was the animosity that it created between supervision and workers, but also between relatives and friends. I had one relative that came here and would speak to my wife and would not speak to me. And I have never forgot that. We've forgiven that person—I have, anyway—but I have never forgot it and I never will."

Leo is not sympathetic to the notion of striking, and he traces his views to an incident in his childhood, when his dad, a boilermaker on the railroad, was out on strike and men were arming themselves with shotguns. "When people get to that point, it's just horrible. My biggest problem with trying to understand those things is, when you have a company that's providing employment and you want to get as much money from your job as you can, the only place that can provide that is the company. So when you both want the same thing, why do you fight? And that's the long and the short of it. The objectives should be the same."

Had he been allowed more say in Wilson's management, he would have done more to bring those objectives in line. "I tried to interest our company—not at that time, but in later years—in giving the workers some kind of stock options, or some kind of remuneration that lets them know they are part of this company. The fellow that I wrote it to was the top dog, and I know that he received it, but it just evidently wound up in File 13. I always believed in fair treatment, but that's in the eye of the beholder, of course."

He would also give employees more say in how the work is done. "My philosophy was always this: The guy closest to the job usually knows it best. You don't have to do what he says, but you're stupid if you don't listen to him." Employees work better, too, he believes, if they see just how their work contributes to the company's productivity and how that, in turn, affects their own income: "If you weren't competitive, you

were just at a disadvantage all around. That's why I appreciated these people. I'd be as honest as I could possibly be with
them on things of that nature, because I always figured the
worst thing in the world is if you don't understand what the
problem is. Usually, if you understand what the problem is,
you can do something to correct it."

Leo's solution to labor grievances is simple and individual-
istic, one that he practiced in his own life by leaving his first
adult job when the boss refused him a raise. "My idea about
that is that unless you owned the place, why then you should
do what they expect you to do; and if you're not satisfied with
the money you're getting, then you should do something for
yourself and not have to answer to that boss. My dad always
said, 'If you can't give the man you're working for a day's work
for what he's giving you, then be man enough to tell him you're
going somewheres else to get a job.' And that's exactly the way
I lived my life."

He did join the union when he was a production worker,
but he was reluctant to get actively involved. When others suggested that he run for secretary-treasurer, he turned them
down. There is a history behind this: "My brother had been in
a union in the American Gas, and I seen what happened to
him. He got blackballed all over town. He couldn't get a job. I
finally talked to my boss, and he talked to the employment
man down there, and he got him a job in the smoked meat department. But if I hadn't vouched, I don't know what he would
have done. They were really rough with him. He could get a
job here and there for a day or two, but it didn't last. So I didn't
come up with a very good feeling toward unions."

The American Gas strike had the opposite influence on Chuck
Lee. Among the family treasures he displays in his basement

are one of the porcelain "snowballs" used to break windows, and the original 1937 charter of the local Ironworkers Union, an independent union that later affiliated with the United Steel Workers. Chuck briefly explains how he came by these souvenirs: "Dick Hagen, who was the head of the Albert Lea Trades and Labor Assembly, which is all the organizations, he had some of these old documents and stuff, and he called me and said, 'I want you to have this because your dad's name is on it.'" Chuck's father, Simon Lee, was president of the Iron-workers, one of the unions directly involved in the situation at American Gas. Though Chuck was only nine at the time, he has one clear memory: "You know they had quite a fracas up there at the old American Gas building. As a result of that, they arrested the officers of the local union. Our neighbor a couple blocks up the street from where we lived, Gus Westrum, who was a policeman and a friend of the family's—we'd known him for years—he had to come down and arrest my dad and take him to jail. Now of course they didn't want to arrest anybody. He said, 'We have to put you guys in jail for your own protection.' I don't remember how long they were in, but then the governor come down and got them out."

Chuck enlisted in the Navy at sixteen, after a brief stint in the packinghouse. My dad remembers picking Chuck up in his cab shortly after he was discharged from the service. He was dressed in uniform, on the way to his girlfriend Tootie's for a date. When he returned to the packinghouse, at nineteen, his father's union leadership "maybe kind of rubbed off," and he, too, became active. It was a risky time to be closely involved. The following year, 1948, after a hard-fought strike that was never properly settled, nine union officers were "left out" and not allowed to resume their jobs in the plant. "Wilson's took the position that they made no effort to control that problem they had at the gate. There was some violence, there was some cars tipped and some rock throwing and what have you, but I don't know how nine guys were supposed to control a thousand people. That was kind of a loss situation," Chuck explains, "to the extent that the strike was called off and we went back to work without a contract. Of course that was the reason that those fellows lost their jobs. There was just nothing that we could pursue to get them back. We had to more or less reorganize, and we had a difficult time getting the company to do anything, or give us recognition. Ultimately we went through another election, and the ballots from the National Labor Relations Board proved that the people wanted a union. Then of course we had to sit down and try to get a contract."

His part in this effort won Chuck the presidency of Local 6 at the tender age of twenty-three, and he held that post for another twenty-three years. It was not until 1960 that the UPWA made the office of local president a full-time paid position. The stop-and-start negotiations of 1959 had required the officers to be released from work again and again. For his first nine years in office, Chuck worked as a gutsnatcher on the hog kill and his wife Tootie worked in bacon. To the comment that pulling out the hog's insides is a heavy job, he says only, "Ya, that was a tough job. But it was like any other job in that packinghouse. It was all tough work."

While Chuck served as president, the day-to-day business of the local was managed by its financial secretary, John Wolden, a white-haired old man with a thick Norwegian accent who had gone to work at the Albert Lea Packing Company in the 1920s and led the first efforts to organize a union there. "He was a square shooter," Chuck recalls. "Boy, he'd get mad at me. He had that old crank mimeo machine, and he could write a really blistering bulletin, but he'd take after the company in the wrong vein once in a while. One day I come up there after work, and John was putting out a bulletin and I was looking at it, and here was a big statement, 'Don't eat pork. It causes cancer.' I said, 'John, what are you doing here?' He said, 'Well, that's a fact. I just read it.' And I said, 'Well, you can't put that in the bulletin,' and he said, 'Well, it's already in there.' I said, 'Well, you're not putting that bulletin out. They'd sue us.'"

Though they had their tussles, the old organizer and the young strategizer found plenty of common ground in their frustration with Wilson & Co., whose "attitude in general was that they just didn't recognize the fact that the employees decided through an election that they wanted a union and should have the right to have a union. They never did subscribe to it. Wilson's just took the position that, 'We'll tolerate it, but only to the extent that we can get by.' They were difficult to get along with. Even though they negotiated a contract, it was a constant fight all the time. They'd just make up their own rules. So it was constant bickering and fighting in between contracts. That's why, over the years, there was a lot of walkouts in that plant in Albert Lea. You know, they'd just take completely unfair advantage of somebody, fire people—either that or implement some goofy program or change that just didn't make any sense. Things would blow up and the whole place would just walk out. That was because of Wilson's attitude. We'd have turmoil in the plant where there really shouldn't have been any."

In times of turmoil, Chuck would have to face off with Leo O'Neal, whom he describes as "real hard-nosed and tough. That's why they made him plant superintendent. He just wouldn't give in to anything, really." Yet the two of them worked out a means of settling disputes at the local level as often as they could. "Leo admitted on several occasions," Chuck asserts, "that if they'd leave him alone from the upper echelons, he could do a lot better job running that place."

Much of Chuck's effort went into improving the union's relationship with the community, which had been tense ever since 1948. "It seemed like there was always some animosity amongst the people—not all people, but some people. There always has to be some. They felt that the packinghouse workers, even though we were paid very little, were overpaid. As far as the business community was concerned, they didn't have any—very few of them anyway—didn't have any time for unions. And as a result, we just didn't participate in a heck of a lot, as far as the community was concerned." When he talks about the most outspoken antiunion businessmen, those who believed that workers went on strike just to cause trouble, his calm demeanor ruffles a bit. "It's amazing, the beaucoup of those people that convinced their employees that we were way overpaid to begin with. See, they'd say to their employees that they should be against that because those guys are making problems for this community. 'They're making too much money. They're getting too many benefits. And as a result, it hurts everybody.' You know, that's a bunch of crap. If it was that good a deal, they could have went out to the packinghouse and got a job."

The tension began to ease after the strike was settled in 1960, Chuck observes, without claiming personal credit for the improvement, "because there was a lot of bitter feeling in a lot of different places. It screwed up a lot of families. I had relatives that went in there. It takes a long time to heal after this situation. And there was a lot of hard feelings amongst some of the business people. Some of the guys that worked in the plant didn't treat some of the business people very good either. You know, they run up bills and were given credit, and then after-wards they never took care of their obligations the way they should have, so it took a while and some fence-mending. So we tried to get along and get involved in different things more so than we had ever done before, because we realized that if we were going to have other problems again, we needed some friends."

Besides winning friends for the union, Local 6's fence-mending also won praise for Chuck Lee's leadership. "Albert Lea was fortunate to have someone of the stature of Chuck Lee at the head of the union," Dr. Niles Shoff, mayor from 1958 to 1969, attests. "People respected him. Whenever I called him or the city manager called him or the chief of police called him, he always had time to listen to you." The UPWA recognized his skills, too, and hired him on staff, in 1974, as an international representative; he was responsible for organiz-ing, negotiating contracts, and generally helping out the union locals in an eight-state region. Though he traveled a great deal—never internationally, he is quick to point out, despite his job title—he continued to live in Albert Lea for the ten years he served in that post.

Both Leo and Chuck are retired now, and they have had coffee or lunch together on occasion. Leo is enjoying his leisure, fishing and bowling as his health allows, often with his former employees. He confesses to being a homebody who prefers his wife Beans's cooking to restaurant lunches. Chuck and Tootie take a regular morning exercise walk through the mall, and Chuck has become active in a member-run cemetery association, formed after a con man who sold burial plots skipped town with the perpetual-care fund. A cradle-to-grave union man, you might call Chuck Lee.

The Breaking Point

The few strikes that have made it into history textbooks—Homestead, Pullman, Republic Steel—are remembered for their deadly violence. Never mind that the shots were fired by police or armed security forces serving the employer; the onus of uncontainable rage fell on the striking workers themselves. Blue-collar workers, many more-privileged people believe, are prone to fistfights, drunken brawls, wife beating, motorcycle gang rampages.

This is not what I know to be true. My family, like others around us, settled peacefully into the daily routine of being on strike. We were angry, yes, but we kept our anger subdued, believing that a wary patience would better serve our cause. We had been through this before, after all, in far less settled times. In 1948, temporarily homeless, we had moved in with relatives; now we had a fully furnished house of our own, and the savings and loan had agreed to a temporary suspension of mortgage payments. Then Mom and Dad had three young children to feed and clothe and keep healthy; now there was only me, and Mom was free to work as much as she needed. Then I had been too young to understand the disruption in our lives; now I was trained in the virtue of delayed gratification. Leafing through catalog photos of bulky knit sweaters and desert boots satisfied me almost as much as hanging new clothes in my closet.

Dad, never content to sit still, hired himself out for repair and remodeling jobs and often earned enough to forgo the union's $18 weekly strike benefits. The union had set up a job-finding service and encouraged striking workers to show how enterprising they could be. Detractors who said, "They just don't want to work," would be proved wrong.

We had more to eat than I had expected, but now some of our food came in boxes that Dad and I picked up from delivery trucks unloading in the Union Center parking lot. Trucks came from as far away as South St. Paul, where Swift was back at work, and Local 9 in Austin brought us our Thanksgiving turkey. So far, we enjoyed Albert Lea's good graces, as well. Two hundred local businesses donated "everything from cash to snuff." No man need break his snoose-chewing habit because of the strike.

Besides staying away from work, the only pressure tactic the union exercised was a boycott of Wilson products, promoted by leaflets and buttons bearing a lampooned version of the company's advertising slogan. "The Wilson label protects your table" became "The Wilson label disgraces your table." Of course, this was an aggravation, and Wilson's quickly responded by filing a $500,000 damage suit against the UPWA. The court ruled in Wilson's favor, and the union dropped the slogan, though no one was sent out to collect the offending buttons. The boycott continued, sloganless but still fairly successful. In Albert Lea, only one small grocery store, Wayne's on South Broadway, advertised Wilson's meat.

Wilson & Co. was on the offensive, and its strategy, ever since the first shutdown in June, was to take its complaints straight to court. Choosing a sympathetic judge in another county, the company sought and won a temporary restraining order against the union for alleged acts of coercion and violence on the picket line. Though a local management witness testified that pickets had not prevented anyone from entering the plant since the first day of the strike, company officials in Chicago continued to claim otherwise and to accuse Local 6 of promoting violence.

Only nine union members crossed the picket line, but Wilson's had no intention of slowing production. There were rumors that black people rounded up from the day-labor employment lines in Chicago would be moved to Albert Lea to keep the plant open. There was a historical basis for the rumor. The big meatpackers had done just that in the 1910s and 1920s, recruiting black farmworkers from the South to fill the Chicago plants where white workers, native-born and immigrant, were attempting to organize a union. That tactic had ultimately backfired on the companies. As a result, the UPWA was a racially integrated union with a platform of full racial equality. It was involved early on in the emerging civil rights movement, and had even donated $11,000 in seed money to help establish the Southern Christian Leadership Conference.

Nevertheless, a mass migration of African-American strikebreakers to Albert Lea, a white town where "Mexican" was a loaded term, would have inflamed hatreds and maybe even buildings. Wilson's was mean, but not suicidal. The scabs who answered Wilson's far-flung newspaper advertisements were not of another race, let alone—as I would readily have believed—of another species. They were mostly farmers with surplus livestock to sell, wet corn rotting in their fields, and a lower than usual cash flow. And they were distressingly like us, with Norwegian and Danish names, Dutch names, German names, Bohemian names. Though many came from across the border in Iowa, some actually had kids in the Albert Lea schools.

What turns a strike to violence? When does the strikers' peaceful persistence, their controlled anger, give way to explosive rage? I know without doubt when and how that shift occurred in Albert Lea. Evidence of that moment—a sequence of two moments, actually—is preserved in a brown folder tied with orange string that spent thirty-seven years in a drawer of the mahogany desk that had once been our family's only "good" piece of furniture. Among a few other mementos of the strike are two Dear John letters on Wilson & Co. letterhead with its familiar logo: a barred red W, like a cattle brand. Both are signed by Vice President John Cockrill.

The first letter, dated November 25, 1959, two and a quarter pages of single-spaced type, ends with this sentence: "We hope to fill these jobs with our present employes, but, *unless you return to work by Monday, November 30, you run the risk of being replaced*" (Wilson's emphasis). The second, dated December 5, accuses the UPWA leadership of spreading rumors that a strike settlement is close at hand, reiterates the company's refusal to negotiate unless its two conditions are met, and closes, "Many of the strikers have now been replaced by new employes. You must understand that each day that you fail to return to work increases the chances that a new employe will have replaced you. If you are interested in working for Wilson & Co., Inc. I suggest that you return to work at once."

Up to this point, we thought the scabs a nasty incon-
venience: thoughtless opportunists who turn up to make a bit
of extra cash by filling in, robbing the regular workers of their
only leverage in contract negotiations, economic pressure on
the employer. "Scab" was, at the time, the only word I knew
for a strikebreaker. It was, I thought, a purely denotative
term, like "thief" or "pirate." I couldn't imagine why any sane
and moral person would choose to be one. Now these scabs
had been hired on as "new employes," "permanent replacements" for striking workers. If the company truly made good
on its threat to replace everybody who didn't return, the plant
would be operated entirely by scabs. Staying away from the
packinghouse until a contract was signed meant losing your
job there forever. In effect, the union's lawful right to strike
had been revoked.

The first letter created a stir, though it didn't bring workers
streaming back across the picket line. Instead, it lifted the lid
on their anger and turned a few of them to the violence the
company had already accused them of. In the dark of night, a
bag of paint was slung against a scab's house, sugar was poured
into gas tanks, a corncrib slashed, a tractor damaged. Several
scabs reported being tailed home from the plant by cars with
scowling faces in the windows. With the restraining order in
place, anyone caught in these acts was charged not only with
vandalism, but also contempt of court.

The union leadership read the Dear John letters as a bluff.
"Don't be a sucker for their phoney threats," Chuck Lee wrote
to the Local 6 membership. "They cannot replace the years of
skill you have in your head and hands. They cannot put out a
first class product with fourth class butchers. If you have been
in court, you have seen what a crummy lot they are hiring.
Don't let the number of cars in the parking lot panic you.

Those characters maybe can drive cars, but they cannot put out meat."

Nevertheless, the very notion of full-scale replacement was an insult too outrageous to ignore. It violated the workers' dignity as well as their rights, and brought hundreds of strikers and sympathizers to the plant gates at shift-changing time to see who these "new employes" were and to show them whose jobs they had stolen. There were, of course, taunts, name-calling, obscenities exchanged.

As the winter solstice nears in Minnesota, afternoons turn dark and cold. After four o'clock, it's hard to see who's who, to distinguish body from shadow, to tell whose arm is raised, which of the men in hooded parkas are on your side. In this murkiness, judgment falters, panic builds. On December 9, a car attempting to leave the plant through a gauntlet of angry people, some yelling, spitting, pounding on the windows, struck and knocked down Conky Stanek, a nineteen-year-old laborer and Golden Gloves boxing champion. He was treated at the hospital and released, but the incident was injury enough to draw retaliation. Had it not happened, some other provocation would have sparked a riot.

That night, and the following night, the scene at the plant looked like primitive warfare. Some strikers had come armed with baseball bats. Others combed the yard of the concrete company, next door to the packinghouse, for rocks and shards of concrete and fired them through the air or smashed them against car windows. They rocked and overturned cars, spread nails in the driveway, and shouted threats after cars that got away. Since the plant sat outside the city limits, the city's only jurisdiction was its Main Street boundary, the main entrance to the plant. Sixteen policemen patrolled that area, while the county sheriff and his two deputies tried to contain the rest of the melee. Chuck Lee used a bullhorn to urge the crowd to calm down and go home. "Use your common sense," he pleaded. "We are!" one of the rock throwers shot back.

Though I can call back the tense mood of those two nights, I didn't see any of this myself, except on the TV news and in newspaper photos, which were subsequently flashed across the country to a public all too ready to accept the surface story: union laborers behaving, once again, like hoodlums. I couldn't ask Dad for an eyewitness report. True to his own work ethic, he was out at my uncle Cliff's, finishing a new basement rec room. I knew Dad had seen plenty of violence in 1948 and didn't find any glory in it, though he relished telling one story: The police chief, aptly named Big Ole, had been watching a group of strikers struggle in vain to tip over a car. Finally, he ambled over and stretched out his arm, as if to stop them. Instead, he leaned down, reached under the car, and, with a big grin on his face, gave it the helping heave that overturned it. Now, in his forty-seven-year-old wisdom, Dad regretted that his fellow workers had let themselves be provoked. He knew, as he assumed Judge Cooney did, that violence easily turns public sentiment against a strike, no matter how just the cause. It was mostly the young guys who fell for it, he said, the ones with no families to support and little seniority to lose.

The tumult at the plant was pretty much off-limits to a teenage girl, at least one trying as hard as I was to be "nice," but it was enticing to hormone-driven adolescent boys. Photos reveal the white sleeves of Albert Lea High letter jackets in the shadowy crowd. Though I didn't know it until many years later, I had a surrogate on the scene, Morris Haskins, like me the child of a striking laborer, but two years ahead of me in school. It was a righteous anger like mine, a loyalty to family like mine that caught him up in the fury those two nights, though he also admits that the plant was "where the action was." What he experienced both excited and unnerved him. He joined in the yelling and pounding, but was struck by how crazy it all seemed. He watched while a bunch of angry men tried to drag the personnel manager out of his car and pull off his shoes. He knew this man, a neighbor, as a nice guy who enjoyed matching eager workers with suitable jobs, and they, in turn, thought well of him. Yet his backlog of good will was no protection against the fact that he was now responsible for hiring "replacements." In middle age, Morrie looks back on this scene from three vantage points. As a beef kill employee in his twenties, he learned firsthand how rigorous the work was, enough to "make a young man old real fast," and how committed or desperate you had to be to stick with it. As a National Guardsman, he learned about the "mob mentality" that takes over in chaotic situations, how you "lose your identity" and finally "just don't give a rip" what damage you do to others or to yourself: "It takes one person to ignite it, and pretty soon everybody's at it." Finally, as an Albert Lea police officer, he understands how torn the policemen must have felt. Blue collar themselves, they had relatives, neighbors, and longtime friends in the crowd, people they would have to get along with the rest of their lives.

From my girlish distance, I tried to make what sense I could of the violence, and I wondered how easily I would have been drawn in, had I been a boy. I had not thought of myself as having violent tendencies, nor of my family and neighbors as hot-tempered, unruly people. Yet, when I mulled over what had happened at the plant, I could feel the indignation, the throbbing sense of injustice that can tighten a fist around a rock. I began to gather in the evidence that we were, after all, savages deep down. I recalled the thrill of being hunter and hunted in our neighborhood games of cowboys and Indians, cops and robbers, war. Once, I had even helped dig a foxhole that we would fill with water and cover with a blanket and grass, to ambush a girl we didn't like that day. Luck and our ineptitude kept the scheme from working.

Guns were familiar household objects, seldom hidden away. On the edge of town, where we lived, people used pellet guns or birdshot to scare away animals—sometimes even the neighbors' dogs—that strayed into their yards. Boys graduated from cap pistols and cork guns to BB guns at nine or ten, and got their own hunting rifles by thirteen or fourteen. Playground fistfights were common enough in grade school, despite certain punishment. I had heard that high school boys sometimes fought with brass knuckles, and they wore their dads' steel-toed workboots to football games against Austin, just in case. It wasn't unusual to see a couple of cursing drunks stagger out of a bar and grab each other's shirtcollars before someone stepped in to break them up. Once I peered through the stairway rails at my grandparents' cafe while one man knocked another clear across the room with a fist to the chin. There were other rumbling feuds, too, but they were rarely allowed to turn bloody. I knew that men sometimes hit women, but the police car screaming through the night to break up our neighborhood's most obvious "domestic" set heads shaking the next day. A drunken, violent husband, I learned, is not worth putting up with.

Some habits of violence lay far beyond my imagination: the horrors the war vets—both world wars and Korea—carried in their memories. The drinks they tossed back at the American Legion, the VFW, or at Harley's, Eddie's, and Pete's, the bars across from the plant, were supposed to erase the violence, not incite it, though alcohol was known to backfire on those who craved it. And there was the packinghouse environment itself, its brutal thrusting and sawing, its death squeals and gushing blood. Are people who stun or stab or gut one living creature after another day after day, year after year, violent beings? Did people who worked on "gangs" become "gangsters"? They dared to speak the work's plain language. "Kill," they said, not "abattoir," "guts" not "offal." Rather than let the work get to them, they dispelled its power in the mock violence, the black humor Dad told about in his stories. How long a stretch was it from a pig toe tossed playfully at a coworker to a rock heaved at a scab? If these people swarming the plant gates were violent, maybe the work they did at Wilson's had made them that way.

Chuck Lee was offered free radio time to appeal for calm. "Take every precaution to avoid trouble," he urged. "For example, many people carry guns in their cars all the time for hunting. Please take all guns out of your cars until this is settled." The violence was not all one-way, however. One morning in a search of strikebreakers' cars entering the plant, the sheriff confiscated five shotguns, two rifles, nine pistols, and a knife. Police and union scouts patrolled Chuck Lee's block after his wife received threatening phone calls and saw strange cars idling in the alley behind their house. Mayor Shoff's wife kept the curtains pulled. Nor was all the violence by men. After one striker punched a fellow worker who had crossed the picket line, the scab's wife appeared at the striker's house and refused to leave. A scuffle ensued and the two brought charges against each other. The man pled guilty to the original assault, but the charges against the woman were dismissed. The court "did not feel it could find a woman guilty of assault and battery against a man."

The most dramatic story told to me about the violence came from Leo O'Neal, the plant superintendent, who describes the strike as "one of the saddest parts of my life." Tears came to his eyes as he told about the phone call he received one evening.

"This fellow says—he wouldn't tell me who he was, but he says, 'I'm at the union hall right now. They're going to come to get you tonight.' I says, 'Well, do you have any idea what time?' and he says, 'Sometime after twelve o'clock.' I set out in the backyard where them swings are, and he'd told me how they were going to come. And he said, 'They'll turn their lights off.' So, here comes the car, and it turned its lights off, just like he said, and it come right around over here and it stopped right there. But I was laying out there in that vacant lot there, and I had my shotgun, with six shells in it, and they were slugs. And I had made up my mind that if they do anything to this house, then I'm going to let them have it. No matter what happens to me, that's what's going to happen. Fortunately, I raised up. I had the gun pointed at them, and evidently, when I raised up, the lights from the streetlight showed me with that gun and they took right off. God, I'm glad I raised up. That would have been the most devastating thing that could ever happen to me. That's how the mentality gets when you've got to defend your own home."

We, too, were geared up to defend our home, as I recall. Dad fed shells into the shotgun, kept sheathed in canvas behind the vacuum cleaner in the front closet, just in case anyone should come around to bother Mom and me. He says now that the gun was never loaded, but I remember trying to imagine my flustered mother fending off intruders at the front door with a gun neither of us knew how to use. We were both more likely to hide than to defend ourselves. "Struggling will only get you killed" was the axiom we females memorized. Suppose it had been up to me to defend our home. What sign would have alerted me to grab the gun? A face in the small glass panes in our front door? Harsh voices? A flame flickering in shadow on the wall? Could I have lifted that heavy gun and held it steady against my shoulder? Could I have fired it, and at whom?

Owning up to violent feelings shook my teenage-girl pacifism, but I had less trouble gauging the depth of the insult that provoked the violence. Tell a hospital surgical staff that surgery will henceforth be performed by pharmacists, and how will they react? Putting a whizzard knife in the hands of an off-season farmer and expecting a quick, lean cut of meat is just as absurd—to those who know and take pride in that work. When Wilson's first announced, in November, that it was keeping up production with management employees and a few temporary laborers, the union's strike newsletter joked about the quality of the product:

"In Cedar Rapids, for example, five cows were killed, four of which were tanked, and the fifth, we hear, went to feed the foremen and office workers. . . . Just heard from Omaha that the company is now holding classes for their white collar people. Subject—how to use a steel and sharpen a knife!!"

The hiring of permanent replacements was not to be taken so lightly. This was a humiliating blow to laborers who had struggled to find employment in the Depression, risked their lives and livelihoods in the war, or even just finished high school successfully without the means for any further education. They staked their pride, their identity, on work well and honorably done. Hard work would win them the respect of their employers, their families, and the community in which they lived and shopped, went to church and sent their kids to school. Hard work, like other forms of suffering, built character through endurance, but it also developed skills. Even the repetitive jobs on the line called for the steadiest stance, the sharpest eye, and the most efficient stroke. If people were as easily interchangeable as the Dear John letter implied, then its message was, *There's nothing to this work. Anybody who walks in off the street can do it.*

I had eavesdropped on the women of my family enough to know how they measured a man's value, and I knew that my dad passed the critical tests. "Gordy's not afraid of hard work," they said. "Gordy's a good provider." I admired my dad for pulling himself out of bed every morning without complaint. In winter, if the snowplows hadn't yet made it through our neighborhood, he'd wade through the drifts to the highway and hitch a ride with my uncle Ted. When even the highway was drifted-in, he bundled himself up and trudged across town to the plant, joining the many others who had managed to find their way through the snow. This image of my dad came back to me when, reading archival material, I ran across a clipping of one of Wilson's 1959 ads for replacements: "Have openings for experienced plant maintenance millwrights." As though Gordy Register could have been replaced.

Inevitably there were those who came to work late, or drunk, or not at all. Turning these slackers into faithful workers was a joint task of the local management and the union. Both Leo O'Neal and Don Nielsen describe the disciplining of these workers as a give-and-take process. O'Neal says, "When I had some bad characters, I'd suspend them indefinitely, and then I knew that I'd hear from the union. I'd tell them my side of the story. Usually what I wanted to do was hurt them in the pocketbook a little bit to get their attention. And then I would take them back. The union didn't like that, but they knew that's how I operated." As Nielsen tells it, "If somebody wasn't doing their job, they'd probably get fired somewhere down the line, and then, of course, we'd have to go to bat for them. There was one particular case of a guy Leo liked pretty well, but he never showed up for work. We'd say, 'He's a good worker.' 'Ya, he's a good worker,' Leo would say, 'but he ain't worth a damn when he ain't here.' We always got him back to work." The object for both sides was to get him there. "I think the people that get up and go to work every day in their life," O'Neal says, "I think they're the salt of the earth."

It was the salt of the earth that Doug Hall, the UPWA's Minnesota attorney, meant to portray in compiling his defense of sixty-five workers charged with violating the company's restraining order by milling around the plant gates on December 9 and 10. Wilson's had stationed cameramen on the roof of the plant and had management employees scan the photos and film to identify faces. In addition, one of the regional television stations had erected a platform outside the gate, "ready for a big show," as the mayor put it, and their film caught people not visible from the roof. Many of those who were identified and charged claimed to have been peaceful onlookers only, and a few insisted they weren't even there. Hall listed not only their names, but their ages, family status, and years of service to the plant, for example:

"Fred Carmichael, age 55. 31 years at Wilson."

"Leonard Higgins, age 40. At Wilson 23 years."

"M. E. Schuhmacher, age 25. 2 children. 4 years at Wilson."

"Clarence K. Aldahl, age 67. Wife invalid. 17 years at Wilson. Arrived close to 5. Had come to get groceries at store near car lot. Left around 6, got groceries, went home."

"Donne Rygmyr, age 31. 3 children. 6 years at Wilson. Heard of events at line on radio at 5:30 P.M. . . . drove over. Stood on viaduct where police officer Weigel was."

"Alton Horvei, age 34. 3 children. 13 years at Wilson. Working on his new house all day."

"Frederick Zensen, age 43. 14 years at Wilson. Spent entire day fishing 50 miles away from Albert Lea." (Zensen's witness list includes his foreman on the hog kill.)

But no one spoke more eloquently to the issue of loyalty than the voice preserved in this resolution, adopted unanimously by the membership of Local 6 on December 13, 1959, two days after the National Guard was called in to maintain order:

> We the members of this Union have an investment in the Wilson Company of many long years of loyal service. Most of us have spent all of our years of productive service as Wilson employees. Most of us were born here in Albert Lea. Our children were born here. We have raised our families here. We will perhaps die here. We own our homes and have our roots deeply imbedded in the soil of this community. We have always been part of the community and have acted as law abiding citizens, and have abhorred lawlessness.
>
> The fact that the Company has refused to grant to us the same benefits put into effect by all other packers has made us angry and has bewildered us.
>
> The fact that the Wilson Company has brought strike-breakers into its plant to replace its employees provoked Wilson employees to the breaking point of human emotional endurance.
>
> We believe, and we believe rightfully so, that we have a property right also in Wilson & Company as a result of devoting most of the best years of our lives as employees.

Our jobs, our homes, and the welfare of our families are at stake. We urge Wilson & Company, in the name of common sense and decency to sit down in negotiations and work out an agreement similar or equal to that of negotiations with all other packers.

We urge the Wilson Company to agree not to reopen its plants until negotiations are completed, and if they do this we will join in with them in asking the removal of the National Guard from the City of Albert Lea.

English Lessons

It was not primarily reading and writing we were to learn in Miss Sybil Yates's ninth-grade English class, but the necessity of rules: rules of grammar, rules of pronunciation, rules of etiquette, rules of propriety, all of which served to enhance the refinement of human behavior. This was a perplexing challenge for the ungainly children of farmers and laborers. Lessons in the usage of "shall" and "will" were lost on teenagers who said, "Me and him coulda went with if we woulda wanned ta."

Yet Miss Yates was determined to ed-u-cate us in every manner possible. If we were to make our best impression on society, she instructed us, especially that which lay beyond our limited horizons, we must pay careful attention to the rules of pronunciation. The dictionary might list two or three *accepted* pronunciations for each word, but only the first was *preferrrred*. Strange as it may sound to our benighted ears, this was the one we were to use. And so she drilled us: "ape-ri-cot, boo-kay, koo-pon, soph-o-more, to-mah-to, Tyews-di."

We were somewhat more appreciative of her frequent readings from the great works of English and American literature. Poe and Dickens were favorites. A female Vincent Price, she hissed the "sinister" in Richard Harding Davis's *The Bar Sinister* so that we would never forget its meaning.

Miss Yates claimed more purview over our behavior than is normally covered in English class. Using books for plates and pencils for knives and forks, she pulled our utensils free of our ape-like grasps and taught us to nestle them in the crease of our thumbs and forefingers. Before our first ninth-grade dance, she had us push our desks to the wall, so that the boys could practice being gentlemen, politely inviting the ladies onto the dance floor and then returning them to their places with a nod and a thank-you. Never mind that Albert Lea girls danced with each other while the boys only huddled around the gym entrance, snickering.

We thought Miss Yates at best an exotic, displaced bird, with her hoity-toity mannerisms and her peculiar priorities. At worst, she was a hag who had sprung fully aged from a grammar book, e-nun-ci-at-ing clearrr-ly. We found her dedication to teaching strangely obsessive. In her thirty-fifth year in a junior high classroom, she still remembered the names and faces and behavior of siblings and even parents she had taught years and decades before. We didn't know how embedded she was in this culture whose habits she tried so fervently to displace. It was many years later, reading graduation bulletins in an archive, that I learned she was an Albert Lea girl herself, a 1921 graduate, raised not in the parlors and porches of Fountain Street or Park Avenue but across the tracks on South Broadway, where the town petered out into cornfields.

It is still baffling to me that I also remember Miss Yates as a rule breaker. One day she simply asked us, quietly and discreetly, to put our heads on our desks and cover our eyes. Breathing eraser dust, our cheeks numb against the cold metal desktops, we waited for the next instruction.

"Now," she said, "if you have a parent out on strike at Wilson's, please raise your hand."

There was to be no mention of the strike in the public school classrooms, the superintendent had decreed, and any students found conversing about it on school property would be disciplined. I stretched my hand high, regretting that my classmates couldn't see it and that I had to miss this chance to identify who my allies were.

Miss Yates, a die-hard Republican, was the only one of my teachers at Southwest Junior High to risk acknowledging the present condition of our lives. I don't remember if there were consequences. I got the A I felt I deserved. She never mentioned the strike again, and so we missed hearing the preferred pronunciations of the words we added to our vocabularies that year:

ar-bi-*tra*-tion
bay-o-net
black-jack
boy-cott
con-*sesh*-ons
goooon
in-*junk*-shen
lock-out
mi-*lish*-a
night-ri-der
re-*strain*-ing or-der
scaaaab

shut-down
sit-down
strike-break-er
Taft-*Hart*-ley
wild-cat strike
yel-low dog

Under Siege

I had seen plenty of soldiers before, but they were always a novelty, always a grand and gut-churning thrill. Some neighbor kid would come pedaling fast up the road on a dewy summer morning yelling, "Army trucks! Army trucks on Highway 69!" We'd pour out of our houses and run down the clover-covered slope and hop the spongy moss at the bottom of the ditch to line up, our toes just short of the highway's gravel shoulder. Much of the fun was counting the vehicles out loud. How many canvas-covered trucks? How many jeeps? We hated having to chant a number over and over when a string of ordinary Nashes and Studebakers broke into the procession. Those cars ruined our game of pretend: the Yanks were coming to liberate us.

It was only a convoy of Iowa National Guardsmen, our folks insisted, probably on their way to a bivouac up north at Camp Ripley. But the soldiers themselves played along with our fantasies, smiling and waving and hollering just like victorious GIs.

Words like "convoy" and "bivouac" helped me hold the fantasy in place until they came back through again, wearily heading home.

I slept through the real drama, the arrival of the Minnesota National Guard—225 troops who came to liberate us from our own worst instincts in the predawn hours of Friday, December 11, 1959. I doubt they were smiling or waving, having been ordered out into the cold just past midnight to enforce an edict they may or may not have supported in their civilian lives. But for now and the indefinite future they were under command of Governor Orville L. Freeman, who had ordered the Wilson plant closed and placed Albert Lea under martial law. The state safety commissioner had urged him to intervene, and Albert Lea's mayor and police chief and the Freeborn County attorney and sheriff had recommended closing the plant for a cooling off period. "Egress and ingress of persons and vehicles to the plant is so repugnant to the persons outside the plant," they wrote in a formal petition published in the paper the next day, "that its continued operation is a threat to the peace of the city and county and the safety of the citizens therein." The city and county couldn't muster the resources to control the growing violence. Soon there might be casualties.

Years later, I collected some firsthand reports about the convoy's arrival. Don Nielsen, then a union steward, remembers the entrance of the National Guard as orderly enough. "They just got out of their trucks, and they had their guns with them, and they just took over. There was a lot of screaming and hollering when they came, but there was not much you could do but let the guards come in. They didn't bother the pickets, as long as the pickets stayed over by the picket shack." Morrie Haskins remembers busloads of guardsmen pulling up along

Main Street, a sign that the situation really was serious. Once martial law had been enforced, he believes, those who had taken part in the melee felt relief at the excuse to calm down. "They had their two days with everything hot and heavy. We got to smashing windows and chasing people. I think it started to scare people: how bad it was going to get or could get."

Leo O'Neal was not relieved, but saw the calling of the guard as a political favor to the union, which generally endorsed DFL candidates. "I was so damn mad I could have hit Governor Freeman right in the nose. I was sleeping in my office down there, and they come over and announced they were taking over the plant. It was the adjutant general of the National Guard and another guy. 'Leo, may I speak to you in your office,' he says. I figured that was all right. I was so mad I didn't care. 'Look,' he says, 'I have a job to do. I don't like it any better than you do, but we have to do this.' 'Well,' I says, 'I guess you got the guns to do it with.'"

They had guns, all right: rifles and bayonets, tear gas, and ball ammunition—copper-jacketed metal bullets that kill by penetration. This was no practice bivouac. Those guns could be fired if need be, but, like the nuclear bomb that had us covering our heads in the school stairwells and stocking canned goods in our basement fruit cellars, they were meant to deter violence, not provoke it. Whether the presence of troops in Albert Lea looked like liberation or an invasion or an embarrassing blotch on the community's image depended on where you stood. A reporter on the scene that first morning heard someone say "It sure makes a beautiful picket line" and tapped that phrase into the teletype serving the national press. It was printed over and over with allegations that Freeman was in collusion with the union. The union's reaction is carefully phrased in a teletype sent from Local 6 to the Chicago office of the UPWA: "You will understand that while this local does not like to be under martial law any more than anyone else does there is still a certain amount of satisfaction being expressed here in seeing the scabs sent home."

When Linda Melting and I went uptown that Friday night, Albert Lea looked like a setting for a World War II movie. There were soldiers posted in front of the Interstate Power Company and on the busy corner by the dime store; they wore their helmets and had rifles strapped on their shoulders. There were jeeps parked all around the Armory, normally the site of teen dances and home builders' shows. This movie set was more suited to a Danny Kaye musical than an Aldo Ray drama, however. The soldiers' uniforms were clean, their faces scrubbed and shaven. Instead of blazing, bombed-out ruins, there was Santa Claus waving mechanically in Skinner's window, tipping his head back in an openmouthed, tape-recorded "Ho Ho Ho." His elves hammered along in a creepy slow motion. Only ten more shopping days till Christmas, ten more days to stretch the meager strike benefits into passable gifts. The Salvation Army lady, Ruth Jenson, wearing her black bonnet with the big ribbon at the side, gave more exuberant blessings than ever to the passersby who dropped their loose change in her pot.

I loved nighttime Christmas shopping. Those last ten days when the stores stayed open every weeknight until nine brought a bustle and hubbub to Broadway that transported me to New York's miraculous Thirty-fourth Street or, if the snow was falling lightly in huge, wet flakes, to the Victorian London of Christmas cards. I loved the tinny Christmas carols that rang out from loudspeakers, the green cellophane garlands strung across the street, the oversized fake candles mounted on light posts, the snow-flecked stormcoats and billowing scarves on passersby. Yet the sight of young men outfitted for war, men who smiled faintly at our curious glances, reminded me instead of Little Rock, of hostile civilian faces with lips pursed to spit, of shouted curses. Could this be real? What would become of our Christmas spirit?

In fact, martial law was not meant to disrupt our lives, but to put them back on an orderly course. No school or church or community activities would be canceled, no stores closed. There would be no curfew—as long as we remained on our best, most civil behavior. As Linda and I walked down West William and turned the corner on Washington, we read the sign outside the Palm Garden announcing that Whoopee John's polka band was playing that weekend. "Whoopee John *Willfahrt* and his band will *play*," we joked, and it was just as funny as the last time. The movie *A Summer Place* had finally opened at the Broadway. I had been slowdancing myself around our basement rec room to its instrumental theme song for months, it seemed. We made plans to go to the show Sunday afternoon, martial law or not. The movie turned out to be yet another object lesson about teenage pregnancy. Troy Donahue or no, the characters didn't move me, spoiled rich people that they were. I longed to see a movie about an ordinary union family like mine, and I wondered why we weren't fit subject matter for Hollywood, except for an occasional dark, grimy movie like *On the Waterfront*.

To judge from the national press reports broadcast on TV or reprinted in the Albert Lea Tribune and the Minneapolis papers, or quoted in union newsletters, we really did lead dark, grimy lives of violence and corruption. Just as Dad feared, the violence outside the plant had turned public opinion squarely against us. "Mob rule" became the shorthand term for what had happened in Albert Lea, and the "mob" was made up of "labor goons," "hoodlums," and "union gangsters." "In a town with the improbable name of Albert Lea, Minnesota," the New York *Herald Tribune* wrote, "it is somehow lawful and proper to throw rocks, but it is unlawful and improper to get in the way of them." The city officials and law enforcement personnel who failed to stop the violence were called "spineless" and "craven." Some editorialists wrung irony out of the names "Freeborn County" and "Freeman." The turn of events, they claimed, looked more like Russian communism than freedom.

These shocking portrayals made Albert Lea's normally contented middle class recoil in shame. Albert Lea was a calm and neighborly city, a nice place to raise a family, a hometown to be proud of. Newcomers found the civic pride a little on the smug side. A high school administrator who ushered prospective teachers around town was given to describing Albert Leans' sense of make-do comfort with this parody: "We don't have a swimming pool," he would say, "but we have something almost as good as a swimming pool: we have a beach. We don't have an ice arena, but we have something almost as good as an ice arena: we flood the parks in the winter." He summed up his presentation in typical Scandinavian-American understatement. "Albert Lea is almost as good a place to raise your children as you can find." Now that good enough image had been cracked by violence, and who was to blame but the ruffians at the packinghouse?

Joyce Kennedy, a teacher who spent ten years in Albert Lea, remembers the mood of that winter: "There was this daily feeling of dread that just permeated everything, even though on the surface it was still this lovely little town sitting around a couple of lakes. All of this violence didn't fit with the self-image of the town. It was a dissonance, and everybody felt that. One thing about people in Albert Lea: they did know how to be guarded. Well, this was a situation in which no matter how guarded you were, the fact of something wrong was there. Every now and then something will happen in which you realize how delicate that whole social balance is."

Though the editor and the publisher were hardly friends of labor, the *Evening Tribune* covered the many controversies with admirable journalistic discretion. The strike story was a professional boon to a couple of up-and-coming reporters, Pete Vanderpoel and Lindy Davis, whose bylines became familiar to those seeking daily, on-the-spot information. The editorial page practiced nonpartisanship by declining to publish "inflammatory" letters about the strike, but editor Ken Allen's attempt to describe the situation in neutral terms did not sit well with union households:

"Wilson employes are entitled by law to strike, to picket, by peaceful means to persuade people to support them. Wilson & Co. is entitled by law to keep its plant open, to hire whom it will, and to attempt by peaceful means to persuade people to buy its products. That is the law. As Americans we are required to obey. If it is unjust we are entitled to attempt to change the law, BUT WE MUST NEVER BREAK THE LAW."

The deprecation implicit in the capital letters fell, we understood, on the rebellious employees. It surely didn't apply to the company that had stalled negotiations, made false accusations to win an injunction, or challenged the right to strike by hiring permanent replacements.

I puzzled over this seemingly one-sided "law." Wasn't there a broader morality that went beyond what "the law" decreed? Why is it a crime, I wondered, to steal food, but legal to hold wages down so that even people who work hard have to scrimp? Why is it a crime to vandalize property, but legal to demand work that injures the people who do it? I was not free to ask these questions in school, where discussion of the strike had been prohibited, and confirmation and Sunday school never addressed issues like this. Luther, of course, had nothing to say about strikes and plant closings.

One Sunday incident the following year has taken on new meaning, as I've learned more about the strike. My Sunday school teacher was the county sheriff, Everette Stovern, who had been roundly criticized for not enforcing the law and dispersing the crowd at the plant. One of the Bible verses we were to memorize was "Judge not, that ye be not judged." "How can *you* do your work if you're not supposed to judge people?" we absolutist teenagers demanded to know. "Isn't it a sin, then, to arrest people and put them in jail?" The sheriff was speechless. He shook his head. "I don't know," he said, and I, for one, looked upon him with skepticism that ranged dangerously close to sinful judgment: how could they let him teach Sunday school if our simple questions stumped him? I have since come across an enlightening reference to Sheriff Stovern in a report drawn up by an investigator for the U.S. Senate's McClellan Committee who had been sent to Albert Lea to hunt for Communists. (He didn't find any.) One of the civic leaders he interviewed was Sheriff Stovern. In his report, the investigator puzzled over the sheriff's handling of the strike violence. He had arrested only one person, a teenager whom he set free again with only a warning. That teenager, I know now, was policeman-to-be Morris Haskins, who was warned to stay away from the plant for his own good. The sheriff's rationale to the committee was that he didn't have enough manpower to make arrests. I wonder now whether the late Sheriff Stovern mulled over that Bible verse as he watched his friends and neighbors erupt in violent anger at the loss of their livelihoods, and I regret that First Lutheran Church was not then a place for candid talk about moral judgment.

In the meantime, I had to decide for myself what was right and wrong in this case. The question debated all over town was, *Who should make decisions about the way the packinghouse operated?* Who had the greatest stake in those decisions, the people who worked there or the people who owned it? I engaged in this debate as though my life depended on it; I truly believed it did. One evening in the public library, where I had gone to work on a research paper, I nearly lay across the sturdy oak reading table to whisper my arguments to a classmate who whispered hers back with equal fervor.

"It's the owners' money," she insisted. "They can do whatever they want with it."

"But what if they've only inherited it, without lifting a finger?" I retorted. "And what about the people who have worked every day for years to bring that money in? Don't they count?" To keep the volume low, we pushed our words out in sputtering bursts of air.

"Those people at the plant are never satisfied," she said, echoing words I was sure she had heard somewhere else. "They make plenty of money."

"Money's not the only issue," I argued. "There's overtime and job security . . ."

"If they don't like their jobs, they can just go someplace else," she hissed at me.

"Oh yeah, where?" I seethed, exhaling the "h" Miss Yates insisted we pronounce in "where" . . .

The salty smell of a wooden tabletop still fires me up.

Conversations like these left me feeling under siege, not by an occupying militia, but by cold, uncaring people with no comprehension of how hard and how loyally my dad worked for his living and in what vile surroundings. Judge Cooney off in Chicago was too distant an adversary. The bewilderment I felt over his implacable contempt for the union transferred to my classmates and neighbors. Why didn't they get it? How could they be so cruel? I began to see Albert Lea as a town composed of two hostile camps governed by self-interest rather than Christianity's command to "love thy neighbor as thyself." If ever anyone was ripe for communist influence, at least Marx's theory of class conflict, it was fourteen-year-old me.

All my life, I realized, I had lived in a divided world: boys and girls, farmers and town people, Republicans and Democrats, Catholics and Protestants, Norwegians and Danes; I had taken these categories as givens, as though God had divided us up into teams for some cosmic game. I was wary of Republicans, but didn't dislike the ones I knew. Boys were puzzling, but I figured someday I would marry one. Catholics intrigued me, and farmers and Norwegians were only dumb and backward, I thought, not evil. But this new division was troubling: people either supported the right of workers to decent treatment or they didn't.

Only Linda and a few other kids I knew well seemed exempt from this generalization. Her dad, a meat salesman, was ineligible for the union but didn't really get the benefits of management either, as far as I could tell. He too worked long hours and was often away from home for days at a time. My dad actually felt a little sorry for these people: the salesmen, the "girls" in the office, and especially the foremen—who, when promoted, had to give up the only salvation in this kind of work, membership in the union. If they honored the picket line, they'd be fired. But when they crossed it, they blended in with the scabs. Linda kept her feelings reined in, and I tried to control my zealotry in her presence. Of course, that was often impossible, as strong as my convictions were and as sure as I was of their righteousness. Many years later, Linda told me that her parents had sat her down to talk about my situation and assured her that they would treat me fairly and not oppose her friendship with me. Their words were careful and deliberate, as though they had talked through this problem themselves and worked out a team approach to it. Linda, in turn, trod warily at my house and, more than I knew, around me. "I remember feeling hurt," she told me recently, "that it didn't seem like you saw me as a person anymore, but that you saw me as someone who wasn't involved like you. It probably wasn't something you were conscious of, but I felt kind of judged. You felt so much more deeply about it than I did, but in your deep feelings about it, it kind of brought out a family loyalty directed toward me, and I didn't like that, because then it meant we had stress."

I had indeed begun to sort out who was on our side and, by elimination, who the villains were. My evidence was mostly circumstantial, but I watched and listened carefully. We shopped at Clifton's, a grocery store that not only stopped carrying Wilson products but extended credit to regular customers out on strike. We bypassed Wayne's Grocery, which advertised its support of Wilson's, but then we had never shopped there anyway. Our Pastor Knutson preached to us about the sin of violence, while the Presbyterian minister, Lloyd Peterson, traveled to Chicago to persuade the two sides to negotiate. A Catholic priest in Austin had gone so far as to call strikebreaking "morally evil." Teachers were hard to figure, since they weren't allowed to talk about the strike at school. I tried to decipher pro- or anti-union hints in what they taught us, but they were too careful. The DFL mayor, Niles Shoff, respected the union. The chamber of commerce was by definition probusiness, and predictably voted to demand that the plant be reopened. Farmers were not all alike, I found out. The Farm Bureau sent a brigade to St. Paul to ask the governor to reopen the plant, so they could sell their livestock before it passed its prime. The Farmers' Union, on the other hand, stood by the UPWA. Doug Hall, Local 6's lawyer from the Cities, became a witty, outspoken, workingman's hero, while Ralph Peterson, the local lawyer for the company, was nicknamed "Jughead," after the clueless character in *Archie* comics. His secretary, however, was Linda's kind and understanding mother, Dolores Melting.

The dividing lines were not as clear as I would have liked them to be, and I risked crossing them unawares myself. If only we could have worn blue and gray caps, like the boys in grade school who reenacted the Civil War. Even the chamber of commerce could not have settled on one uniform; the vote to demand that Wilson's be reopened was sixty-three to forty-three, far from unanimous, and the discussion was heated. Fred Jacobsen, the minister at Trinity Lutheran, owned up to being a socialist in his youth in Denmark and called the chamber members "snobs." Dad still gets tears in his eyes when he tells how old Charlie Upin, the owner of St. Paul Clothing House, reminded his fellow storekeepers that they owed their success to the Wilson employees—good, steady customers who paid their bills. Even though most of them lived in Shoreland Heights, we thought of the Jewish merchants as friends of labor. It would be ten years or more, however, before I learned about the significant presence of Jews in the history of the labor movement. These compassionate storekeepers may well have had family ties to the sweatshops of the early 1900s.

Sam Romer, the Minneapolis *Tribune* reporter assigned to cover the strike, dubbed the tension in Albert Lea a "Cold War," but he drew the lines differently than I would have:

"City officials and civic leaders are reluctant to discuss it and some are inclined to deny its reality. But it is confirmed in conversations with the barber and the baker, the main street merchants and the fellow sitting next to you at the lunch counter. . . . There have been some observers who, noting the tense attitude of the townfolk, have written of Albert Lea as a 'town divided.' This is true—but it is a town divided between those who are pro-union and those who are neutral. Persons ready to defend the company are hard to find." I doubt, however, that he had surveyed Southwest Junior High, where I had thought I felt them swarming.

While I was caught up in the accusations of lawlessness lobbed our way, and assumed the newspeople had come to town to sensationalize the strikers' bad behavior, their rancor was directed primarily against Governor Freeman. As the National Guardsmen took their posts in Albert Lea, Judge Cooney himself boarded a train to St. Paul to plead his case with the governor. When Freeman refused to surrender control of the plant, Wilson's filed suit in federal district court, a move supported by editorial writers all over the country. The inviolability of private property was the rallying call, and a government seizure of private property fed rampant fears of Communism. Even the notorious witch hunter Westbrook Pegler chimed in. Newspapers in the South took some pleasure in equating Freeman's action with Orval Faubus's seizure of Little Rock High School. Orville and Orval made a clever parallel, and a handy opportunity to challenge liberalism's interpretation of civil rights.

Even setting my pro-union sentiments aside, I was pretty certain that Freeman had acted correctly, but to confirm my opinion I tested it with a homely analogy. "If two kids are fighting over a toy," I asked my mom, "shouldn't the mother take it

away from them till they calm down?" "That's right," Mom
said, with a force meant not so much to affirm my good sense,
I suspect, as to avoid discussing complicated issues with an ar-
gumentative teenager. Even as I made the analogy, I guessed
that ownership and sharing were tough matters even for mothers to negotiate.

Throughout this commotion, Albert Lea was pelted by a driving rain that froze on the trees and road surfaces. On the
wettest, most bone-chilling night, the Guard opened the plant
for several hours so that a contingent of strikebreakers, management personnel, and union observers could go in and finish processing perishable meat. TV newsfilm of officials duck-
ing in and out of the plant, while thunder rolled and the rain
refracted the lights outside, looked like a scene from a
Frankenstein movie. The packinghouse made an appropriate
house of horrors.

When the rain turned to snow and the snow softened the
lay of the land again, life resumed something like a normal
rhythm. I went to school, relished French class, tolerated algebra, and passed notes and flirted in science. I gave up *American Bandstand* long enough to practice a play in which Kathy
Wicks and I played twins named Flora and Dora, roles that required us to dye our hair flaming orange. One day after play
practice, I spotted Mom sitting in the Pontiac outside the door
nearest the school's theater. "You have a brand-new nephew,"
she announced. Joey had given birth in a hospital in Mankato,
and she and Rodger would be bringing little Jeffrey Alan to
Albert Lea for Christmas vacation.

The shortage of Christmas presents would be more than
offset by a new baby, the first member of the family's next generation. Nancy and Rog came home from Michigan, too, and

the tension in the house was broken by baby cries and adult laughter. The guys spent much of their time hanging out at the Union Center, listening to stories over glasses of tap beer, while we females indulged ourselves in our new baby, whose downy little raisin face made sucking motions even while he slept. Visitors appraised him with the odd but familiar line, "He's so homely he's cute."

There was yet one more saving grace in our strike-burdened Christmas. Local 9 in Austin had collected the names and ages of all the children in Albert Lea's striking families and distributed them among its members. Each of us—1,700 kids in all—was to get one Christmas gift from a Hormel worker's family. They were delivered and sorted at Skateland roller rink, where we were to come on the Tuesday before Christmas to claim them.

I had never been to Skateland before. Much as I would have enjoyed roller skating, I understood that hanging out at a roller rink would taint the good reputation I needed to do well in school and to win the scholarships that would help me out of town. Skateland, a huge room with a chicken-coop roof, was now aflutter with noisy little kids. My friend Mimi and I stood in line, trying to maintain our fourteen-year-old dignity and feeling a bit miffed about being counted as children. Union sons and daughters fifteen and up had been offered a much better deal—one five-dollar bill apiece—and their line moved quickly because there was no matching to do. Mimi and I groused about our bad luck in being born too late and worried aloud about what strangers might choose for us. With a five-dollar bill, we could at least buy something we really wanted.

We had checked in at the door and been handed slips of paper with numbers that corresponded to our names on the list. At the head of the line, I handed over my numbered slip, now curled and sweaty, and the man who took it headed toward a pile of gifts along the wall. He returned with a rectangular package about five inches by three inches and I clutched it in my hand while he found a bigger present for Mimi. We carried our gifts off to a corner to open them. Hers was, as we feared, a poor choice. The single man who had signed the tag on her gift was obviously unfamiliar with teenage tastes and sizes. He had bought her a butterfly-bedecked sweater in a child's size fourteen. I ripped at the flap on the end of my present with growing apprehension. My heart thudded to my stomach when I saw what it was: a blue jewelry box with gold embossing on the top. Green, blue's mismatch, was my favorite color, and I seldom wore jewelry. I carelessly flipped open the lid. Inside was a five-dollar bill.

That moment of grace, an undeserved act of generosity from a family whose name I believed, in my youthful complacency, I would always remember, has stayed with me throughout my life as a restoration of faith in goodwill. It shocked me then that such kindness could come to me from Austin, the town we had learned to distrust. It surprises me now to think how little we teenagers expected from the common bonds of work and social class and union membership.

The jewelry box has stayed with me, too, a priceless souvenir of that long strike and a symbol of solidarity and compassion. In it I keep my other childhood treasures: the watch Grandpa and Grandma Petersen gave me for Confirmation the following spring, the one remaining cuff link from the beautiful melon-and-rust plaid dress my mom sewed me for the ninth-grade party, my first two-dollar bill, my high school class ring, my school honor pins, and the mink earrings Joey let me wear when I played dress-up. Whenever I open the lid, the memory spills out, and I am always pleased to relive it.

The Associated Press sent out a wire about the Christmas gifts at Skateland, and a file in the UPWA archives contains clippings of the AP story from around the country. The 1,700 names had been snapped up in less than an hour at Local 9 headquarters. The cost of each gift was to range from four to six dollars, and I doubt I was the only child whose benefactors broke that rule. "This act of human kindness will never be forgotten by these children," the Austin *Unionist* newspaper reported. This is one assertion I will not submit to fact-checking, but take as given on the strength of my own experience.

"Dear Governor Freeman"

(Documents from the files of Governor Orville L. Freeman, in the Archives of the State of Minnesota, Minnesota History Research Center.)

> Mrs. James H. Tuberty
> 431 Columbus Ave.
> Albert Lea, Minn.
> Dec. 15, 1959

Dear Gov. Freeman,

I thank God for a truly Christian man who placed life & decency above property damage and big business.

My husband has worked for Wilson & Co. in a skilled labor dept. for thirty years and my father worked in the same compacity when I was a little girl. Never before have I seen such a situation become so out of hand & the company's office help & officials along with their scabs certainly did aggravate this to the point where the Union men could stand no more of it.

If it were not for a man like you who put your position & life above all these material things I am sure their would have been blood shed.

I do not want you to feel that this letter is from some radical person.

We have a son Capt. James Tuberty who is now attending Command & General Staff College at Ft. Leavenworth, Kansas. A son a Dr. of Optometry in Mt. Vernon, Iowa & Sister Edith the head of the Psychiatric Dept. of Nursing at the College of St. Catherine's is our daughter.

It was a long hard struggle for us to give to our children the educations they each received but we were always entertaining high principles & did not wish to see our children have to work as hard as their father had to make a living.

I want you to know we admire your high principles & will do everything in our power to support both you & your party in the coming election.

One of Wilson's men from Chicago was here (who used to live in A. L.) called up one of our friends & the first question he asked her was if she voted?

Please do not make public in any way my name as my husband only has six years to go before retirement & he hopes to get back at Wilson's.

Let me assure you also no rock throwing or acts of violence were ever forth coming from this home.

Sincerely,

Mrs. James Tuberty

Dec. 15, 59

Governor Freeman,

We want to thank you for calling in Natl Guard at Wilson's at Albert Lea. Wish it had been sooner. You see, my husband, has been unable to work for nearly 3 yrs, just recently purchased a truck from his former boss, the man financing it for him.

Just before posting the Guard, he took a load of cattle to Albert Lea, unloaded, and started out, the strikers forming a line trying to stop him but he kept driving, they had to let him throu then, but some of them followed him out to Geneva, where he stopped for coffee. While they were inside they slashed a tire on his truck, a new one, used about 2 mo. cost $90.

He has a "copy" from the sheriff & Deputy of the incident—

The insurance won't cover it so just out $90 and that's quite a set back just starting out with 9 children to support. The Welfare says they can't help us now—he being employed— Jan. 1st, $210. for license, and trucking so slow since 1st of Nov—so I hope you'll continue the Natl. Guard—just think of all the other damage citizens have to stand expense for their "vandalism".

Again thanks.

Mrs. J.R. Watkins
Randolph Minn.

Back to Work

January is Minnesota's most confining month, cold enough to freeze skin within minutes, dark before the end of the day, with snow piled high along shovel-wide walkways. It is a savagely beautiful month, with its bold blue Arctic skies, the sun glinting so brightly off the snow's crystal surface that you have to shield your eyes. A frozen lake becomes virgin terrain to young explorers, and their legs leave postholes in the broad sweep of snow. Even the adults who hurry from one doorway to the next listen for the distinctive crunch and squeak of below-zero snow under their boots. The wind wraps veils of snow around them and their breath leaves ice clinging to the scarves they pull over their numb faces. Still they pause briefly to look at the bare, filigreed profiles of oak and maple against that brilliant sky.

January of 1960, though, seemed unusually long and dreary, marked by nervous waiting. The year had turned, had signaled a new decade, but it brought no promise of a strike settlement. In fact, the company and its scabs now enjoyed special protection from the courts. A panel of three federal judges had ruled on December 23 that Governor Freeman had exceeded his authority. "It would be a shocking reflection on the stability of our state government," they wrote, "if the state could not quell the mob action in Freeborn county without declaring martial law and decreeing the deprivation of constitutional rights of those who are victims of lawlessness." The packinghouse was reopened on December 28, with a large complement of strikebreakers, and half the National Guard troops were sent home. Sheriff Stovern had sworn in fifty-five special deputies, and Minnesota Attorney General Miles Lord took command of them while Stovern went off for a New Year's vacation. The last one hundred Guardsmen pulled out on January 6, even though the nightriding had not subsided. Both strikers and scabs were armed and on edge. The county commission offered $100 rewards for information leading to the conviction of anyone committing violence, "whether involved in the current labor dispute or not." The city council threatened to impose early curfews and shut down bars and restaurants to prevent "explosive discussions of strike issues in public places" and "aimless driving and roaming of the streets." Now that martial law was officially over, the need for it seemed greater than ever.

There were spirit-boosting displays of strength and solidarity, the rallies and marches that make stirring photos for history books. UPWA members from Minnesota and Iowa amassed in Albert Lea for a regional meeting on January 30, and a parade of 2,500 marched twelve deep down Broadway at 7:30 that morning. Wilson's kept the plant closed that Saturday, and the entire police force was on duty, but the demonstration was peaceful. Two weeks later, 5,000 supporters, members of various unions from all over Minnesota, rallied in and around the Armory, and 1,000 of them marched through town. They brought $17,000 in cash and donations of food that weighed 180 tons and filled three warehouses.

Before each of these events, rumors flew: Austin's hardware stores had sold out of pickax handles, the *Tribune* reported. All those outsiders coming to town were surely planning to riot. Wilson's claimed they had been tipped off about a plot to blow up the plant in the middle of the night. This bit of news seemed preposterous, probably a scare tactic devised by the company. Yet there was a nugget of truth in that rumor, put on record years later: a plan hatched in the fantasy of Frank Ellis, the old and somewhat dotty Hormel worker who had organized the Independent Union of All Workers back in the 1930s. He even had dynamite. Calmer minds managed to persuade him that the brothers and sisters in Albert Lea were counting on a place to work when the strike was over. The only riotlike behavior was an excess of public drinking that prompted the mayor to close the town's sixteen bars for part of a Saturday evening, a highly unpopular move that nearly *sparked* a riot.

Hard as I squeeze my eyelids, I can't call up one bit of January's organized excitement. At 7:30 on a Saturday morning, I was likely curled under my chenille bedspread, dreading the blast of the alarm clock—rather than shivering on Broadway while a parade passed by, let alone marching in it. Still, all those strangers roaming around uptown after my Confirmation class should have left an imprint. No, if history photos were to capture that midwinter time-biding as I remember it, they would show dads shoveling snow off roofs or watching daytime TV as the windowpanes crackle and squeal, and moms scowling at their kids for whining over a supper of unfamiliar canned beef stew. There would be photos of men in billed caps, their parkas unzipped, drinking coffee and smoking cigarettes, just waiting and waiting.

Negotiations were stuck at an impasse over who was entitled to work at the packinghouse. Wilson's had recruited its strikebreakers with the promise of permanent jobs, and the management was reluctant to break that promise. Many of those replacements came from farm families who sold livestock to Wilson's. Betrayal of the promise might drive that stock to Hormel or Armour or Swift. Even if the company were to negotiate the other issues on the table and agree to a settlement, it insisted on the right to hire at will: to keep its scabs in place and call back the striking workers only as they were needed. The union, of course, would never sign a contract that put its membership out of work. A suicidal move like that would not only destroy the union but cause an upheaval in the community. You might as well shove a giant spade into the ground underneath Albert Lea and flip over the soil. Its roots would dry in the air, and the place would soon be crawling with worms and weeds.

A few cautious, measured voices beyond the union began to appeal for a settlement that restored rather than wrought havoc on community stability. Early in the strike, an ad hoc committee of eleven public officials and civic leaders had formed to keep watch over the town's well-being. They delegated one of their members who declared himself neutral on labor matters, the Reverend Lloyd Peterson of First Presbyterian Church, to plead with both sides to resolve their differences. While Peterson spoke on behalf of the citizens of Albert Lea, his intervention would affect Cedar Rapids, Omaha, and the other Wilson locations as well. He had traveled to Chicago at his own expense just days before the violence erupted in

December, and he walked the thirteen blocks between the company offices in the Prudential Building and the union's headquarters on Dearborn Street. As on subsequent trips, he stayed at the YMCA and avoided spending money on taxis so that he would not be accountable to either side for financial support.

Reverend Peterson was in his early fifties, and had served for sixteen years as pastor of Albert Lea's single Presbyterian Church, where Cliff Cairns, the plant manager, worshiped alongside his employees, more white collar than blue. Peterson had no experience in labor negotiations, but he was respected throughout the state for his leadership in youth programs. A family scrapbook now in his son's possession contains a February 1959 issue of a Presbyterian publication, *Social Progress*. The lead article, "The Church and Labor," outlines the history of the labor movement and the rationale for unions and collective bargaining. The article acknowledges that the Presbyterian Church has had relatively few working-class members and that some congregations had even shown hostility toward labor activism. This, then, was an effort toward greater understanding and tolerance. Compared to the newspaper editorials of the day, the tone of this article is temperate. Peterson no doubt found in this piece theological support for his nonpartisan efforts. He had a delicate balance to maintain given the divisions in his own congregation, as well as the sensitive task at hand. He learned how easily his intentions could be misread the Sunday he invited Governor Freeman into his pulpit to appeal for calm. Some parishioners took this as an endorsement of Freeman's decision to close the plant and were angered that their church had been put to political use. Others wanted to see Peterson as a friend to the downtrodden worker who chose to follow Christ's example of ministry among the poor and oppressed. In fact, he was neutral, and his "calling" in this case was mediation of a conflict that threatened the peace of his community.

Peterson soon realized that the dispute over who was to work at the packinghouse called for a creative negotiating strategy, one that did not rely on the usual, by now exhausted and maybe embittered personnel. A rumor circulated—a rumor that lives on in Albert Lea—that the strike had become a "grudge match" between Cooney and the UPWA's Helstein. Some Austin clergy suggested that Peterson contact Frank Schultz, the former president of UPWA Local 9 then serving as a vice president of the international. Peterson remembered hearing him speak one time and, like the Austin clergy, he had been impressed with Schultz's calm, persuasive manner. Since Schultz was already on the scene in Chicago, Peterson recommended that he approach Cooney directly. In a 1977 interview on file at the Minnesota History Center, Schultz recalled that he turned the invitation down, thinking it would be "a real slap in the face" to Ralph Helstein. Helstein, though, was willing to let Schultz settle the strike any way he could. Reverend Peterson set up a meeting with Cooney at Wilson's headquarters, and the effort proceeded from there, a long series of meetings that lasted from a few hours to an entire day.

Schultz: "I'd have to walk about a city block through all of these desks and all—everybody sat out in the open at Wilson's office. [The vice presidents] sat in glass cubicles. Everybody could see them, and they could see everybody else. They could make sure that everybody else was working. This was the kind of setup Wilson had. Except for Judge Cooney, he sat way off in the corner in an enclosed office. Nobody could see the old judge. I always felt horrible, I felt like a traitor in the enemy camp, you know, our guys out on the picket lines. Finally, I deliberately let him create a father-son relationship. If he suggested going to lunch, I'd let him. When we went to lunch, I'd let him order. He was quite gracious. He would hold my coat for me, hold the doors for me. He told me how much money he could make by breaking the union in Albert Lea. It was umpteen thousand. He told me exactly how much they'd pick up in workers' pensions, and he had a good espionage system, better than ours. He knew everything that was going on. Finally one day we were having a conversation, [and] he got to talking to me about scabs. This is what he called his loyal employees who were in there working, he called them scabs. He said, 'If I would agree to put those scabs [out of] work, I could never again buy any hogs or cattle from their fathers and mothers.' I said, 'Well, if that's your problem, don't put them [out of] work. Why don't you arbitrate it?' He thought that was a good idea, that was a way out for him."

The union drew up a plan to submit the question of rehiring strikers to arbitration, and Cooney signed it immediately. Schultz reflected on how nervous he felt about this unusual one-on-one negotiating process:

"You know, I used to get goose bumps walking over there, thinking of the responsibility I had, just one guy, and they put that much trust in me. I thought, well, what if something goes wrong and we lose all those thousands of people, over 5,000 people? How are you going to live with that? Already the Albert Lea guys are saying they're going to kill me if we lost it."

Schultz brought a contract proposal to Albert Lea on February 18 and went through it point by point before a "turbulent" rank-and-file meeting in the high school auditorium. Submitting their job security to arbitration was both risk and insult to many in the crowd. And why *should* they approve a contract they might never get to work under? "This really isn't a question of victory or defeat," Schultz argued, but a matter of "facing the realities in front of us." The vote on the proposed contract, plus arbitration, was six-to-one in favor in Albert Lea. Only one local, Omaha, voted it down, but with votes from all the locals tallied, the ayes prevailed. The strike would officially end February 23, though only those the company specifically invited back would return to work for now. It had been 109 days, the longest strike yet in the meatpacking industry. Judge Cooney was quick to proclaim victory. None of the "objectionable" provisions, those he said infringed on management prerogatives, were included in the settlement, he told reporters.

That night, while the long rank-and-file meeting was still raging, an armed robber held up Wayne's Grocery, then jumped into a waiting car and disappeared, never to be caught. The store had been singled out for protest during the solidarity march on January 30, and a graffiti painter had gotten as far as SCAB LOV on Wayne's window before being chased off. Even unfinished, it clearly spelled out a motive for robbery, but that night the usual suspects had a good alibi.

If Dad expressed either joy or relief or disappointment over the vote to settle, I don't remember. I only recall my shock at learning that the clerk on duty at Wayne's, the one who had faced the gun and turned over the money, was the sixteen-year-old sister of my most recent crush. Was she a scab by association, and her brother too? I would have to be more careful, I thought, even find a way to check out loyalties before making friends or setting my sights on a boy. What if I mistakenly fell in love with the opposition? Leaping ahead into an imagined future, I told myself that I could marry a Catholic or a Jew or even a Negro, but never someone who crossed picket lines or ignored boycotts.

We were waiting again. The fates of 5,600 striking Wilson workers and 3,000 strikebreakers were placed in the presumably judicious hands of a three-man arbitration board: Rabbi Jacob Weinstein, Ralph Helstein's rabbi, was likely to favor the union; Edward Bullard, an attorney for Wilson, would mainly endorse the company's position; so it was really up to the third, Federal District Judge Sam Perry, to make the decision. Dad's conversation during the next three weeks often turned to Judge Perry, to speculation about what kind of guy he was and how he might look on this or that situation. "There was some press that he was kind of a flighty character," Chuck Lee recalls, "and you didn't know where he was going to come from. The best shot anybody's got going into arbitration is fifty-fifty. A chance is better than not any chance, but if they hadn't done something there would have been war. There probably wouldn't have been a plant there."

Others in town were not only speculating about the outcome but hoping to influence it with letters and telegrams. Members of the county welfare board wrote that they "sincerely believe that if the strikers are not returned to their jobs with Wilson & Co., it will have a tragic and devastating effect upon the economy and welfare of this community, and could breed hatred and bitterness for many years to come." Even A. K. Grinley, the municipal court judge who had heard the cases of people charged with contempt and vandalism, pleaded with the board to hire the strikers back: "First, in my opinion, this is a matter which goes beyond the bare legal concept 'that the employer has a right to hire or re-hire its employees as it sees fit'. I believe rather that this question should be decided on the much broader basis of the fundamental equities existing between the various parties involved, including the regular Wilson employees, the replacement employees, Wilson & Co. as the employer, and, finally, the community of Albert Lea and Freeborn County."

In the meantime, Wilson's began calling back its regular employees, a few at a time, to complete the workforce and to fill positions some of the replacements had abandoned. One of the first back to work was electrician Don Nielsen. His regular job in the battery shop was occupied, so he was assigned to do electrical troubleshooting around the plant. "It wasn't a very pleasant place to come into," Nielsen remembers. "I went into a plant with some twelve or thirteen hundred scabs in it. I basically stayed by myself. I had my own tools." Nielsen's skills were apparently so vital to the plant's operation that the company dropped a contempt citation it had filed against him.

Leo O'Neal has his own key memory of that first day. The "economic replacements" were angry about the strikers coming back and some of them stopped the hog kill in protest. "And so my division man called me up and I came up there and I told them, 'I have no jurisdiction over what the judges have said we have to do. I have to carry out what they say we're supposed to do. They're coming back, and I can't do a thing about it, so you either get back on the chain or get out the door.' They went out the door, and I hollered up to start the chain up. I went in and I started heading hogs. And Leroy Tostenson came in and I handed him the knife, and the line was going the same speed when he came back as it was when he left."

On March 10, nearly three weeks after the settlement, the arbitration board issued its two-page ruling that both striking workers and replacements were legitimate Wilson employees, and that "all employees are to be treated as if the strike had not occurred." Jobs would be assigned by seniority. Those not placed—virtually all of them strikebreakers—would be on lay-off until positions opened. The changeover to the more senior workforce was to be completed by March 27. The wire services spread the story, and news and business magazines weighed in on its meaning. *Business Week* opined that the ruling gave the union "one reason to be encouraged about the outcome of an otherwise lost strike." Without the promise of permanent jobs, it would be harder for companies to hire replacements during a strike. The Albert Lea *Tribune* called it "one of the most far-reaching decisions in labor–management history."

Though it had surrendered some long-sought benefits, the UPWA had pulled off one significant victory: affirmation of workers' property rights to their jobs. The city of Albert Lea, too, had reason to rejoice. The outsiders could go home, the resident breadwinners could return to work, and the economy and social order could settle back into normalcy. Yet there were no parades, no public celebrations, just quiet expressions of relief.

I came home from school the afternoon of the arbitration ruling and walked in on a sight I never expected to see in my family's lifetime of restrained hopes and endured disappointments. Dad was sitting at the table, his head in his hands, sobbing so hard that his shoulders shook. Mom stood behind him, her face blanched white, tears in her eyes. "What's the matter?" I stammered, dreading to hear who had died. "Dad lost his job," she said, her mouth quivering. "They won't take him back."

The arbitration ruling didn't apply to "employees involved

in unlawful or unprotected activity," and Dad's name was on a list of those alleged to have violated injunctions or picketing rules. There were 124 such people in Albert Lea. The charge against Dad was a total surprise: obstructing the main entrance to the plant on November 3, the first day of the strike, his only day of on-the-line picket duty. He had walked across the driveway to offer Marion Toot, his picketing partner, a cup of coffee from his thermos. A management employee had driven up in a pickup truck, rolled his window down to say a few words, then had backed up and turned around and driven to another gate. Wilson's had stationed an employee with a movie camera on top of the building, and he had caught this scene on film. The driver of the pickup claimed that he'd been threatened and ordered to leave.

More puzzling to me than the charge against Dad was his reaction to it. Defiant anger would not have surprised me, nor would relief at a sound excuse to leave Wilson's and look for another job. Sour grapes would have tasted sweet to me just then. But this was grief—a deep, soulful grief that I had never yet witnessed. Just two years before, Grandpa Register had died of uremic poisoning after a fairly brief illness I never guessed would be fatal, though others knew. Dad was stoic through the funeral, as befits a responsible oldest son. If he cried, he did it in private, too softly to be heard through a closed door. The only tears I had ever seen him shed were the sentimental ones he wiped away during *Gunsmoke*, or the proud ones that glistened in his eyes when Joey won the Miss Albert Lea pageant and Nancy graduated from college.

My inherited share of the grief wells up as I write this, with the image of Dad hunched and shaking vivid in my memory. Like others of his generation, he put aside the youthful dreams he couldn't afford to pursue and settled into what work there was, devoting himself to it with the same vigor he would bring to work he had aspired to. At fourteen, I had already learned from his example that talents are to be used to their fullest, even if the stage is small, the audience sparse, and the applause miserly. We believed in the virtue of work well done, knowing the reward was usually just more work to do. Now even that had been taken away. One false accusation and the ungrudging overtime, the perfectly threaded gears, the plucky ingenuity counted for nothing. I won't name the man in the pickup, who brought the charge, a man Dad swears he never treated unkindly. His act was petty in comparison to the larger betrayal: the company's coldhearted disregard for its employees' loyalty.

These days, Dad scoffs at the whole ordeal, though he never quite forgives and forgets. When the arbitration board saw the evidence, he says, they threw the charge right out. It was obviously trumped up, a waste of their time. Yet that's not what the official record shows. "There is insufficient basis," the board's ruling reads, "to hold guilty of physical acts of violence the persons whose names are hereinafter set forth. The arbitrators do find such persons guilty of making threatening remarks or aiding and abetting therein, and are of the opinion that the company was justified in bringing these charges to the attention of the arbitrators." Rabbi Weinstein dissented, saying that "it seems that some demonic powers have hovered over these flimsy charges to make them more ominous by the mere passage of time."

Dad never got to appear in court to confront his accuser or explain his actions directly to the arbiters. The union's lawyers entered affidavits, or "appidavids" as I heard the word, on behalf of the entire "crap list." Dad and Marion Toot, along with Gilbert Haskins, Morris's dad, and several others, were returned to work two months later without back pay. Those found guilty of more serious offenses were kept out longer. By December, everyone was back at work, except for five men held responsible for inciting the violence on December 9 and 10. In the meantime, on March 4, Judge Cooney was replaced as president and named chairman of the board, with responsibility for long-term planning. We liked to say he had been put out to pasture, though there were some who would rather have hauled him up on the beef chain.

Throughout this crisis and for many years after, my friend Linda and I never acknowledged to each other that her mother must have known of Dad's fate all along. As attorney Ralph Peterson's secretary, she probably typed the list. But she, too, was a loyal worker who took her job seriously, and she kept these matters confidential forever.

Dad returned to work in May, Minnesota's most pleasant month. The spring rain plumps the leaves on bushes and trees and brings out all the subtle variations in hue of yellow and green. Soon the tulips and apple blossoms, the lilacs and spirea trust the sun's warmth enough to open and fill out the rest of the spectrum. Spring in Minnesota is a burst of joy, a brief season of bug-free contentment before the sweltering heat of a prairie summer sets in again.

Back to work. Back to "work," as human endeavor, as obligation, as source of worth. In the years since I walked in on Dad's sorrow, I have come to understand why his job meant so much to him. Recently, I had the unexpected pleasure of meeting the men who won it back for him, Eugene Cotton and Irving King, Chicago labor lawyers who argued the union's case before the arbitration board. Cotton, who says his hair literally turned gray from worry about the five thousand families dependent on his legal skills, delivered the general argument, while King handled the individual cases of those, like Dad, who were not hired back. I have also had a conversation with Ralph Helstein's daughter Nina, with whom I felt instant rapport. What binds us all, besides our common history, is a shared sense of the value of work that does not depend on level of income or social status, the supposed rewards of upward mobility. Nina was sixteen at the time of the Wilson strike, and, ever curious about her father's work, she sat in on the arbitration hearings. She remembers Eugene Cotton's presentation as "brilliant" and "gripping," "a long, wonderful, and passionate explanation of the importance of seniority and what it means to people. My father said it was the best description and defense of seniority that he had ever heard. He related what he was talking about to people's daily lives."

Job security meant a great deal to my parents. Their measures of worthwhile work, I believe, have been security, skill, and utility. They sought steady work that kept them safe from the need they had known earlier in their lives, but they also wanted work that tested their abilities and gave them the satisfaction of feeling competent. Their work had to have purpose and had to be of some benefit to others, not in any grand metaphysical sense, but useful at its most basic. Dad's work provided food; Mom's, clothing. They tried to pass on these lessons to me. As I tested out college majors, they wanted to know, "Can you get a job with that?" and "What use is that?"

There is an element missing here that has been at the center of my own search for worthwhile work. First on *my* list is vocation—the certainty that I am doing the work I am most suited for, the work I am meant to do. It was vocation—in my case, writing—that called me away from home. Now it has brought me back. Mom and Dad never turned away from their own true callings, I see now, but followed them outside of work: he in politics and public service, she in the creativity and beauty of the sewing she did on her own time. Their families' financial struggles had taught them to bank on security. I, on the other hand, have risked security for vocation, and have been lucky enough to find work that neither assaults my senses nor puts me in danger. Skill and utility matter as much to me as they do to my folks. Joan Didion defines a writer as "a person whose most absorbed and passionate hours are spent arranging words on pieces of paper." I arrange and add and delete in a search for words honed as sharp as the knives on Dad's skinning machine and for sentences as smooth and even as Mom's seams. But most of all, I want my words to make the dim and misunderstood events of my childhood ring clear and true.

Faith in the Face of Reality

"This isn't really a question of victory or defeat," Frank Schultz told the members of Local 6 before they voted to end the strike, but of "facing the realities in front of us." His statement could apply to any strike, and to the entire course of labor history. It is never really a question of victory or defeat. All victories are potential defeats, as the opposition devises fresh strategies to undo them. The one constant is that there are always realities to face, the usual injustices and unsettling new ones.

The UPWA came away from the Wilson strike with one memorable victory: the arbitration board's ruling that the workers out on strike retained their seniority. The arbitrators did not address whether Wilson's was right or wrong to hire permanent replacements. The United States Supreme Court had ruled, in the 1938 case of *National Labor Relations Board v. Mackay Radio and Telegraph Company*, that hiring permanent replacements was not in itself an unfair labor practice.

The arbitration ruling could not override a Supreme Court decision, but it set a precedent that made it impractical, at least, for companies to promise permanent employment to strikebreakers. This union victory, like others, was temporary. Seniority did not protect the striking PATCO air traffic controllers in 1984, when President Ronald Reagan, in a dramatic display of executive power, fired them all.

Regardless of what the UPWA sought in its continually thwarted negotiations with Wilson's, it spent most of its efforts avoiding penalties for a strike it believed the company had instigated. Winning back the union members' jobs became the most pressing need, and its immediacy makes that victory look substantial. But this particular threat to job security was not initially the most vital issue on the table. For the union, it was job security in the longer run: protecting livelihoods in the face of the most threatening reality, automation. For the company, it was control over an efficient and profitable automation process: the right to eliminate and redefine jobs—to lay off workers and reduce wage rates—without union interference. Who won, finally? The UPWA gave up its identity in a merger with its rival, the Amalgamated Meat Cutters and Butcher Workmen, in 1968. Wilson's went bankrupt fifteen years later. Today's meatpacking industry hardly offers evidence of progress toward safe, clean, and well-rewarded work. What, then, is the point of a strike—or of a union, for that matter?

That is not a question I have ever really thought to ask, since history shows that workers rarely get fair treatment without joining together to advocate for themselves. Fairness, I learned as a child, is the supreme virtue governing human social life. If ever compassion replaces greed as a human motive, fairness will prevail and all will be well. Labor unions, in victory and defeat, help keep that vision alive.

I grew up with an against-all-odds faith in social progress that I like to trace to Great-Grandpa Ostrander's prairie populism, one example of the great wave of progressivism that fueled the social movements of the late nineteenth and early twentieth centuries. I see this faith, too, in Grandma Petersen's ability to send troubled visitors home laughing. If I probe deeply enough, I can find the Petersen counterpart to prairie populism in N. F. S. Grundtvig's Danish folk movement, which turned us into "happy Danes" rather than the "holy Danes" associated with religious pietism.

In my review of documents related to the 1959 strike, I saw a similar faith at work in the UPWA. I understand now how deeply ingrained it is in my family and others like us, though we had no name for it, other than "union." "Democratic unionism," it is called in a 1959 pamphlet published by the UPWA to answer a charge by the House Un-American Activities Committee that the union was infested with Communists. Of course there were communists active in its foundation, the union admits. Given the economic and political climate of the 1930s, "it would have been strange indeed, if there were no communists, socialists, single-taxers, technocrats, and utopians in the ranks of our union." The union can best guard against Soviet-style totalitarianism, the pamphlet explains, not by coercion and purges, but by remaining faithful to the democratic process, which values freedom of speech.

The UPWA was equally committed to industrial unionism, to including packinghouse workers of all skill and wage levels in its membership. And faced early on with the reality of racial divisions, it declared itself a force for racial equality and played an instrumental role in the civil rights movement. The active participation of its members was crucial to the union's governance. "There is no spirit of 'let the business agent do it' in the UPWA," the pamphlet boasts. "The philosophy that the union belongs to its members, that the officers must be the servants rather than the masters of the membership, is our very foundation."

The true measure of union democracy is, of course, taken among the rank and file. "The UPWA was a union that give more voice to the people," Chuck Lee believes, "and was run by the people a lot more so than a lot of the other unions. And that was a big sticking point, too, when we started talking merger with those different unions, because it seemed to us that some of the top people in those organizations run it the way they thought it should be run instead of listening to the rank and file. We felt that the UPWA was a better, open organization. It give real consideration to the people." As an example, he cites the "chain" method of organization. In addition to each local sending several delegates to conferences and negotiation sessions, representatives of the workers in each company met separately as the "Wilson chain" or the "Armour chain." This gave workers from each of the plants an opportunity to bring up issues very specific to their own working conditions and to make sure they were addressed in the master contract.

The fact that only one man—and a lawyer at that—presided over the union for its entire twenty-five-year existence might make these claims to democracy seem a sham. But Ralph Helstein did not fit the stereotype of the union boss. "Ralph was a good leader," Chuck Lee says. "He was the one that always wanted things open and felt that they should be. And he was real concerned about not only the union people, but anybody who had difficulty." Helstein came into the presidency as a compromise candidate, after representing the Packinghouse Workers' Organizing Committee in its first successful contract negotiation, between Austin's Local 9 and the George A. Hormel Company.

Ralph Helstein undoubtedly stumbled from time to time over his clay feet, but he has impressed *me* with his commitment to a vision of union democracy. The line in the 1959 document about the officers being servants of the membership was one he could have authored. His daughter Nina has a favorite story that illustrates his understanding of servanthood.

"When we were quite little, he used to sometimes on a Saturday bring us to his office. We'd play with paper and pencils and he would get stuff done. I really had no idea what he did, at all. When I was in fourth grade, a boy said to me at school, 'Your father kills pigs.' I came home very upset and said, 'Is that what you do at the office, Dad? Are you killing pigs?' I remember *exactly* what he said, because it was so typical of him and so wonderful. He said, 'Well, what if I do? You eat ham, you eat bacon. Someone has to kill the pig.' And I thought about that, and then he said, 'As a matter of fact, I don't, but I work for the people who do.' And that, too, was very typical of him, or at least of what he was trying to teach me, because he saw himself as working for the membership."

Nina traces his beliefs to two early influences. Born in Duluth, Minnesota, in 1908, he grew up in an Orthodox Jewish family in Minneapolis that was, in her words, "completely observant." Though he gave up the strict religious practice when he left home, the ethical values of "prophetic Judaism" remained at the core of his identity and motivated his work. The second influence was, and I smile as I write it, the Farmer-Labor Party, which firmed up his political beliefs. Farmer-Labor Party doctrine shows through still in the UPWA archives, in leaflets and newsletters that appeal to livestock farmers to make common cause with the people who process their animals into meat.

I was both fascinated and envious as I listened to Nina Helstein talk about four of her father's friends and associates who helped him apply his vision of labor democracy to life's realities: Myles and Zylphia Horton of the Highlander Folk School, which ran educational sessions for union delegates; community organizer Saul Alinsky, with whom he debated organizing strategy; Martin Luther King, with whom he met monthly for two years. Chuck Lee remembers hearing King speak at several of the UPWA's annual conferences.

I would like to think that these prominent reformers had a trickle-down influence on my life. I can guess, by my conversations with Chuck Lee and Don Nielsen, that the officers of the union locals received an education in civics as sound as anything they would have learned in college classes, had they been fortunate enough to go to college. The UPWA was a training ground where people with little power or social status had their value affirmed and learned to keep working for what was only fair. We who grew up in the light the union cast over our families benefited too, if we paid attention. Nina Helstein's memories confirm this:

"The union had a convention in Washington, and we got to go to the Rose Garden and meet President Kennedy. And I went. Dad said I could. I enjoyed meeting President Kennedy, but the thing that was most interesting to me about the trip was that the membership was getting prepared to do lobbying, and I went with the delegation from Louisiana and met with Senator Ellender. We talked about meat inspection and wages and something about health care. That was an extraordinary experience. There was a man named Chester Driver, I think, who was from Louisiana. He was an older man. He was a black man from the bayou, and very smart and very knowledgeable, and he kind of led us. Everybody was very polite to the senator, but wouldn't budge. They had prepared for this for a long time, and they knew what the issues were and what they meant to them, and they stayed with it. My memory of that time is that people were very well informed. I would go to all the conventions too, and I would sit through the meetings, because I was so interested. I was just always really impressed. People had thought out opinions and they were substantive opinions."

Digging through the hundreds of file boxes in the UPWA archives, I can easily mourn the loss of this democratic, progressive organization. Fortunately, there is another repository of memories where the spirit of the UPWA is not enclosed in cardboard but displayed on the walls and kept alive in proud stories. The Illinois Labor History Society, a three-room suite on the tenth floor of an old office building in Chicago's Loop, is a labor of love overseen by Leslie Orear, an amazingly youthful man who went to work in Chicago's Armour plant in 1932 and was active in the Packinghouse Workers' Organizing Committee from its very beginning.

I met Les Orear on the Internet. He wrote in answer to a query I sent out and told me he might have a few pictures from the 1959 strike on hand. I arranged to visit the ILHS office a few weeks later. He met me at the door, smiling and full of energy, and showed me around his gallery of posters and enlarged photographs, pointing out all the figures I might know. Then he led me into the library room and pulled a manila folder out of a file drawer. He spread it open on the table and began sorting through the pictures. "That's Emil Mazey, the secretary-treasurer of the United Auto Workers," he said. "He visited all the packinghouse locals during that strike." "And that," I shrieked, pointing to the man drinking coffee across the table from Mazey, "is my uncle Ted!"

Next, he brought out some yellowed copies of *The Packinghouse Worker* and showed me a double spread on the arbitration hearing, with photos of a young Eugene Cotton arguing the union's case at the arbitration hearing, his arms outstretched like a master orator.

"We used to get *The Packinghouse Worker* at our house," I said, slipping into my ardent-teenager voice.

"Oh?" he responded. "I edited that paper for a bit."

"You *did?* When?"

"From 1952 to 1968."

"For a bit?" I shot back. "Then you were the editor during the strike."

"Yup, I was," he said modestly.

"What does it mean to edit a paper like that?" I asked. "Does it mean you write most of the articles, too?"

"Yup," he said. "I wrote it."

As his modesty gave way to pride, I asked him how *The Packinghouse Worker* compared to other labor newspapers, and his answer was consistent with the democratic character of the union itself. "It was decidedly unprofessional," he said. "It breathed a lot of excitement, and it was not put out by anybody who'd ever been trained as a detached newsman. It was just enthusiastic all the time about everything. And we had this unusual feature of a center spread with pictures of workers on the job. It had a very rank-and-file foundation. Its focus was sharply on local activity. Another thing important about this paper is that Helstein kept his hands very much off. This thing was just not a canned ersatz house organ. It was sort of like a voice of the people."

The circle of faith was drawn tight around me in that little office within rumbling distance of Chicago's elevated train. The realities in the meatpacking industry today are grim indeed, but I have to believe that someone will step forward to face them, "breathing excitement," just as Les Orear and his coworkers did so long ago.

LEGACY

How to Make History

A woman of the kind I feared becoming—a Wilson sausage worker—has been my silent collaborator on this book. Her name is Hazel Gudvangen, and her photo sits on the window-sill by my computer. Whenever I doubted the value or wisdom of what I was doing, I looked at Hazel to remind myself why it mattered. The figure caught in the photo is about the age I am now, and short and stocky with a curly permanent, a familiar type in the supermarket aisles of Midwestern towns. For this picture-taking occasion, she is dressed up, in a red winter dress, and posed on her davenport alongside the pole lamp that marks the era. It's Christmas, and she has no doubt been crocheting tree ornaments and making bleach-bottle Santa Clauses for her grandchildren.

I never met Hazel in person. She died young, only sixty, just five years after retiring on disability from a full work life in the packinghouse. I know her only through the precious gift she left behind. It sits in a high cupboard in the Local 6 office in

Albert Lea's Union Center. Each time I came to see it, Deanne, who works at the front desk, would stand on her chair to reach it and then carry it down the hall to a conference room, as gingerly as if it were an Egyptian papyrus. There I sat alone, while cars streamed by outside the Main Street window, and paged carefully through Hazel Gudvangen's five-inch-thick scrapbook of the 1959 strike.

Hazel's daughter, Marlene Hammero, remembers the scrapbook lying on a card table in the corner of the living room all through the strike. Every night Hazel clipped articles out of the newspaper—any item that had to do with the strike, even a tiny two-line classified ad from the For Rent column: "Clean six rooms—$55.00. Phone FR 3-4840. No scabs." If she was too busy to paste them in, she tucked them inside dated envelopes, to keep from upsetting the chronological order. Among the clippings are other mementos no newspaper file would contain: Hazel's picket-duty card, with punched holes that demonstrate her loyalty to the strike; union leaflets and reports to the membership; the company's Dear John letters; a typed list of scabs the union could identify, along with the acreage they farmed or violence they either committed or suffered.

Here, too, are a warrant for Hazel's arrest on a charge of assault and battery, various court documents, and letters from neighbors called to be character witnesses. Hazel has the distinction of being the only woman prosecuted for strike-related violence. (One other was charged by the company with spitting on a car but the arbitration board did not regard this as a crime.) She is the only female striker to appear in the public record, and even then her role is obscured. The *Evening Tribune* reports that "ten men" were called to give depositions in Wilson's attempt to get a permanent injunction against the union. One of those ten men is identified as Hazel Gudvangen.

All ten refused to appear and were fined $50 each. Nine had their fines reduced or suspended. Only Hazel had to pay in full.

What Hazel did is still unclear. She was present at the scene of a brawl involving a carload of scabs from Iowa. That much is certain. In the melee, she allegedly grabbed and slapped a woman in the group. She pled innocent to that offense, then changed her plea to guilty. In court again, she retracted her guilty plea and explained that she actually meant to protect the woman from harm. Someone else in the crowd was about to hit her with a board, and she had merely pulled her out of the way. The woman, misinterpreting the gesture, kicked her and Hazel slapped her back.

Marlene and her husband, then living in Austin, heard her name on the television news, packed their kids in the car, and rushed to Albert Lea. They found Hazel at the bowling alley— it was her league night—and she didn't seem worried at all. There was nothing to the charge, she told them, and it was sure to be dismissed. She described how the crowd had scattered when the police came, and though she was not the only union woman involved in the action, she was the only one caught. "It's the most excitement I've had in a long time," she laughed. "So what if I have to go spend some time in jail?"

A few days in jail would have been a quick and easy end to the story, but that's not how it developed. In fact, this lone woman was punished with dismaying severity. Like my dad, she was denied reinstatement at Wilson's after the strike was settled. Though the arbitration board referee who heard her case recommended that she be exonerated for saving the other woman from more serious harm, the board's verdict was "guilty with provocation." She was one of the last three striking workers to be hired back. The others were men, one a union officer who was stripped of his seniority. Hazel was out of work, with no pay, for thirteen and a half months, starting with the lockout in November.

"Hazel never took any guff from anybody," is how my dad remembers her, though there seems to be plenty of guff in the legal proceedings. He got to know her because the disk machine she used to make sausage casings frequently broke down. She was a nice person to talk to, easygoing for the most part, but she was known to stand up for herself when she felt slighted. "She fought for what she believed in," her daughter concurs. "She basically got along with people, except she was pretty headstrong when it come to the union."

Hazel's was not an easy life. Divorced at an early age, she moved from Austin to Albert Lea, where her widowed mother lived, and rented an apartment on Charles Street. She had worked at Hormel's and now found a job at Wilson's, in bacon, to support herself and her young daughter. It was a "woman's job," contracted on a separate, lower pay scale than the men's jobs. The UPWA was formally committed to racial equality, and women in the union raised the issue of sex equality as early as its founding days in the late 1930s, but with little success. The reasoning was, of course, that men had families to support.

"My mother was a *very strong* union person," Hammero says. "She believed very deeply in the union." Hammero's father had helped to organize the union at Hormel's, and Hazel got involved as soon as she went to work there. At Wilson's, she kept up her active participation and was elected union steward of her mostly female department. The leadership of Local 6 was and always had been exclusively male, so Hazel had to speak forcefully. She was a visible presence throughout the 1948 and 1959 strikes. In addition to her picket duty, she cooked meals at the Union Center and went along on bus trips to other meatpacking towns to leaflet their plants.

Even after she remarried, Hazel continued to work full-time. She was a hard worker, both at the plant and at home, a high-energy person who seldom sat still. The work took its toll, and carpal tunnel syndrome, pervasive in the meatpacking industry, made it impossible for her to continue her sausage job safely. Surgery left her with no feeling in her thumbs, and though she continued to work on her crafts, she held her coffee cup with both hands for safety's sake. Reassigned to a gofer job, delivering orders from the office to various departments, she took pleasure in her freedom to move around the plant and to wear her housedresses to work.

These are the bare outlines of a life I would have recoiled from at eighteen. In middle age, as my own life has settled into the routines of single-motherhood and household tasks, and as I shed some of my grandiose dreams, I feel more akin to Hazel than I ever expected. Our work is vastly different: hers repetitive and governed by the speed of the line, mine self-disciplined and as varied as imagination allows. But I would guess that the ideals we attach to our work and the responsibility we take for it are similar. I learned my work ethic in Hazel's community, after all, so I did not entirely escape the influence of the women on the processing lines.

What draws me to Hazel most of all, and what makes our strange collaboration possible, is her sense of history. She believed that her life and the events she was caught up in mattered enough to keep a permanent record. I know that scrapbooks were popular at the time. My mom clipped and pasted the news of local boys killed in World War II and my sister memorialized movie star Betty Grable. I started a Jeanne Crain scrapbook as soon as I could be trusted with scissors. Yet I have never seen a scrapbook as thorough and meticulous as the one Hazel Gudvangen kept through the strike and beyond.

It starts at the beginning, as though she anticipated a story worth telling, and it continues a full year after settlement, with post-arbitration analyses and strike-averting measures at Wilson's, including the hiring of Pinkerton Guards for plant security. It ends only with the city's victory in the annexation dispute. Personal artifacts mingle with news accounts, evidence that she treasured her role as an actor in this history. Hazel Gudvangen's priceless scrapbook offers the most thorough and reliable coverage of the 1959 Wilson strike I have found. Even its gaps are useful guides, springboards to other sources.

If only she had kept a diary, I thought with longing as I paged through the scrapbook. The sad news is that she *did*, but her husband burned it shortly after her death. The scrapbook was spared because she had already offered it to her daughter, who suggested that she take it to the Union Center, where it might be of some use. What I wouldn't give now for the daily log she wrote on calendar pages and in ledger books, year after year. Every day something happened that mattered enough to record. I might have learned how many hours she worked, the amount of each paycheck, her bowling scores, what kind of pies she baked, and who dropped by to visit.

I don't mean to romanticize Hazel Gudvangen as either union maid or dogged worker. Though the specter of women's work at the packinghouse no longer frightens me, that may be true only because my escape was successful. Yet I eagerly celebrate Hazel as the like-minded neighbor I never knew, one of many unsung women who shaped my life in ways I can only see in retrospect. Hazel knew, and so do I, that any life has meaning which knows its connection to the world. Any life has meaning which is lived not in sour isolation but with purpose that lasts beyond its own numbered days.

My Vengeance on the Wienie Moguls

I feel the anger as a catch in the breath, a tightening of the jaw, pressure building inside my chest. No doubt I look like I have a chip on my shoulder. I try to brush it off myself—it's such an aggravation—but some other excess or insensitivity will soon come along to rile me up. Calling myself "angry" feels affected. It's one of those ritzy words I had to learn to use when I went away to college. At home, we just got "mad." This "madness" of mine has been implacable since the strike, which turned my misgivings about people who grow rich on the labor of others into a raw but unfocused hostility. Unsure where to direct it, I've tried, like my dad, to keep the safety on.

I watched the daily effort Dad made to live with the discontent produced by hour after long hour of grueling, dangerous, and sometimes loathsome work—*skilled* work, admittedly, to which he had pledged his life and loyalty. It was a good living, after all, among the best in town. A steady paycheck was nothing to complain about. Dad kept his indignation contained in the pretense of moral superiority. We, the honorable "little guys" were a different species from those greedy "rich people." For half my life, he had me convinced that rich people aren't happy. There was little need to work up anger at people already suffering the boredom and emptiness of their material excesses. A cold disdain was more livable.

Besides, the people who got rich off packinghouse labor never showed up for the fight. The whereabouts of the Wilson heirs was a mystery, and Judge Cooney, whose name oozed out between Dad's curling lips, kept himself ensconced in the Prudential Building in Chicago. The big stockholders hid their identities behind investment-company names. They were, we concluded, too racked by guilt to face us; and guilt, we Lutherans knew, was the greatest cause of unhappiness known to mankind.

Nor was it easy keeping clear lines between a stable blue-collar "us" and the middle-class "them" who pass for rich in a town with no real wealth. Familiarity caused additional complications. As I moved from my working-class elementary school into the more encompassing community of junior high, even my image of Shoreland Heights began to blur. Grouped with other students of college potential, I got to know some of the rich kids: daughters of dentists and lawyers who had grown up on drought-stricken farms, grandsons of Jewish refugees from Eastern European pogroms. They had no evil intentions toward me that I could detect.

Since leaving home, I have picked up a few more subtleties about social class, but I have certainly not shed the fascination that was encouraged on our family's rides through Shoreland Heights. I still scout out the rich folk wherever I go, cruise past their houses, and scoff at their self-indulgence. Ridiculing the unhappy rich no longer keeps the lid on my anger, however. Their freedom to hide out and hold themselves aloof from the consequences of their greed works me into a froth. Ordinarily, I am cool as a Scandinavian autumn, far too low-key and mild-mannered for the task I have set myself. Only contempt for the rich—for their luxuriant oblivion of the rest of us—rouses the passion I need to think and write about social class.

I know enough now to distinguish between the nouveaux riches, belittled from both sides, and the firmly moneyed, who hold themselves beyond judgment. I may have some petty quarrels with the lean, blond suburbanites who invade my Minneapolis neighborhood in their oversized sport utility vehicles to eat pasta salad at the yuppie café that replaced our local greasy spoon, but my wrath is reserved for the truly and deeply rich, those so embedded in the habits of wealth they no longer need to show off.

While rich people may, indeed, be unhappy, just as Dad claimed, they have the resources—the means for leisurely travel and guilt-shedding philanthropy—to ease the melancholy that is our common human condition. Travel and good causes are the two uses to which I, too, would put my excess money, if I had any. Instead, I have been on the receiving end of philanthropy, and have not kept a purist's moral distance from the rich. It was a rich man who sent me to college. A banker from an old East Coast family, he took delight in hand-picking, from a list of University of Chicago applicants, the two per year who would receive the scholarship he had endowed. The other beneficiary in my class was a girl from Cicero, Illinois, a tough town, home of Al Capone, where the labor unions were said to be infested by mobsters. Maybe she was better equipped than I to handle this blessed giving. When it was clear that my grades would satisfy my benefactor's expectations, my adviser encouraged me to write him a letter and tell him all about my first year and, of course, express my gratitude. Having been assured that he took a strong personal interest in his students, I wrote him a chatty letter about my studies, my aspirations, my home, my family. He never wrote back. All I know about him I read in *Who's Who.* I could as well be one of those hollow-eyed Third World children urging "Please sponsor me" in glossy-magazine ads.

As a writer, I pride myself on my independence and self-discipline and my sometimes inspired exercise of free speech. Yet, short of a best-seller, writing is also mind-and-finger work for which even minimum wage would be a substantial raise. Writers—the self-selecting genteel poor—are seldom rewarded directly for their time and effort, but must scrounge out a living however they can. My work has been financed, in part, by rich people. For example, I once submitted an essay about my working-class heritage to an anthology underwritten by the Rockefeller Foundation. When the check arrived—a generous $500—I bought myself a Maytag washer. It really ought to bear a bronze plaque, I think, commemorating John D. and all his kin. When I pull out the dial to start up the wash cycle, I imagine the machine gushing crude oil and the Rockefellers rushing in to reclaim it under some lifetime lien on mineral resources.

I don't take well to philanthropy, though I take what I can get. I would like to live more honestly, like the union workers of Wheeling, West Virginia, who, eleven years after the deadly Homestead steel strike of 1892, urged the city to refuse the gift of a Carnegie library. "There will be one place on this great green planet," they vowed, "where Andrew Carnegie can't get a monument to his money." But I know I would have balked at supporting that protest. Without Carnegie's endowment, what would we common folk read?

Shortly after I began writing up my memories of the packinghouse, I was accepted for a residency at the Ragdale Foundation, a writers' and artists' retreat in Lake Forest, Illinois. Here I would be comfortably housed and well fed for two weeks while I concentrated wholly on my writing. Lake Forest, I knew, would feed my fascination with rich people. The rich were everywhere, parking their Audis and Ferraris along the architecturally noteworthy town square, treating their dayschool-uniformed children to bags of exotic bulk candy at Sweets. ("Here you are, Judson. Now, what would you like, Tucker?")

In the mornings, I walked the prairie preserve behind Ragdale House for inspiration; but to clear the words from my head after a day's work, I went for a ride. The streets on the Lake Michigan side of Sheridan Avenue, an area so exclusive you are not allowed to park your car along the curb, offered far greater cause for astonishment than Shoreland Heights. Lake Forest is beyond rich, a city of multiwinged brick mansions and chemically enhanced lawns behind stockade fences and wrought-iron gates. It is wealthy, affluent, opulent.

"Do you know who lives here?" my new friend Jessica, a San Francisco painter, began as we plundered the Ragdale refrigerator for lunch one day. "It's wienie moguls."

"Who?" I asked, doubtful of what I had heard.

"Wienie moguls. Hot-dog kings," she tried again. "Meatpackers. The Armours and the Swifts and the Cudahys. They're all here. Lake Forest is built on Chicago stockyard money."

Now why was Jessica privy to an epithet that I, by rights,

ought to have known? I wondered if she, born into a literary family, pronounced it with aristocratic distaste rather than the righteous anger I would have loaded it with.

Jessica didn't yet know that I was writing about packing-house life, so what she told me was serendipitous information. I went to the phone book to check, forgetting, in my eagerness, that the richest of the rich might keep their numbers unlisted. I found five Armours, five Swifts. There were Wilsons too, as there must be in every American phone book. A high school classmate of mine who also went to the University of Chicago on scholarship spent a summer living on the third floor of the former Wilson mansion in the Kenwood neighborhood. It had been saved from demolition and refurbished by a member of the faculty. Unfortunately, he moved out before I had a chance to get inside, and it was not the safest area for slow cruising. Across the street, armed guards protected Elijah Muhammad's mansion from insurrections within the Nation of Islam. The Wilsons had moved away, but I had no proof that they had joined the rich white flight to Lake Forest.

I asked the woman who managed the Ragdale office if I could photocopy the phone book's city map, and while she did this for me I chitchatted about the famous names I had spotted.

"Oh," she perked up. "Are you writing about the Armours?" She spoke the name with the respect due a benefactor.

"Not exactly," I said, feeling an unexpected sheepishness.

With the map on the seat beside me, marked with Xs, my diversionary evening ride became a spy mission. Looking for-ward to peeping in on the wienie moguls at rest after a long day of doing whatever they do, I set out, first, for a home likely to have lake frontage. I followed a street that curved and wound around wooded plots and across ravines to a bluff above the lake, a neighborhood more secluded than the row of ostentatious manors along Lake Avenue. The street I sought was only one block long, and the odd-even house numbering pattern helped me locate the house on the lake side, although there was no number in front to identify it. The mailman knew where to go, I figured. The street dead-ended at the edge of a lush ravine and I sat there with my foot on the brake, gawking.

I can't begin to describe the house. I never saw it. The only evidence of habitation was two driveways leading into a thicket of trees, one of them marked "service entrance." These were people so accustomed to their wealth that they felt no compulsion to display it to passersby. I waited for a dog to bark or a child to come riding home in the dusk on a bicycle, but it was completely still. As the engine idled, my compact car quivered and my emotions seethed. The pressure building in my chest could only be relieved, I guessed, by the toss of a brick, the strike of a match, or a well-aimed glob of spit. But spitting into the trees brings little satisfaction.

I drove back to Ragdale feeling both angry and deprived. I wanted to see just what a century of packinghouse labor had bought. I wanted a visual image to go with my literal understanding of what it means to "live high on the hog." My Ragdale compatriots suggested that I deliver a pizza or simply show up at the door with a movie camera and film my own version of Michael Moore's *Roger and Me*. I wished I had that much audacity. Anger unrelieved can take ridiculous shapes. I even began to fantasize about charging into Sweets and collaring Judson and Tucker as they blithely pointed to one candy jar after another. "Do you have any idea whose hard work is buying you this candy and what it costs them? Let me tell you . . ."

In moments of heightened anger, my memory flashes to the image of Dad sobbing at the table after he learned that Wilson's refused to take him back. This is one humiliation I would like to fling back at the wienie moguls if I ever do flush them out of hiding. Yet I don't know which explanation I would rather believe: that Dad was the victim of a nasty frame-up masterminded by the wienie moguls and executed by their lowly henchmen, proof of the inhumanity of those who make their living off the labor of others; or that Dad, one cold winter day, let the lid slip off his anger and planted himself in front of a provocateur pickup. Together with Marion Toot, whose bib overalls hanging from the clothesline made an awesome sight, he could easily have blocked that gate. I would take it as proof of his human frailty, and a safety valve for mine.

My imagination continues to fume over the treasures stacked up behind the wienie moguls' shrubbery. This is not a pleasant emotional state to live in, nor does it accord with my self-image, that of a tolerant, rational being capable of subtlety in her observations of human behavior. But this anger—whether residual or fresh—is undeniably real. When I get "mad" like this, my lust for vengeance drifts into dreams of the absurd. To dispel the rage, I have to send the Armours or the Swifts or the elusive Wilsons on a humbling Sunday-evening ride through Albert Lea. I want the wienie moguls to be as curious as we are about life on the other side of the average household income. Firmly rich as they are, they would probably choose discretion and take one of the midsize American cars they keep on hand for such tooling around. My fantasy, however, keeps shooing them into a huge silver Mercedes.

They make quick business of Shoreland Heights, baldly nouveau riche, and take time to cruise the generically named Northside and Southside before heading out west past Wal-Mart and the half-empty Skyline Mall, to the 1950s housing development where I grew up. Up behind the Bel-Air Motel, they come upon a neatly maintained white rambler with an R on the Rusco screen door, a planter of softball-sized begonias flourishing on Miracle-Gro, and a country mailbox rigged with a crafty spring-and-string device that shows whether the mail has come and eliminates fruitless trips outside. Their eagerness to peer inside the house will be disappointed. The drapes are pulled across the picture window to keep the sunlight from fading the furniture, and the front door stays locked most of the time to keep too much coming-and-going from tracking dirt on the beige carpet.

It's difficult to idle discreetly at the edge of an unfenced and unhedged yard, so the wienie moguls have to swing into a driveway up the street, back out, and make another pass. This time an aging woman in a curly permanent steps out to gather the throw rugs airing out over the railing on the front steps. She spots the rare Mercedes; and once she's back inside, the drapes part slightly. On a ladder propped against the edge of the roof, a broad-backed, elderly man leans in to scoop up leaves and twigs that the summer storms deposited in the eaves troughs. With bare hands, he stuffs the soggy debris into a plastic Hy-Vee grocery bag, causing the squeamish Judson to shudder, then climbs down a rung at a time, favoring his left knee. He walks across the yard and up the hand-poured cement driveway toward the single-car garage. His beefy shoulders roll forward, pulling his polo shirt free of his pants, which droop and cling against the back of his legs in the humid air. His legs look too thin to bear the weight of his torso.

The mogul dad turns off the air-conditioning and presses the button that lowers the car windows. This should be a full experience for the boys, he decides, with sounds and smells and the feel of the air, slightly putrid from his industrial plant's smokestack across town. Judson and Tucker hear crickets

chirping, thinly, their song less vibrant than the music of the ci-
cadas so abundant in Lake Forest. As the old man stops at a
window box to pull dried petunia blossoms and drop them in
his bag of humus, a mourning dove coos in the distance.

Acting with the sort of boldness that comes naturally to a
man of his station, the mogul dad gives a teeny tap on the horn
and waits, with a kindly smile on his face, for the man to turn
around in acknowledgment. He doesn't know that the man is
hard of hearing, that an old tune plays on inside his skull: the
hiss of steam pipes, the lurching clatter of the overhead line,
the whine of saws grinding bone. Mogul dad, his left foot resting firmly on the brake, gives the gas pedal a nudge with his
right and guns the engine. Still, the man walks on at a steady
pace, his weathered body never flinching, even at the finely
modulated hum of a Mercedes. He opens a door in the breezeway beside the garage, steps in and lets it fall shut behind him.
He has his own work to do now.

Mellowing

I passed my driver's license exam—on the second try—in a hot car. I had flunked abruptly the first time when our 1948 Pontiac jumped the curb and nicked the parking meter as I pulled into a diagonal space by the courthouse. Beside me, in the passenger seat, was the tense, unsmiling examiner. He had already lost confidence watching me lean into the turns—a hundred pounds of girl struggling to subdue a ton of automobile with one arm while the other stretched out the window to signal the direction. Our new car, a white 1960 Mercury with a sky blue interior, had power steering and a turn signal with a soothing *blink-a-blink-a-blink* that is fixed in my memory as the archetypal sound of driving pleasure.

The car wasn't really stolen. Dad had checked out the registration papers and everything looked legit, he assured us. The price was low, the payments affordable for a family who had just survived a strike—because it was a demonstrator model. He had bought it, however, from a cousin who had done time for dealing in stolen car parts. Any guy who could chop a car and sell the parts could probably reassemble one too, I figured, and forge papers besides. The thought that I might be driving a stolen vehicle suited my frame of mind. Everything I had taken for granted—the virtue of work, the expectation of deserved rewards, the right to decent treatment and respect, the evil of violence—had been upended in the turmoil of the strike, which came to a close just two months before I turned fifteen, the legal driving age. The Mercury's quiet hum and that lovely *blink-a-blink* lent a sweet harmony to my roiling anger.

As if to put suspicion to rest, Dad quickly put the car to good use. He fastened across its roof, with straps and suction cups, a one-by-four as long as the car was wide, bearing the names KENNEDY–HUMPHREY–FREEMAN. Few Democrats, anyway, would begrudge us the first new car we had owned in my lifetime. Though I followed the rules in the driver's manual, I drove that car, when Dad would let me, in an attitude of defiance.

"Kennedy!" our Mercury shouted. In a town with six Lutheran churches and one Catholic, you could expect rumors about the pope conspiring to overtake Washington, even among the Democrats. Kennedy's faith was no problem for me. I pretended I was Catholic whenever I wore my confirmation medal, though engraved on the back, lest I forget, were the unequivocal words, *I am a Lutheran*. Nor was his wealth a problem, strangely enough. An heir to fortune who chose to be a Democrat had to be a person of integrity and conscience. The prototype, of course, was FDR, whom I had learned to venerate as a child. I felt cheated that he had died only a couple of weeks before I was born, but I had seen Eleanor Roosevelt in person, speaking on behalf of Adlai Stevenson at a banquet in the high school cafeteria. I was in sixth grade and shamefully proud to be the only kid in the audience. If Kennedy took up the Roosevelt legacy, then we were headed for a Brand-New Deal.

The name Humphrey was hardly a threat anywhere in Minnesota. We kids recognized Hubert Humphrey as the talkative guy who promised us his loyalty from the back of a flatbed truck in Morin Park, jumped out of his convertible to shake hands at the Dairy Days parade, patted our heads when we stopped by the DFL booth at the county fair, and drank coffee with our folks at the Union Center.

The name on the sign sure to evoke the most passion was FREEMAN. It seemed that every Albert Lean of voting age either adored or despised the governor. Those who felt indifferent or confused, or afraid of confrontation, kept silent. The unprecedented action Freeman took to calm the violence in the Wilson strike had made him, to some, a champion of labor who enforced ethical business practices, and, to others, a weak-kneed liberal buckling under pressure from a mob of union outlaws. To me he was a hero whose courage in the face of injustice was just short of divine. Even John F. Kennedy had blessed Freeman by inviting him to make the presidential nominating speech at the Democratic national convention. There he was on TV, our very own governor, our wounded World War II hero, speaking to all the nation through the unparalyzed corner of his mouth.

Everyone knew that Freeman had sacrificed reelection, although the labor vote would probably carry Albert Lea and Austin. On newspapers' two-shade post-election maps, Freeborn and Mower Counties usually line up side by side like annoying Democratic buckteeth in the smooth Republican face of southern Minnesota's corn belt. Hauling the name FREEMAN around town on top of the car was not simply campaigning; I meant to taunt those who would deprive my family of our financial security.

I looked for that cherished KENNEDY–HUMPHREY–FREEMAN sign in 1996, when we sorted through a half century's accumulation of household goods to prepare for Mom and Dad's moving sale. Dad remembered shoving it up over the rafters in the garage, but it must have wound up as an ordinary board in some construction project. My interest in Orville Freeman had been reawakened a couple of years before, when I stepped inside the stately new Minnesota History Center one day to pass the time between appointments in St. Paul. I had signed myself into the archive reading room under the pretext of doing local history, but my real plan was just to browse on the computer index and see if anything piqued my interest. The woman behind the reference desk recognized me right off as a computer illiterate and walked over to my terminal to offer help.

"I'm looking for material about Albert Lea," I blurted. The evasive "just looking" I say to wandering clothing-store clerks didn't seem to fit this situation.

"Anything specific about Albert Lea?" she pressed.

"Um, Wilson's meatpacking company."

I moved aside as she deftly tap-tapped on the computer keyboard.

"Well, we have something in the Governors' Archives, under Orville Freeman. It's a box labeled 'Records relating to the Wilson Company strike in Albert Lea.' Would you like to look at it?"

The cardboard box sat on the dolly beside my table, radiating like a shrine of holy relics. I unfolded each item carefully and made sure to return it to its exact place in one of the seven file folders. I perused grainy newspaper photos for familiar faces, and found them: Chuck Lee, the young, curly-haired president of Local 6; Sheriff Stovern smoking his ever-present pipe and displaying, on the table before him, an array of weapons he had confiscated from strikebreakers driving into the plant. The men in the crowd massed at the plant gate all *looked* familiar, though I couldn't name a single one. The lowered earflaps on their winter caps and the parka hoods cinched to the eyebrows obscured their identities.

I made several more trips to the History Center, each time sighing in astonishment or chuckling with delight at what my random visit had uncovered. Here I was, reading our household hero's mail: the letter of December 11, from four city and county officials, formally asking the governor to assume responsibility for law enforcement in Albert Lea; a letter from Judge Cooney relaying rumors of "a well-organized plot" to destroy the Wilson plant with dynamite and acid; a touching, eloquent Christmas wish from a steelworker at Queen Stoves who ushered on Sunday mornings at my church; carefully phrased words of criticism from my best friend Linda's next-door neighbor; a letter from a resident of Homestead, Pennsylvania, recalling the fatalities in that city's 1892 strike and praising Freeman for saving lives; letters from business executives threatening to leave Minnesota or promising never to locate there; pro telegrams from Freeborn County farmers, con telegrams from Freeborn County farmers.

The public debate about Freeman's action during the strike had been mostly critical and sometimes vindictive, but it reads like reasoned conversation in the shadow of the hate mail. "Your fascistic action could be expected from a nauseating Democrat," one letter spews. "Union men must be beaten back when they jeopardize the sanctity of private property.... I will do everything in my power to censure this insanely totalitarian action. . . . You are in effect a damn state dictator." The angry words get scarier when the writer identifies himself as a history professor and threatens to teach his point of view in class. His slashed-out typos make his brief letter look like a death threat. Most heartless of all were the newspaper clippings mailed anonymously from Texas with marginal scrawls addressed to "Little Boy Scarface."

Freeman explained his actions in a letter written in response to a critic: "It would have been very simple for me to send the National Guard in, to arm them and direct them to eliminate forcibly the disturbance which was contrary to established picketing regulations. If I had done so, I'm sure someone would have seriously been hurt and possibly killed. It would seem to me that the use of power with moderation and judgment, making allowances for people's weaknesses instead of running over them roughshod, is much more difficult than the naked use of power which is so easily abused." An eloquent statement, I thought, insightful and carefully composed. Yes, we could be allowed some weaknesses in the heat of anger, and yes, our lives were worth saving, even if the Chicago Tribune had challenged that rationale, asking, "Are these sentiments really as fine as they are meant to sound?"

On sheets torn from a four-by-six notepad, I read phrases the governor had jotted down in the long night after he phoned his orders to the National Guard:

- "history of bitterness"
- "In indust Amer what can the worker do caught between big bus labr"
- "what of community, who can speak for community & people who live there   what are community rights   livelihood of people & future of town"

- "Worker with 10-20-30 years on job has no rights   If
  he feels grieved by company & protests, should he have
  protection"
- "What of company—may it act in harsh & arbitrary
  manner—with brothers city & farm— Does it owe something, how should it be restrained"
- "Also practical is the integrity of one of Minn. finest communities— Legitimate objective to minimize antagonism where
  city country, farm worker & even inter-family bitterness
  takes place—casualties to flow from this are long & real"

The casualties *have* been long and real, and that turbulent
event needs a story to fix its bitter, flowing antagonisms into a
coherent, comprehensible, and salutary shape. It's too complicated a story to tell, I thought, and I might have tucked the
notes back into their file and never looked at them again, except for this one, apparently addressed to his secretary:
"Jean— I have some notes on this and they may be historic
someday." *Only if someone who cares about this moment in history puts them to good use*, I thought, barely daring to imagine
that it might be me.

Orville Freeman did not disappear into obscurity after his defeat as governor. President Kennedy appointed him Secretary
of Agriculture, the one post he had said he didn't want. His
eight years struggling with farm policy and the economy of
food production led him into a new career in international
business, and then to a law practice in Washington, D.C.

The strike had generated a new career for my dad as well.
Although he lost his bid for union trustee, he forged ahead
into city politics. The year I left home, he ran for city council
and floated to victory on the gallons of coffee he drank while
going door-to-door in his mostly working-class ward. He

proudly billed himself as the first workingman elected to the city council. At least two Wilson employees had held the office before, but they were foremen. Ten years later, he made the leap to the county commission. His retirement from that post in 1982, at age seventy, didn't toss him into a life of leisure. He took on volunteer activities, served on the county welfare board and the Trades and Labor housing committee and drove "old" people to the Mayo Clinic for medical care. Only ill health—my mother's—could slow him down.

Dad had been crying wolf for a year or more, pleading for our help and then rejecting whatever we offered. The desperate phone calls were becoming repetitive:

"Mom says she has to go home because her folks are worried about her, so I took her out to the cemetery but she still won't give it up. Will you tell her once and for all they're dead?"

It's not the sort of message you want to deliver to your sweet, confused mother, especially when you don't know which year of her life she's reliving at the moment.

"Don't argue with her," we urged. "There's no place in her brain to store that information. Just take her out for a Dairy Queen or something to distract her." It was easy advice to give from one hundred miles away, to a man who already outdid the rest of us in his new mastery of cooking, cleaning, and laundry.

After Dad's second false-alarm heart attack—"stress," the doctor diagnosed, offering no advice on how to ease it—we stepped up our search for a solution. Nancy, the family's natural-born administrator, had designed for our folks a new life in Minneapolis. Mom would go to adult daycare and Dad would go to an Alzheimer's support group, join the Gray Panthers, help tend the flowers in the Lake Harriet Rose Garden, and work on political campaigns. I was hesitant to uproot him from his four-generation hold on Freeborn County. How would he thrive without the Union Center and the Eagles, without a chorus of "Hi Gordy. How ya doin' Gordy?" following him through the Skyline Mall, without the *kong ka ree* of red-winged blackbirds? But how was he thriving now, afraid to leave Mom alone for more than a few minutes? Joey was trying hard to stay detached, to avoid giving advice that she knew wouldn't be followed anyway. Still, she wasn't spared the frustration and worry.

Mom and Dad's occasional trips to the Cities in their gleaming white Chevy Lumina became less and less frequent as the tensions took their toll. On one such visit, Dad pulled a newspaper clipping out of his pocket and handed it to me. It was an ad for Walker Place, an independent-living facility with a nursing home attached, an ideal place, it would seem, for an alert, active man and his declining wife. I jumped on the impulse before it flitted away and we drove the five minutes to Walker Place and asked for an impromptu tour. The apartments were roomy, the public areas beautifully furnished, and there were plenty of amenities, even an exercise room and a hot tub. I thought it a bit plush for their tastes, but Dad seemed to like it and left his name and number. Back home in Albert Lea, he grew reluctant again. One bedroom or two? Whichever size apartment became available, it was either too big or too small.

In one of those too-small apartments, Nancy and I had a talk with the Walker sales representative. Dad could afford a place like this, we told her. That wasn't the problem, though his tightness might be. Because of his accident at work, he had investments to draw on, including a foot-high stack of U.S.

Savings Bonds. The equity in the house, still in near-perfect shape, would cover the buy-in fee. Yet I had misgivings. He was a laboring man unused to hobnobbing with doctors and lawyers, except the liberal ones he had gotten to know through the dfl and his years in public office.

"My worst scenario," I told the sales representative, "is that he'll move in here and then find out that everyone else is Republican."

"No, no, it's a good mix," she assured me. "Do you remember Governor Freeman? He and his wife just moved in on the eighth floor."

Nancy and I looked at each other and started to giggle.

"They're delightful people," the woman continued. "They've been living in Washington for thirty-five years but decided to retire back home, near their children and grandchildren. He goes over to the Humphrey Institute at the university every morning on the city bus. He could ride in a limousine if he wanted to, but he takes the bus."

"This will sell him for sure, " Nancy sighed, and I tried to explain without telling the whole story. "Orville Freeman was close to sainthood at our house," I said.

Still, it took another false heart attack to persuade Dad that he could no longer postpone the move, wrenching as it was. He never told us how he felt, of course, except obliquely. The people who bought the house were "real nice" and would fit in with the neighbors, but what if they let the roses freeze all to hell over the winter?

Mom and Dad's departure from Albert Lea was clouded by a sadness that grew thicker as each familiar object passed the card table where we took turns sitting with the cash box. It was the first time any of us had seen Joey in a wig since she started chemotherapy for the lung cancer that would soon take her life. All the commotion in the house agitated Mom greatly, and she kept putting towels back where they belonged and hiding other items in the closets. Dad, who was concerned about getting a decent price for his tools, had never quite gotten around to putting price tags on them. Now and then he would pick one up and add it to the assortment he planned to keep.

We watched a cross section of Albert Lea's working class stream through, familiar types I rarely see in my gentrifying Minneapolis neighborhood: overweight women with greasy ponytails who holler at their kids to keep them in line; elderly women with tight permanents who hesitate over twenty-five cent knickknacks and artificial flower arrangements; baby-boom laborers—bearded Vietnam vets in well maintained pickup trucks; Mexican migrant families, the best customers, who load up on blankets and towels, pots and pans. The cousin who sold us our Mercury came, too. As he left, Dad asked if we had noticed how low his pants were riding. "I had eight of those big cow magnets down on the workbench, and after he walked through they were gone." We hadn't seen any of my precious old Wilson stomach magnets come through the checkout line. I still regret that I didn't get to them first.

The first few weeks at Walker Place passed without even a glimpse of the governor. Dad was holding his own among the retired professionals, and Mom's mood was calm enough to let her smile and make small talk with these strangers. A posting on the bulletin board told about the good-bye dinner the Freeborn County DFL had thrown for Dad, complete with commemorative plaque and a key to the city. It also listed his public-service accomplishments, which immediately got him elected vice president of the Walker Place residents' board.

One morning he called to tell me that they had met Mrs. Freeman at an exercise class down in the party room, and she had invited them for dinner the next Tuesday, downstairs in the dining room open to residents and their guests. I waited for their phone call that Tuesday evening until my patience ran out. They were back in their apartment, watching The Nashville Network, when I called.

"So how did your dinner go?" I asked, eager for the detail-rich story I knew Dad was capable of telling.

"Pretty good," he said. "The roast beef was okay, but they don't give you much. About a thimbleful of mashed potatoes . . ."

"But what about the Freemans?" I pressed. "What are they like?"

"Oh, they're real nice people," he said. "They wouldn't let us pay for a thing. She's quite a talker. He doesn't say a whole lot. I told him somebody'd probably been killed in that strike if he hadn't stepped in. He thought so, too. Here's Mom."

I made conversation with my mom, struggling as always to stay in the moment and not ask questions that tested her memory. I could hear Dad's voice in the background, prompting her to tell me what he had forgotten to mention: Orville Freeman would like to talk with me.

Making phone calls to people I'd like to interview always seems abrupt and intrusive to me. I worry about dropping my big question on someone who's just had an argument with his or her spouse or is trying to meditate away a bad case of heartburn. So I wrote to Orville Freeman and got a quick return phone call from Mrs. Freeman, who said he was very eager to talk to me. Could I please send copies of some of the documents I had mentioned in my letter, just to refresh his memory? We scheduled an evening a month away, after their vacation up north.

In the meantime, I refreshed my own memory by reading the photocopies and notes from my encounters with the box in the History Center. I also read a recent magazine profile that portrayed a politician shrewder than the morally driven hero of my childhood seemed to be. This man had helped purge the newly formed DFL of its Depression-era radicals and had narrowly won his first term as governor by buying up total, statewide television coverage for a campaign speech on the eve of the election. I was glad to have this more complex portrait of Governor Freeman. It would help me be the historically inclined writer he was no doubt expecting and not the awestruck kid I was afraid I might regress to as I stepped in his apartment.

He was waiting for me by the elevator, dressed in the plaid sports shirt and cardigan sweater that seem to be the retirement uniform of men who spent their working lives in suits and ties. I was struck by how old he looked, how thin and frail, but I know my parents' youthful appearance has set my standards off-kilter. He shuffled a bit as we walked around the corner to his apartment, where his wife Jane, a petite, sparkly woman with dark hair, settled him into his "comfy" chair and brought us coffee and cookies.

I felt apprehensive when our opening exchange didn't quite make sense, but the interview moved along smoothly once I asked him to tell his story about closing the plant and declaring martial law. A story it certainly was, with a shape molded over many retellings:

"I was all alone, with just my driver, and I was speaking at a

commencement exercise at a small high school. At the conclusion of this, as I prepared to leave, someone came and said,
'There's an urgent telephone call for you.' Someone was calling at eleven at night and I said to myself, 'Now what in the
devil could that be?' And on the phone was O. Russell Olson,
the Freeborn county attorney, and he said to me, 'You asked
me to keep in touch about this strike, because of the activities
and because of the threats there, because of the use of force,
and if anything is out of order, out of line, in connection with
it, why let you know.' I had alerted a number of people because I wanted to be informed in case it was necessary for me
to do something. And he said, 'If that plant opens in the morning, someone is going to get killed.' Bang, just like that, someone is going to get killed. I said, 'Tell me more.' I don't remember now exactly what he told me, but the essence of it was
that this was getting completely out of control.

"So, I got back about midnight and thought, What can I do?
What should I do, and what are the consequences both ways?
The decision needed to be made in a very short time frame. I
didn't have anybody even to discuss it with, and I was not familiar with the law in that connection. I just concluded that it
wasn't worth taking a chance on someone being killed. And so
I went back to my office and got a hold of the commanding officer of the National Guard, General Joe Nelson, and I just
told him the circumstance. I said, 'How long will it take you to
get down to Albert Lea and close that plant?' But the General
said to me—we were good friends—'You can't do that.' I said,
'Goddamnit Joe, I didn't call you up to ask your advice. Get
the troops down there. I want that plant closed by daybreak.'
Olson had said, 'In my judgment, if that plant opens in the
morning, someone's going to be killed.' That made it all really
quite simple, in that you just had to do something. I did do

something. It was a hard decision. It was the toughest decision I made in the period I was governor."

As the interview progressed, I learned that he was still intent on proving the legality of what he had done, looking for precedents in other uses of the governor's executive powers. Floyd B. Olson had closed the Munsingwear plant in the 1930s and was also called into court, but in that case the judges ruled in his favor. One of those judges was still serving on the court that ruled against Governor Freeman. Mrs. Freeman reminded him of this fact: "That's what you never could get over. They found for him and against you, in very similar factual circumstances."

Alert at the beginning of the interview, he began to tire and fade a bit once the chief story had been told. He searched for names and facts in the far reaches of his memory and sometimes retrieved the wrong ones. Had he been to Albert Lea half a dozen times to talk to key people in the community, or was it just once or twice, as his wife remembered? Before long, I had switched the microphone from Low to High to make sure the recorder caught her corrections. He deferred to her more and more and grew quieter, apparently weary of the effort that my questions required of him. I couldn't help but wonder what course Jane Freeman's life might have taken had she come of age at a time more congenial to women in politics. For someone absorbed in raising two small children at the time of her husband's fateful decision, she had a stunning command of the circumstances in which he made it.

My final question roused him back to the world of politics where sharp answers are critical.

"Thinking back on it, would you have done things any differently, or do you feel vindicated?"

"I don't feel vindicated," he said with a wry smile, "because I don't think I did anything improper."

Mrs. Freeman got the last word. "I thought his answer was going to be H-E-L-L no. That used to be what I heard when he was asked questions like that. He's mellowed." We all laughed at that, and I packed up my recorder and said my thank-yous and good-byes.

"Mellowed" has become our pleasant-sounding euphemism for the decline in energy and enthusiasm, the loss of fighting spirit that comes with old age. As I rode the elevator downstairs after a brief check-in with my parents on the fifth floor, I took with me a revised image of Governor Freeman, a man of astute intelligence now retreating into memory loss—a consequence of both Parkinson's and Alzheimer's diseases, I learned later. There was something eerily familiar about the shuffling gait, the weary look that stole over his face, his quiet demeanor as his wife picked up slack in the conversation. A stealthy, unexpected grief snatched at me as I climbed into my car in the parking lot. Many times over, I had bemoaned my mother's loss of memory, shared her frustration, tried to ease her confusion. But now, for the first time ever, I felt my own sorrow at the loss of my mom.

With that new grief, I mourned the passage of time since 1959 and all that it has swept away: my sister Joey, my parents' vigor, my beloved grandparents, the house I grew up in, the ceramic black panther and all the other 1950s knickknacks we sold too cheaply at the moving sale, my neighborhood slough paved over for Wal-Mart, the pitch-black soil of Freeborn County turning dry and brown, the thriving businesses along Broadway now given over to short-lived specialty shops. I even mourned the kills standing empty at the packinghouse, no longer echoing with squeals and moos and the grinding and clanking of machines. The silence I imagined there was unnerving.

I can't live with grief for long without it either immobilizing my work or turning me dreadfully sentimental. I have to smile now as I picture the governor and the packinghouse worker mellowing under the same roof: my dad the skilled mechanic showing JFK's Secretary of Agriculture how to set the controls on the exercise bike; my mom extolling the view, again and again, from the Freeman's top-floor balcony; my gregarious dad and the energetic Mrs. Freeman discussing upcoming elections; my mom and the governor arriving home in the afternoons, he with his briefcase, she with a spoon pilfered from the adult daycare center in the pocket of her sweatpants.

"Life is short," Grandma Petersen said to me once, as she encouraged me to take a trip I didn't think I could afford. Then she tossed her head back and roared with laughter: "Life is *short*? I'm ninety-two years old!" I have to remind myself to keep her perspective. As deeply rooted as I like to feel, we are a people on the move. Grandma was a girl in Denmark, a mother in Alden, an old lady in Albert Lea. Our five generations in Freeborn County on the Register side took up a mere 140 years, hardly a month by Asian standards. The children of rural Minnesota grow up and leave home. Their ancestors did the same. What matters is that we take the heirlooms with us when we go: our sense of justice, our loyalty, our honorable actions. We also come to treasure the surprises, the unintended residue: the ancient, dank memory of a Danish peatbog, the moist breeze riffling through a cattail marsh, the deep green of a cornfield, even the soothing fragrance of a packinghouse that reminds us of home.

Acknowledgments

This book has been long in coming, and I have accumulated many debts of gratitude along the way. First off, I thank my family, who offered their memories and checked mine: Gordon Register, Nancy Register Wangen, Roger Wangen, the late JoAnn Squires, and Rodger Squires. I'm sorry that I waited too long to benefit from my mom's memories, but she, Ardis Register, has been an inspiration anyway. As I watch her fold her napkin at cookie time, carefully matching the edges and smoothing the creases, I am amazed at how the habits of work endure in our bodies' own memories. Many high school classmates reminisced with me by phone or letter or in person over the last eight years: Peter Cooper, Dennis Dingemans, Bill Emstad, Susan Evenson Williams, Ron Hansen, Virginia Jacobson, Diane Knudson Gulbrandson, Linda De Beau-Melting, the late Kathy Narverud Hockel, Judy Chrisinger Ohm, Herbert Ohm, Linda Petersen Zimney, Tom Petersen, Larry Phillips, Janet Reichl Heidinger, Bob Roscoe, Linda

Schue Williams, Dorothy Stowell Rees, Steve Thompson, Mary Tuchtenhagen Buzay, Bill Yost, and my good friend Geraldine O'Leary Macias, who passed away in 1992. I apologize to those I've forgotten to name. Those I've named may not even remember talking to me. Thanks also to Lois Kriesel Claypool, whom the luckiest among us had as our sixth-grade teacher.

A very special thank-you to those, friends and strangers alike, who let me probe their memories, record them on tape, and donate the tapes to the Freeborn County Historical Society for use by other researchers: Eleonora Carey, Eugene Cotton, Linda De Beau-Melting, Marlene Hammero, Morris Haskins, Nina Helstein, Joyce Kennedy, Wallace Kennedy, Irving King, Beatrice (Tootie) Lee, Charles Lee, Donald Nielsen, David Peterson (son of the Reverend Lloyd Peterson), who also let me borrow the family's scrapbook, the late Arlo Oetjen, Leo O'Neal, Leslie Orear, Gordon Register, Dr. Niles Shoff, and six 1995 graduates of Albert Lea High School—Sheila Bock, Tamarae Holt, Susan Lammers, Shari Liebl, Krista Purdy, and Jacques Tran.

As I struggled to bring this project into focus, I showed bits and pieces of it to these fine people, whose comments I took to heart or fretted over or sometimes ignored, to their dismay: Sara M. Evans, Susan Grieger, Paul Gruchow, Tom Heie, Paul Hintz, Amy Kaminsky, Melinda Lockard, Joanna O'Connell, Riv-Ellen Prell, Naomi Scheman, and Richard Solly. A bit further along in the process, the sporadic Essay Group, an offshoot of a class taught by Phillip Lopate, read many drafts and tested out structures for the book: Patricia Weaver Francisco, Brigitte Frase, Patricia Kirkpatrick, Julie Landsman, Margaret Todd Maitland, Jim Moore, and Bart Schneider. Thank you to Bart and Todd for venturing to print a piece of it in *Hungry*

Mind Review (now *Ruminator Review*). I had the pleasure of working with Scott Russell Sanders in the Loft Literary Center's Creative Nonfiction Mentorship program, along with Beryl Singleton Bissell, Barrie Jean Borich, Pamela Fletcher, Patrice Koelsch, and Judith Niemi, all of them superb writers and critics. This was a turning point that headed the book toward home.

I have turned to several research institutions for factual information: the Minnesota History Research Center (special thanks to Deborah Miller for believing in this strange mix of memoir and history), the Freeborn County Historical Society (especially librarian Linda Evenson), the Illinois Labor History Society, and the Wisconsin State Historical Society, where the archives of the United Packinghouse Workers of America are stored. The staff of Local 6 of the United Food and Commercial Workers generously shared their space and materials with me, even when I showed up unannounced. Thanks also to Peter Rachleff and to the members of the H-Labor Listserv who answered my queries.

Ann Regan, managing editor of the Minnesota Historical Society Press, has been both an enthusiastic and a rigorous editor, an ideal combination. I am grateful to Ted Genoways and all the others at MHS who helped bring this book into print, and, in the spirit of TV awards shows, I thank God and Floyd B. Olson.

Work on this book has been funded by a Jerome Foundation Travel and Study Grant, in cooperation with the Dayton-Hudson Foundation; a research grant from the Minnesota Historical Society, a Career Opportunity Grant and an Artist Fellowship from the Minnesota State Arts Board; a Loft Creative Nonfiction Award, and residencies at Norcroft and the Ragdale Foundation. The Loft Literary Center has helped out greatly by allowing me to teach and earn a living, and my students at the Loft have induced me to keep practicing what I preach. Finally, I want to thank my daughters, Grace and Maria De Jong, for their patience with all the delays and disruptions in our family life, and for indulging me in my teenage memories while they were acquiring their own.